EFFECTS OF PARENTAL INCARCERATION ON CHILDREN

PSYCHOLOGY, CRIME, AND JUSTICE SERIES

EFFECTS OF PARENTAL INCARCERATION ON CHILDREN

CROSS-NATIONAL COMPARATIVE STUDIES

JOSEPH MURRAY, CATRIEN C. J. H. BIJLEVELD,
DAVID P. FARRINGTON, and ROLF LOEBER

American Psychological Association • Washington, DC

Published by
American Psychological Association
750 First Street, NE
Washington, DC 20002
www.apa.org

To order
APA Order Department
P.O. Box 92984
Washington, DC 20090-2984
Tel: (800) 374-2721; Direct: (202) 336-5510
Fax: (202) 336-5502; TDD/TTY: (202) 336-6123
Online: www.apa.org/pubs/books
E-mail: order@apa.org

In the U.K., Europe, Africa, and the Middle East, copies may be ordered from
American Psychological Association
3 Henrietta Street
Covent Garden, London
WC2E 8LU England

Typeset in Goudy by Circle Graphics, Inc., Columbia, MD

Printer: United Book Press, Baltimore, MD
Cover Designer: Mercury Publishing Services, Rockville, MD

The opinions and statements published are the responsibility of the authors, and such opinions and statements do not necessarily represent the policies of the American Psychological Association.

Library of Congress Cataloging-in-Publication Data

Murray, Joseph, 1976-
  Effects of parental incarceration on children : cross-national comparative studies /
by Joseph Murray, Catrien C. J. H. Bijleveld, David P. Farrington, and Rolf Loeber.
      pages cm
  Includes bibliographical references and index.
  ISBN-13: 978-1-4338-1743-4
  ISBN-10: 1-4338-1743-8
  1. Children of prisoners. 2. Prisoners—Family relationships. 3. Parent and child. I. Title.
  HV8885.M87 2014
  362.82'95—dc23
                              2013047652

British Library Cataloguing-in-Publication Data
A CIP record is available from the British Library.

Printed in the United States of America
First Edition

http://dx.doi.org/10.1037/14377-000

Family is affected and involved in the prison sentence.
It affects everybody close.

—*Father in prison, England, 2003*

CONTENTS

LIST OF FIGURES AND TABLES

FIGURES

ix

TABLES

FOREWORD

SHADD MARUNA

The APA Psychology, Crime, and Justice Series was designed to serve two related purposes. The first is to demonstrate the potential contributions of a psychological approach to key issues in criminal justice. The second is to demonstrate to the field of psychology the many, fascinating issues that are raised by criminal justice research for a better understanding of our subject. This remarkable new book from Joseph Murray, Catrien C. J. H. Bijleveld, David P. Farrington, and Rolf Loeber succeeds in both of these regards and is therefore a highly fitting contribution to the series.

The book also opens up a neglected new frontier in this area of psychology. Psychologists have long been interested in the psychological consequences of imprisonment (good or bad, but usually bad!) on prisoners. The best of these studies, like Zimbardo's famous Stanford Experiment, also recognize that prison staff are also "doing time" and so will look at the impact of this work on their own lives as well. However, forgotten in most of this work is the fact that, despite the individual-based language of the justice process, the effects of imprisonment are felt far beyond the prison walls. The parents and grandparents, children and grandchildren, spouses and lovers, and even whole communities left behind when individuals are imprisoned are also doing time. They experience the loss of a potential provider and supporter, may suffer shame and ostracization, and have to negotiate difficult interactions with police, courts, and prisons because of a criminal act that they did not commit.

This manuscript is unique in presenting the most rigorous, systematic, and sophisticated analysis, to date, of the crucially important problem of the impact of parental incarceration on the children of prisoners. Murray and his colleagues ask all of the right questions, and they answer them with clarity and precision, utilizing some of the most innovative and sophisticated research studies available in criminology. In a model of comparative cross-cultural research, Murray and colleagues compare and contrast the findings of studies based in the United States, Sweden, the United Kingdom, and the Netherlands, and the differences in outcome are explored in dialogue with a rich array of theory in psychology and criminology.

This is the third contribution to the Psychology, Crime, and Justice Series, and an intriguing pattern is beginning to emerge for the series as a whole. The previous titles—*Rehabilitating Sexual Offenders: A Strength-Based Approach* by William Marshall, Liam Marshall, Geris Serran, and Matt O'Brien and *Cop Watch: Spectators, Social Media, and Police Reform* by Hans Toch—have also opened up new ways of looking at familiar issues. William Marshall's work starts with a familiar topic for psychology, in the sense that there is a huge number of psychologists working in the field of sex offender treatment, but makes a radical case for changing the treatment lens from one of deficits and disease to a strength-based approach promoting good and healthy lives for those convicted of sex crimes. Psychologists have worked less with the police, but when they do, their focus tends to be in helping officers or victims of crime deal with trauma, profiling serious cases, or assisting with witness evidence. Like the latest book from Murray and colleagues, Toch introduces an entirely new angle for psychologists to contribute, exploring the role of citizen observers, spectators, and critics in the dynamics of policing in communities.

Taken as a whole, the Psychology, Crime, and Justice Series demonstrates the utility of psychological theory and research in these justice domains but also illustrates one of the "tricks" of the research trade that I sometimes share with my students. That is, the secret to achieving truly creative and original ideas in the social sciences is often to import ideas that are anything but new in one field of study into another area of research where these well-established theories are much less well-known. The result, in the case of Murray and colleagues' outstanding and pioneering work, is at once the most definitive treatment of the subject of the collateral effects of imprisonment on prisoners' children and a sure catalyst for future innovative research in this area internationally.

ACKNOWLEDGMENTS

Our greatest debt is to the families and children who participated in the studies in this book. They have given remarkable cooperation, trust, and time over many years, and this book would not exist without them.

We have been extremely fortunate to work with insightful and generous collaborators in several countries, to whom we are very grateful: the late Carl-Gunnar Janson, director of the Swedish study in Chapter 5; Steve G. A. van de Weijer, Sytske Besemer, and Victor van der Geest, who worked on the Dutch study in Chapter 6; Dustin Pardini, who worked on the American study in Chapter 7; and Ivana Sekol and Rikke F. Olsen, who worked on the systematic review in Chapter 9. Steve G. A. van de Weijer, Sytske Besemer, and Victor van der Geest kindly helped prepare new analyses of the Dutch study and English study for this book. Yulia Shenderovich helped research background material for Chapter 8 and produced many of the figures throughout this book.

Shadd Maruna gave invaluable encouragement and wise advice from the inception to the long-awaited finish of this book. We are also very grateful to Maureen Adams and the development editors at the American Psychological Association, Harriet Kaplan and Tyler Aune, for their very helpful guidance through this process.

Previously, we published several journal articles about the effects of parental incarceration on children. This book draws together this prior work and presents new findings to provide a comprehensive assessment of how parental incarceration affects children's life chances across four different countries. The previously published individual studies are summarized in Chapters 4 through 7, and new comparative analyses, matching the four studies as closely as possible, are presented in Chapter 8. We are grateful to the publishers of previous articles for giving license to reproduce material in this book. Findings from England (Chapter 4) were previously published by Wiley (Murray & Farrington, 2005), Cambridge University Press (Murray & Farrington, 2008b), and the University of Chicago Press (Murray & Farrington, 2008a). Findings from Sweden (Chapter 5) were previously published by Sage (Murray, Janson, & Farrington, 2007). Previous findings from the Netherlands were published by Oxford Journals (Besemer, van der Geest, Murray, Bijleveld, & Farrington, 2011), and findings from the Pittsburgh Youth Study (United States) were previously published by Wiley (Murray, Loeber, & Pardini, 2012). Our first systematic review about parental incarceration was published by the Campbell Collaboration (Murray, Farrington, Sekol, & Olsen, 2009); Chapter 9 presents an expanded review previously published by the American Psychological Association (Murray, Farrington, & Sekol, 2012).

Funding for the studies in this book is gratefully acknowledged. The Cambridge Study in Delinquent Development (England) has been funded mainly by the U.K. Home Office and also by the Department of Health. The Dutch Study (Transfive) has received funding from Stichting Pro Musis, Hesseveld Stichting, Broedercongregatie OLV Van Zeven Smarten, Aloysius Stichting, and Expertisecentrum Rechtshandhaving Ministry of Justice. Funding for work on the Pittsburgh Youth Study (United States) was provided by Grant 2005-JK-FX-0001 from the Office of Juvenile Justice and Delinquency Prevention (OJJDP), Grants MH 50778 and 73941 from the National Institute of Mental Health, Grant No. 11018 from the National Institute on Drug Abuse, a grant from the Department of Health of the Commonwealth of Pennsylvania, and a grant from the Centers for Disease Control (administered through OJJDP). Joseph Murray received funding for research on parental incarceration from the U.K. Economic and Social Research Council (PhD scholarship; Grant RES-000-22-2311), the British Academy (Postdoctoral Fellowship), SFI Campbell (Denmark), National Institute of Justice (Grant 2007-IJ-CX-0045: 549089), and the Nuffield Foundation (Grant OPD/37411); he worked toward completing this book while on a Wellcome Trust Research Career Development Fellowship (089963/Z/09/Z).

Finally, and certainly not least, we are extremely grateful to our families for all their encouragement, patience, and constant support.

EFFECTS OF PARENTAL INCARCERATION ON CHILDREN

INTRODUCTION

When my dad went to prison it was the worst thing that had ever happened to me. I felt like I had a locked box of tears inside my chest that I couldn't get out and it made me mean to people at my school sometimes and my mum. Please be kind to me when I'm sad or angry and please be kind to my dad.
—Boy whose father is in prison, 8 years old, England, 2013

The arrest of a parent can leave children shocked, bewildered, and scared. Arrest often happens at night or in the early morning, when people are at home with their families. One incarcerated mother in an English study described how "the front and back door were crashed in simultaneously. The house was full of policemen with hammers looking for drugs. It was very frightening, my son was hysterical" (Richards et al., 1994, p. 54). As handcuffed parents are led away, the shadow of the prison looms. To see their parent again, children may need to go through metal detectors, be searched, sniffed by a dog, and led into a crowded visiting room where their mom or dad is clad in orange and not allowed to leave their seat, and may be behind Plexiglas. The prison visiting room may be the only place where children see their parent for several years.

More than 10 million people are held in prisons throughout the world today (Walmsley, 2011). The United States had, as of 2011, the largest prison

http://dx.doi.org/10.1037/14377-001
Effects of Parental Incarceration on Children: Cross-National Comparative Studies, by J. Murray,
C. C. J. H. Bijleveld, D. P. Farrington, and R. Loeber

population (2.24 million; Glaze & Parks, 2012) and the highest rate of imprisonment in the world (743 per 100,000 population; Walmsley, 2011). With such high levels of incarceration, the effects on prisoners' well-being, health, and behavior have become urgent social concerns (Liebling & Maruna, 2005; Nagin, Cullen, & Jonson, 2009; Tonry & Petersilia, 1999b). Equally important are possible far-reaching consequences of incarceration beyond prison walls on recidivism; employment opportunities for ex-prisoners; and children, families, and communities (Clear, 2007; Hagan & Dinovitzer, 1999; Murray, 2005; Murray & Farrington, 2008a; Walker, 1983).

This book is about children whose parents have been incarcerated and how this experience may alter their life chances. For decades, children with incarcerated parents have been relatively neglected by criminal justice systems, social services, researchers, the media, and policy makers. As such, they have been referred to as the "forgotten victims" of crime (Matthews, 1983), the "orphans of justice" (Shaw, 1992a), and the "unseen victims of the prison boom" (Petersilia, 2005, p. 34). Many people might assume that children are made better off when law-breaking parents are incarcerated, but recent research has posed a major challenge to this assumption. There is growing recognition that children whose parents are incarcerated may suffer profound and long-lasting consequences into adult life. In this book, we draw together four of the largest studies to date on the effects of parental incarceration on children. These studies have followed thousands of children through their lives in four different countries: England, Sweden, the Netherlands, and the United States. The findings provide unique evidence about how parental incarceration shapes children's adult outcomes and variation in the effects of parental incarceration across national contexts.

Why should we as a society care about the effects of parental incarceration on children? First, more parents than ever are behind bars, and the number of children affected in the United States is staggering. In 2011, the country's adult prison population was 1.5 million, and its adult jail population was 736,000 (Glaze & Parks, 2012). About half of U.S. prisoners are parents to children under age 18 (Glaze & Maruschak, 2008). As shown in Figure 1, the number of children with a parent in state or federal prison increased from 950,000 in 1991 to 1.7 million in 2007, reaching 2.3% of the nation's children (Glaze & Maruschak, 2008). Given that these estimates are based on surveys of prisoners who may not report that they have children, actual numbers are likely to be higher. The chances of experiencing parental incarceration through childhood have grown dramatically in the United States in recent decades, especially for Black children (Wakefield & Wildeman, 2014). Estimates suggest that, cumulatively, one in 25 White children and a shocking one in four Black children born in 1990 had experienced parental incarceration by their 14th birthday (Wildeman, 2009). As Wakefield and Wildeman (2011,

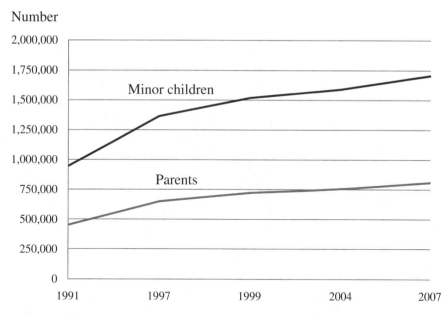

Number

Figure 1. Estimated number of parents in U.S. state and federal prisons and their minor children. Data from Glaze and Maruschak (2008).

2014) cogently argued, this may have caused large racial disparities in child well-being in the United States.

Less is known about how many children experience parental incarceration in other countries, but provisional estimates suggest that the numbers are substantial (Murray & Farrington, 2008a). In England and Wales, approximately 125,000 children have a parent incarcerated each year (about 1% of children under age 18), only one quarter fewer than the number of children who experience parental divorce (Murray, 2007). In Sweden, it is estimated that about 8,000 (Swedish Prison and Probation Service, 2013) to 10,500 (Bryggan, 2013) children have an incarcerated parent, around 0.5% of the nation's children under age 18. Although there are no official figures about the number of incarcerated parents and children in the Netherlands, research on women in Dutch prisons estimates that between 800 to 1,200 children have a mother incarcerated each year (Slotboom, Bijleveld, Day, & van Giezen, 2008).

A second reason why the effects of parental incarceration on children need investigating is that, in a vicious cycle, today's policies of incarceration may harm children and contribute to an even larger prison population in coming decades. If parental incarceration does cause crime in the next generation, this could have implications for criminal justice policy reform.

↑ crime? -

Incarceration policies are commonly justified on the basis of "incapacitation" or "deterrence" effects—incarceration supposedly preventing crime by holding lawbreakers captive and increasing the perceived costs of committing future crime. However, to assess incarceration's true worth, any such benefits (to the extent they exist, which is hotly debated by criminologists) must also be weighed against any costs, including costs to families and children, which have hitherto been ignored (McDougall, Cohen, Swaray, & Perry, 2003; Sampson, 2011). Cost–benefit analyses of incarceration that have been conducted focus mainly on the financial costs of prison operating expenses (e.g., McDougall et al., 2003; Piehl & Dilulio, 1995) and have not included costs to families and children of prisoners (Travis, McBride, & Solomon, 2005). Without quantifying such "unintended effects" and including them in cost–benefit analyses, the overall benefits of incarceration may be overestimated, and policies uncritically employed that enlarge this modern institution.

human rights

A third reason to research the effects of parental incarceration on children is that basic human rights of children are threatened by the forced removal of a parent to prison. As Boswell (2002) pointed out over a decade ago, the United Nations Convention on the Rights of the Child specifically states that children should be protected from discrimination or punishment resulting from their parents' status or activities (Article 2, United Nations General Assembly, 1989). Harmful effects of parental incarceration on children may violate this principle. Article 9 of the Convention also emphasizes children's right to maintain regular contact and relations with a parent from whom they are separated, and this may be denied when parents are held in prison with highly restricted contact opportunities.

vulnerable popns.

A fourth reason why new research is needed on children with incarcerated parents is that a substantial proportion of children in vulnerable populations have histories of parental incarceration. In mental health services in the United States, 43% of children were estimated to have a history of parental incarceration in one study (Phillips, Burns, Wagner, Kramer, & Robbins, 2002). Of children in youth courts, 31% had parents who have previously been incarcerated (Dannerbeck, 2005). Increases in maternal incarceration have been identified as the main cause of the doubling of the population of children in foster care between 1985 and 2000 in the United States (Swann & Sylvester, 2006). Therefore, understanding the effects of parental incarceration on children may have important implications for clinicians working with high-risk youth in various settings.

Stigmatising

A fifth issue of concern, and perhaps one of the most important and troubling, is that parental incarceration appears to be highly stigmatizing for families and children of prisoners (Boswell & Wedge, 2002; Braman, 2004; Sack, 1977; Sack, Seidler, & Thomas, 1976; Zalba, 1964). Poor understanding about the needs of children of prisoners may have contributed to policy failure to identify these children as a vulnerable group and allocate resources for their support (Robertson et al., 2012). It has commonly been suggested that children of prisoners are six times more likely than other children to be convicted or incarcerated themselves (Hagan & Dinovitzer, 1999; Jacobs, 1995; Moses, 1995; Petersilia, 2003; Simmons, 2000; Springer, Lynch, & Rubin, 2000; Van Wormer & Bartollas, 2000). However, having followed the citations for these claims, we found no evidence to support them. Thus, empirical evidence about the needs of children whose parents are incarcerated and their later life chances is important to improve rational debate about services to support them.

Given these issues, we consider it an urgent and important task for researchers and policy makers to investigate the effects of parental incarceration on children and find ways in which any harm may be reduced. A critical issue for research is how to identify true causal effects of parental incarceration, over and above various background circumstances associated with incarceration, which also might propel children toward poor adult outcomes. This is a major challenge, and throughout this book, we discuss the concepts involved and methods used in trying to estimate causal effects on children's life outcomes. Tight causal conclusions will always be hard to achieve on this issue, but various methods of matching, statistical control, and analyzing change in children's behaviors from before to after parental incarceration provide means to move closer to this goal.

In this book, we consider parental incarceration in terms of any kind of custodial confinement of a parent by the criminal justice system, except being held overnight in police cells. Incarceration can refer to confinement in jails or prisons (e.g., in the United States, at state or federal level). We consider how children might be affected differently according to the length of parental incarceration or the number of times that parents are incarcerated and whether mothers or fathers are incarcerated. However, we do not examine other types of parental captivity, such as the effects on children of parents being held as a prisoner of war (e.g., McCubbin, Dahl, Lester, & Ross, 1977; Najafi, Akochkian, & Nikyar, 2007), nor effects of incarceration of nonparental household figures (e.g., siblings, aunts, uncles, grandparents).

Although the United States clearly has the largest prison "problem," "we can learn things about crime and punishment by looking across national boundaries" (Tonry, 2001, p. 3). A cross-national perspective comparing effects of parental incarceration on children across a range of social and penal contexts can help identify where parental incarceration has harmful effects, where such harmful effects are mitigated, and the kinds of policies that might be used to prevent adverse outcomes for children whose parents are incarcerated. As such, this book aims to identify and compare the impacts of parental incarceration on children across four different countries with markedly different social and penal climates. This complements the growing literature documenting the considerable adverse effects of parental incarceration on children in the United States (e.g., Murray, Loeber, & Pardini, 2012; Roettger & Swisher, 2011; Wakefield & Wildeman, 2014).

We chose to study the effects of parental incarceration in England, Sweden, the Netherlands, and the United States both because these countries vary in terms of penal landscape in important ways that could affect children's reactions to parental incarceration and also because of our access to high-quality longitudinal data in each country. Comparing the criminal justice systems in England and Wales, Sweden, and the United States, Mulready-Jones (2011) concluded that children with incarcerated parents in Sweden "are by far the most fortunate in terms of the support services available to them and the effectiveness of those services in minimizing the harm caused . . . by parental incarceration" (p. 5). As will be revealed in the chapters that follow, comparisons of long-term effects of parental incarceration on children between these countries reveal different risks associated with parental incarceration, with more harmful effects found in England and the United States and mitigated effects in Sweden and the Netherlands.

When our studies in Sweden and the Netherlands began in the 1950s–1960s, resocialization was the primary goal of prison, with shorter sentences and lower incarceration rates than in England and the United States (Downes & van Swaaningen, 2007; Marnell, 1972). As Friday (1976) wrote, "Sweden's penal and legal philosophy has developed out of a general social welfare ideology which tends to emphasize the similarities among its citizens rather than the differences" (p. 48). We believe that cultures of universalism, tolerance, and reintegrative penal policies in Sweden and the Netherlands may have protected children from long-term harmful consequences of parental incarceration found in England and the United States. Moreover, evidence suggests that changes in penal culture through time can also alter effects of parental incarceration on children. Specifically, as the penal climate in the Netherlands shifted from being similar to that in Sweden in the 1950s–1960s toward greater punitivism in the late 1970s, effects of parental incarceration on children in the Netherlands got worse. As such, the principles of reintegrative penal policies in Sweden and the Netherlands in the mid-20th century may be taken as inspiration to reform penal systems to support children today and avert long-lasting consequences in the next generation.

The book is organized as follows. We discuss the many practical and emotional difficulties experienced by families and children during parental incarceration in Chapter 1. Chapter 2 reviews key theories that might explain effects of parental incarceration on children, and Chapter 3 lays out key research questions and methods for the remainder of the book. Empirical findings from individual studies in England, Sweden, the Netherlands and the United States are presented separately in Chapters 4 through 7 and then brought together in comparative analyses in Chapter 8 to consider how and why the effects of parental incarceration on children might vary across social and penal contexts. As well as reporting results of this primary research, we also use state-of-the art methods to synthesize all available evidence on the effects of parental incarceration in a "systematic review" in Chapter 9. In the final chapter of the book, we summarize our conclusions and consider implications for policy, practice, and research.

I

BACKGROUND

1

arrest → trial → incarceration → home.

CHILDREN'S EXPERIENCES OF PARENTAL INCARCERATION

Many practical and emotional difficulties can affect families and children of prisoners from arrest onward. In this chapter, we discuss the process of parental incarceration studied from the child's point of view. We especially draw on numerous qualitative studies, which use in-depth analyses of specific cases to provide rich descriptions of children's experiences before, during, and after parental incarceration. This provides an important starting point for the large-scale surveys investigating long-term effects of parental incarceration on children, which we report on in Part II of this book.

PARENTAL CRIME, ARREST, TRIAL, INCARCERATION, AND RETURN HOME

Even before parental arrest and incarceration take place, children with parents involved in crime often have home and community lives that are thwart with trauma and social disadvantage, including poverty, prior family

http://dx.doi.org/10.1037/14377-002
Effects of Parental Incarceration on Children: Cross-National Comparative Studies, by J. Murray, C. C. J. H. Bijleveld, D. P. Farrington, and R. Loeber

disruptions, and violence inside and outside the home. In the United States, 46% of parents in state prisons reported that they were repeat offenders with either a current or past violent offense, and about half (54%) of incarcerated parents were using drugs in the month prior to their offense (Mumola, 2000). As Jane Siegel (2011) stated, "violence is truly ubiquitous in these children's lives. It permeates their homes, their communities, and their schools. Both they and their mothers are victims, witnesses, and perpetrators in these various milieus" (p. 90). Eddy and Reid (2003) suggested that in the context of multiple risks, parental incarceration may serve as a "tipping point" toward more severe problem behavior.

The arrest of a parent can cause children to feel shocked, bewildered, and scared (Fishman, 1983; E. I. Johnson & Waldfogel, 2004; Nijnatten, 1998; Richards et al., 1994). Among 192 incarcerated parents in Arkansas, 40% of parents reported that their children had been present at the arrest (Harm & Phillips, 1998); in 27% of those cases, weapons were drawn. Law enforcement officers explained why they were arresting the parent to just 20% of the children. Handcuffing the parent was postponed until the parent was out of children's sight in only 3% of fathers' arrests and 30% of mothers' arrests. In Kampfner's (1995) study of 36 children with incarcerated mothers, many children reported symptoms of posttraumatic stress disorder, including flashbacks of their mother's arrest (see also Phillips & Zhao, 2010).

Following parental arrest, trial in court can be highly anxiety provoking for families and children. Uncertainty about the outcome of the trial means that families cannot plan concretely for their future (Fishman, 1983). Children cannot be assured of their parent's availability, and they may not understand court processes relating to their parent's trial, leaving them more bewildered by the events that surround them. During the trial, family members often hope for the best, which means that they may react to a custodial sentence with shock and disbelief (Fishman, 1983). Often, alternative care arrangements have not been made for children in advance (Richards et al., 1994).

The incarceration of a parent can be practically and emotionally devastating for families. One mother caring for a son whose father was imprisoned in England stated that

> for a child, losing a parent or carer to the prison system feels a little like bereavement without a body: visitation, letters and phone calls cannot replace a face at the breakfast table, or in the audience at a school play, the shared minutiae of daily life.

Although most incarcerated parents have some contact with their children, in the United States telephone communication can be limited by the high costs of calls, far higher than the costs of calls outside the prison ("Why Does It Cost So Much," 2013). Many families have their phones disconnected within 2 months of incarceration because of these costs (Braman, 2004). Visits can also be limited because of long distance and costly travel, because visiting times can overlap with school hours, and because sometimes incarcerated parents need documented proof of parenthood for the visit to take place (Hairston, 1998; Murray, 2005, 2007). Christian (2005) described the exhausting and costly 24-hour return journeys that some families make to visit their incarcerated relative in New York, with long bus rides and waits outside prison for very limited contact time. Typically, children wait for 30 to 60 minutes in a visitation area with little to do before being called for a 20-minute visit in a crowded, noisy room (Arditti, 2005). Some children cannot visit their incarcerated parent because they have no adult who will accompany them. Children's caregivers might not want to visit the person in prison, or they might think that children would be adversely affected by visiting their incarcerated parent (Arditti, Smock, & Parkman, 2005; Nesmith & Ruhland, 2008).

Moreover, prisons are generally not child-friendly places, and children can find visitation distressing (Hairston, 1998; Nesmith & Ruhland, 2008; Richards et al., 1994). To enter the visitation area, children might have to pass through a locked door and a metal detector, be sniffed by dogs, and sometimes be searched. Children can be scared of these procedures and the officers who enforce them. One female prisoner reported that "[the officers] are very insensitive to what kids go through and what it means to kids. They don't understand how threatening they are with their uniforms and such. My daughter is very intimidated by officers" (Richards et al., 1994, p. 34). In many prisons, inmates are restricted to their seat (bolted to the floor) during visitation, and sometimes physical contact between prisoners and visitors is prohibited. Comfort (2003, p. 101) argued that the way the prison imposes on families' lives is a form of "*secondary prisonization*, a weakened but still compelling version of the elaborate regulations, concentrated surveillance, and corporeal confinement governing the lives of ensnared felons." Although visitation conditions vary by prison and jurisdiction (Robertson, 2007), it seems that normal visitation environments do not facilitate the close contact that could reassure children of parental availability (Poehlmann, Dallaire, Loper, & Shear, 2010). In fact, in Poehlmann's (2005b) study of 54 children ages 2 through 7 years with incarcerated mothers, it appeared that children who visited their mother in prison had less secure attachment representations of their mother than children who did not visit.

Another difficulty for children during parental incarceration can be changes in caregiving arrangements and reduced quality of care (Kjellstrand & Eddy, 2011a, 2011b). Prisoners' partners can be left depressed, overworked, lonely, and struggling under the burdens of child care and providing support for an incarcerated partner (P. Morris, 1965; Richards et al., 1994). As one caregiver described, "it was just hard . . . taking care of them by myself . . . I went into a big depression" (Turanovic, Rodriguez, & Pratt, 2012, p. 94). According to Comfort (2007),

> the mental health consequences of incarceration, one may argue, extend far beyond the sentenced individual, permeating the daily life of relatives, friends, and even people with no firsthand knowledge of the inmate (for instance, in the case of an infant too young to yearn for a father behind bars, but who still suffers from the imprisonment if the caretaking mother becomes clinically depressed). (p. 282)

As such, supervision of children and attention to their needs might be impaired by the considerable stress that caregivers experience during parental incarceration.

Effects of strained caregiving on children can be exacerbated by loss of family income and home, school, and neighborhood moves after parental incarceration (Bocknek, Sanderson, & Britner, 2009; Murray, 2005; Sharp, Marcus-Mendoza, Bentley, Simpson, & Love, 1997/1998). Financial loss can be a significant challenge to many families when a parent is incarcerated (Arditti, Lambert-Shute, & Joest, 2003; Geller, Garfinkel, & Western, 2011). Prisoners receive meager pay for work, and even children who were not living with their parent prior to the incarceration are likely to experience loss of family income as a result of reduced child support payments (Geller et al., 2011).

Practical and emotional difficulties for families of prisoners can be compounded by social stigma (Braman, 2004; Condry, 2007; Geller et al., 2011). In some cases, the stigma of a relative's incarceration can lead to isolation, peer hostility, and rejection (Nesmith & Ruhland, 2008). For example, one boy with a father in prison in England described how "they bully me, say nasty things. I don't let them know I care, but sometimes I cry on the way home. The teachers don't know my Dad's in prison and I don't want to tell them" (Boswell, 2002, p. 19). The stigma associated with having a family member in prison is likely to explain why some families keep the incarceration secret from friends, neighbors, and work colleagues (Braman, 2004), which can push children into a "forced silence" about their situation, making it even more difficult for them to receive support and reconcile what is happening to them (Arditti, 2005; Bocknek et al., 2009; Myers, Smarsh, Amlund-Hagen, & Kennon, 1999, p. 20).

A related difficulty for some children is that often they are not given honest and developmentally sensitive explanations about their parent's incarceration. In P. Morris's (1965) classic study of 469 wives of English prisoners, 38% said that the children did not know that their father was in prison. In Sack and Seidler's (1978) study in the United States and in Shaw's (1987, 1992a) English study, about one third of children were told lies about the whereabouts of their incarcerated father, one third were told a fudged truth, and one third were told the whole truth. As one mother in an English study stated,

Because [their dad] is a lorry driver, I told them he was working because I didn't know what was going to happen, whether he was going to get convicted, and they accepted that, but they're not stupid. After a couple of months, they started crying saying they missed their dad, when's he coming home, and I thought then, I've got to tell them he ain't. They did get upset then. (Glover, 2009, p. 8)

Children may also worry about the conditions that their parent lives in, as revealed by one child in the study by Nesmith and Ruhland (2008): "You have to stay in a cave. . . . And they don't have no clothes to wear. They only have that orange stuff that they wear everyday. And they eat bad foods. And that's it. . . . [Prison is] bad because I think he screams and yells so that he can get out" (p. 1126). When children are confused or deceived about parental incarceration, even with good intention, they may not be able to understand why their parent is missing, and their absence may be more difficult to cope with (Bocknek et al., 2009; Bretherton, 1997; Kobak, 1999). In a study of 54 young children, those who were given emotionally open and developmentally appropriate information about their incarcerated mother's absence were more likely to have secure attachment representations of their current caregivers than other children (but they were not more likely to have secure attachment representations of their incarcerated mothers; Poehlmann, 2005b).

Moreover, families and children can experience additional difficulties when ex-prisoners return to the community. They may have adapted to new roles while their relative was inside (McDermott & King, 1992; P. Morris, 1965), and ex-prisoners themselves face significant barriers to successful reintegration, which may impose further burdens on the family. From the early 1990s, there have been large-scale cutbacks in prison vocational and education programs in the United States, as well as reduced parole supervision, which means that inmates are left more idle in prison and have fewer prospects for employment on release (Petersilia, 2003). These problems are exacerbated by stigma that reduces ex-prisoners' chances of finding and keeping employment and housing after leaving prison (Pager, Western, & Sugie, 2009; Petersilia, 2003; Uggen, Wakefield, & Western, 2005; Western, 2002; Western, Kling, & Weiman, 2001). Thus, when incarcerated parents do return to the community, they may struggle to provide positive support for their families and children.

In summary, parental crime, arrest, trial, incarceration, and return home can cause profound emotional and practical difficulties for families and children. Accordingly, parental incarceration might have long-lasting harmful effects on children's adjustment. The principal mechanisms that might account for these effects are attachment relations regarding parent–child separation and quality of care, social and economic strain in relation to reduced family income and other kinds of "social capital," reduced parental monitoring and involvement, and stigma and labeling processes. These various theoretical perspectives are discussed in Chapter 2.

DIFFERENT CIRCUMSTANCES UNDER WHICH PARENTAL INCARCERATION TAKES PLACE

Children experience parental incarceration under different circumstances, and their reactions might vary according to which parent is incarcerated, prior living arrangements, the quality of parent–child relationships before the incarceration, children's age at the time of incarceration, the nature and length of the sentence, alternative care arrangements, contact with the incarcerated parent, and how other family members cope with the event, as well as the wider social context (Hagan & Dinovitzer, 1999; E. I. Johnson & Waldfogel, 2004; Murray & Farrington, 2008a; Parke & Clarke-Stewart, 2003). As E. I. Johnson and Waldfogel (2004) put it,

> consider the situation of a child who has been living with a single mother and then, because of the mother's incarceration, is removed from her home and placed with a foster parent or other substitute caregiver. Consider a second child who has been living with both parents, whose father is incarcerated, and who continues to live with the mother. Consider a third child who had already been removed from her parents' home before the incarceration for reasons of abuse or neglect. Surely the impact of having a parent incarcerated will be different for each of these children. (p. 100)

These kinds of differences are important to bear in mind when considering average effects for children found in large studies. Next, we describe what is known about some of the different circumstances under which parents are incarcerated, based on results from national surveys of state and federal inmates in the United States.

Incarceration may have different effects on children depending on whether their father or mother is incarcerated and the prior level of involvement in childcare by the incarcerated parent. The vast majority of children (91%) with an incarcerated parent have a father in prison (Glaze & Maruschak, 2008). However, between 1991 and 2007, the number of children with mothers in prison more than doubled, up 131%, whereas the number of children with a father in prison grew by 77% (Glaze & Maruschak, 2008). Among state inmates, mothers (61%) are more likely than fathers (42%) to have been living with at least one of their children immediately before the incarceration (Glaze & Maruschak, 2008). Mothers are almost three times more likely (77%) than fathers (26%) to have provided most of the daily child care, although nearly two thirds (63%) of fathers report having shared the daily care. About half of incarcerated mothers and fathers provided the primary financial support for their children before incarceration (Glaze & Maruschak, 2008). Incarcerated mothers (37%) are much less likely than fathers (88%) to report that their child is currently cared for by the other parent (Glaze & Maruschak, 2008). Incarcerated mothers are more likely to report that other people are looking after their children: grandparents (45% mothers, 13% fathers), other relatives (23% mothers, 5% fathers), foster home or agency (11% mothers, 2% fathers), and friends or others (8% mothers, 2% fathers).

Of course, parental incarceration may have different effects on children depending on the nature of the offense for which their parent is incarcerated. In a 2004 survey, the most common current offense for inmate mothers was a drug offense (35%), and the most common offense for inmate fathers was a violent offense (45%; E. I. Johnson & Waldfogel, 2002). Most inmate fathers (67%) and mothers (53%) had been incarcerated previously at least once (E. I. Johnson & Waldfogel, 2002). Incarcerated parents are, like other prisoners, at increased risk of mental health problems and substance abuse. Of parents in state prison, 57% have a mental health problem, and 67% have a substance dependence or abuse problem (Glaze & Maruschak, 2008).

The extent of contact maintained between parents and children during parental incarceration may also affect how children cope with the event. Seventy percent of parents in state prison reported exchanging letters with their children during incarceration; 53% had spoken with their children on the telephone, and 42% had had a personal visit during the incarceration (this refers to contact with any child, of any age; Glaze & Maruschak, 2008). Incarcerated mothers are more likely (56%) than incarcerated fathers (39%) to report at least weekly contact with their children.

Children's experiences of parental incarceration are also likely to vary according to wider social contexts, notably nation penal policy and culture regarding prison environments, contact opportunities with families, and stigma associated with crime and punishment. We briefly describe the four countries in which research for this book was conducted (England, Sweden, the Netherlands, and the United States), with more detailed discussions of their settings in Chapters 4 through 8. Incarceration rates (per 100,000 population) are currently 153 in England and Wales, 78 in Sweden, 94 in the Netherlands, and 743 in the United States (Walmsley, 2011). In the 1960s when our European studies began, Sweden and the Netherlands had remarkably liberal and social-oriented penal policies. After the Second World War, visitors from England and the United States were impressed by the humane prison conditions in Sweden and the Netherlands and the possibilities of reforming English and American systems in their style (Marnell, 1972; Salomon, 1976; Ward, 1972). Opportunity for contact with families and children was extensive in terms of uncensored mail, telephone calls, family visits, and home leave (Downes, 1992b; Friday, 1976; Marnell, 1972;

N. Morris, 1966). Thus, children's experiences of parental incarceration—its length and their contact with incarcerated parents, experiences of stigma, loss of family income, and changes in caregivers—may all vary in important ways according to national context.

Three main contrasts between these countries stand out regarding possible differences in effects of parental incarceration on children's later life chances. First, there is the difference between the less family-friendly prison policies in England compared with its European counterparts in the 1950s–1960s. Second, there is the marked difference between the extent and conditions of incarceration in the United States compared with all the European countries, particularly with respect to the phenomena of "mass incarceration" in recent decades. Third, there was a marked shift in penal culture in the Netherlands, away from rehabilitation and toward increased punitivism, from the late 1970s onward (Downes, 1988, 1992b; Downes & Mitchel, 1982; Downes & van Swaaningen, 2007). This shift in Dutch penal culture produced a within-country change that also may have ramifications for children's experiences of parental incarceration.

In summary, potentially important differences exist between children whose mothers and fathers are incarcerated in terms of their living arrangements before the incarceration, offenses for which their parents are incarcerated, alternative care arrangements during parental incarceration, and possibilities for contact with incarcerated parents. There probably are many other circumstances that influence how children react to parental incarceration that have not been documented in large-scale prisoner surveys to date—for example, the quality of care given to children, levels of social support, and family economic resources. There may be significant variation in the effects of parental incarceration on children across these different situations and across national social and penal settings. Investigation of how context matters is important.

2

THEORETICAL FOUNDATIONS

What are the theoretical reasons for thinking that parental incarceration might have adverse effects on children's life chances? Several psychological and sociological theories suggest rather different ways in which the experience of parental incarceration might affect children's development and contribute to long-lasting adverse outcomes. In this chapter, we describe four such theories: attachment theory, strain theory, social learning theory, and stigma/labeling theory. Although these four theories suggest that parental incarceration probably causes adverse outcomes for children, another perspective suggests that this is not the case because children with incarcerated parents were already at risk even before their parent was incarcerated (following Hagan & Dinovitzer, 1999, we call this the *selection perspective*). Finally, parental incarceration could actually protect some children and reduce their chances of adverse outcomes by removing a disruptive or antisocial influence

http://dx.doi.org/10.1037/14377-003
Effects of Parental Incarceration on Children: Cross-National Comparative Studies, by J. Murray, C. C. J. H. Bijleveld, D. P. Farrington, and R. Loeber

from the home (Eddy & Reid, 2003; Hagan & Dinovitzer, 1999; Wildeman, 2010). Ecological theory emphasizes that social context may modify the effects of parental incarceration on children. We think that each of these theoretical perspectives has some plausibility and that empirical studies are needed to assess them. Research on the effects of parental divorce on children is much more advanced than research on parental incarceration, and prior to examining theories about parental incarceration, we draw on the divorce literature to examine themes that may be important to consider.

CHILDREN'S ADJUSTMENT TO PARENTAL DIVORCE: RELATED THEMES

Parental divorce and parental incarceration differ in important ways, but Richards (1992) highlighted the following potential similarities in children's experiences of the two events: sudden and often unexpected departure of a parent; loss of contact between children and their absent parent; reductions in family income; and caregivers becoming depressed, confused, and unable to cope. There are a number of excellent narrative and meta-analytic reviews of research on the effects of parental divorce on children (Amato, 1993, 2001; Amato & Keith, 1991a, 1991b; Emery, 1999; Hetherington & Stanley-Hagan, 1999; Rodgers & Pryor, 1998; Sigle-Rushton & McLanahan, 2004) from which we highlight a few key points that may help consider how parental incarceration might affect children's development and later life outcomes.

The evidence clearly shows that compared with children living in intact families, children with divorced parents are at increased risk for a broad range of adverse outcomes, both in the short and long term. In meta-analyses, Amato (2001; Amato & Keith, 1991a, 1991b) found that parental divorce was significantly associated with children's conduct problems, psychological difficulties, and poor academic achievement, as well as other adverse outcomes. However, effect sizes were generally small, and with a few exceptions, they were smallest among more methodologically sophisticated studies. Interestingly, effect sizes declined somewhat during the 1980s but then increased again in the 1990s. Clearly, social norms and contexts may influence how children react to parental divorce.

Early research on children's adjustment to parental divorce was guided by a deficit model and focused on family structure to explain the association with children's later outcomes. However, increasingly a life-course approach has been taken, emphasizing the importance of various family processes before, during, and after divorce (Hetherington & Stanley-Hagan, 1999). Amato (1993) reviewed five key theoretical perspectives that might explain the increased risk for adverse outcomes among children of divorce. First are theories suggesting that parental absence after divorce explains children's outcomes because of reduced emotional and practical resources available to the child. Research comparing children who experience parental divorce and children who experience parental death has been important in showing the limitation of this perspective: Despite the loss involved, parental death does not carry the same level of risk for children as parental divorce (Emery, 1999; Rodgers & Pryor, 1998). A second theoretical perspective emphasizes the adjustment of the remaining parent. Because divorce is stressful for parents, quality of child rearing might be impaired, and this could explain the risk for children associated with parental divorce. However, Amato (1993) concluded that evidence was inconclusive on this possible mechanism. Third, interparental conflict occurring before, during, and after divorce could be the principal factor explaining children's adjustment, and there is considerable empirical support for this point of view (Amato, 1993; Emery, 1999; Rodgers & Pryor, 1998). Fourth, economic hardship and loss of family income after parental divorce may be important for understanding children's outcomes, although low socioeconomic status also predicts divorce and therefore may act as a confounding variable.

The fifth and most general theoretical perspective about parental absence is the *life-stress perspective*, which emphasizes that multiple stressful events, including those considered previously and others such as house and school moves and new marriages of parents, are important for understanding children's postdivorce adjustment. Although there is general support for this notion, some research has suggested that it may not be the absolute number of stressful events that is important, but rather the particular characteristics of some types of change. Amato (1993) concluded that empirical evidence provided the strongest support for the interparental conflict model, but no single model can fully account for the empirical findings.

A few important considerations should be taken from the more extensive work on parental divorce when examining children's outcomes after parental incarceration. First, the parental divorce literature has indicated that a broad range of outcomes should be examined to delimit and specify the effects. Second, a simple deficit model (effects of parent–child separation) is unlikely to adequately explain the effects on children of either parental divorce or parental incarceration. Third, observed associations with child outcomes might be spurious (caused by factors preceding the divorce or the incarceration), and it is very important to consider factors associated with parental incarceration to try to identify its true effects on children. In the context of parental divorce, interparental conflict has emerged as a particularly important issue to consider. In the context of parental incarceration, parental crime and antisocial behavior are the most obvious background issues that must be considered. Finally, as in research on parental divorce, studies of parental incarceration should ideally include preincarceration measures of children's well-being to examine whether children's problem behaviors actually increase from before to after the event.

ATTACHMENT THEORY

"It's like you have a space in your heart missing" (Siegel, 2011, p. 136). Parental incarceration might cause behavioral and mental health problems for children because of the traumatic separation involved, highly restricted contact opportunities, inadequate explanations given to children, and the pressures on alternative caregivers. Attachment theory, which was developed by the psychologist John Bowlby (1969, 1973, 1980), proposes that secure attachment to a caregiver provides children with a safe base from which to explore their surroundings. On the basis of experiences with key adults, children develop expectations of their caregiver's availability and responsivity, described as *working models* that guide and shape future encounters in new settings (Main, Kaplan, & Cassidy, 1985). In contexts of affectionate and consistent caregiving, children may develop secure working models of attachment. However, insecure attachment can develop following a variety of environmental threats, and through time, insecurely attached children can develop angry and chaotic representations of relationships that may predispose to externalizing behavior problems (Vaughn, Byron, Sroufe, & Waters, 1979).

Several commentators have drawn on attachment theory to predict that parental incarceration may adversely affect children's experiences and expectations of relationships (Boswell & Wedge, 2002; E. I. Johnson & Waldfogel, 2004; Kampfner, 1995; Murray & Murray, 2010; Parke & Clarke-Stewart, 2003; Richards, 1992). Small-scale studies have shown that children show grief, confusion, and a raised level of anxiety during separation caused by parental incarceration (Bocknek, Sanderson, & Britner, 2009; Boswell & Wedge, 2002; Fritsch & Burkhead, 1981; Kampfner, 1995; Poehlmann, 2005b; Sack, 1977; Sack, Seidler, & Thomas, 1976; Skinner & Swartz, 1989).

> You just feel different emotions inside of you and it's just like you don't understand why . . . Is my mom comin' back? Why did she do what she did? . . . [Y]ou have to get attached to the person you're livin' with . . . and I mean it's not always easy to get comfortable with people. (Siegel, 2011, p. 134)

Parental incarceration might be particularly threatening to children's sense of attachment security because of traumas involved in parental arrest, the stigma and silence surrounding the parent's absence, and severe restriction on contact during incarceration (Bernstein, 2005; Poehlmann, 2005b; Shaw, 1987). Thus, children's trust in the accessibility and responsitivity of their parent may be reduced. In Poehlmann's (2005b) study, 63% of children had insecure attachment representations of their incarcerated mothers, and a similar proportion had insecure representations of their current caregivers. Notably, child insecure attachment was associated with unstable caregiving situations during the mothers' incarceration.

Although insecure attachment is not a disorder in itself (Rutter, 1995b; Sroufe, 2005), longitudinal research has shown modest associations between insecure attachment in childhood and later externalizing problems (Fearon, Bakermans-Kranenburg, Van Ijzendoorn, Lapsley, & Roisman, 2010) and internalizing problems (Warren, Huston, Egeland, & Sroufe, 1997). These associations may be stronger in the context of higher social risk (Belsky & Fearon, 2002), such as disadvantaged environments associated with parental incarceration.

Parental absence because of incarceration might be particularly difficult for children as it is often experienced as a form of *ambiguous loss*—loss in which family members become uncertain about who is in or out of the family and who has what roles (Bocknek et al., 2009). Children may have conflicting feelings about trying to understand why their parent is absent if it involves coming to terms with the fact that their parent committed a crime. Grief following such ambiguous loss is particularly hard to cope with and may cause estrangement. In one study of incarcerated young fathers, one man reported of his daughter: "She . . . feels I'm a kind of a stranger in a way. She has that look in her eyes like she's kind of confused whether she should come and hug me. She treats me like a stranger sometimes" (Nurse, 2002, p. 74).

STRAIN THEORY

According to strain theory, which developed in sociology (Agnew, 1992; Merton, 1938), economic hardship and stressful life events give rise to feelings of anger and frustration that cause children to attack or try to escape the source of adversity, use illegitimate means to achieve their goals, or abuse illicit drugs. Children with incarcerated parents are frequently exposed to economic hardship and other stressful events, which might affect them in this way. As the French prison reformer Charles Lucas wrote in 1836: "The same order that sends the head of the family to prison reduces each day the mother to destitution, the child to abandonment, the whole family to vagabondage and begging. It is in this that crime can take root" (Foucault, 1977, p. 268).

In her study of 67 children with arrested, jailed and imprisoned parents, Jane Siegel (2011) observed that

> the social worlds inhabited by the children I met indeed were largely demarcated by their socioeconomic position, which placed them in environments with meager resources and few of the advantages enjoyed by more affluent youth. The children were acutely aware of their families' economic hardships. When asked what they would wish for if they had one wish, the nearly universal response was related to the acquisition of wealth. (p. 73)

Although families often lose a source of income through parental incarceration (Travis & Waul, 2003a), they simultaneously bear extra costs of prison visits, letters, and telephone calls after incarceration. Family poverty significantly increased after incarceration, according to retrospective reports of family members in the study by Arditti, Lambert-Shute, and Joest (2003; see also Ferraro, Johnson, Jorgensen, & Bolton, 1983; McEvoy, O'Mahony, Horner, & Lyner, 1999; P. Morris, 1965; Richards et al., 1994). In the long term, incarceration might also cause fewer educational opportunities and unemployment for ex-prisoners, which may expose children to additional family economic strain. In the Fragile Families and Child Wellbeing Study, incarceration caused fathers to contribute significantly less to families on release partly because of reduced earnings of former inmates, but also because of their reduced likelihood of living together with their children—"the destabilizing effects of incarceration on family relationships place children at significant economic disadvantage" (Geller, Garfinkel, & Western, 2011, p. 25).

Theories of cumulative risk (Appleyard, Egeland, van Dulman, & Sroufe, 2005) have emphasized the particularly aversive effects on children when multiple strains co-occur. Mackintosh, Myers, and Kennon (2006) investigated experiences of multiple negative life events among 68 children with incarcerated mothers. Considering 16 stressors—including, for example, serious illness or injury of a family member, changing schools, or witnessing someone being beaten or shot—60% of children had experienced four or more stressors in the previous year (see also E. I. Johnson & Waldfogel, 2004; Murray & Farrington, 2005; Poehlmann, 2005a). Consistent with a model of cumulative risk, children who experienced more life stressors during maternal incarceration had more symptoms of internalizing and externalizing problems. Thus, parental incarceration might cause undesirable outcomes for children because of economic strain and cumulative negative life events.

SOCIAL LEARNING THEORY

Social learning theory in psychology (Bandura, Ross, & Ross, 1961) also might explain undesirable effects of parental incarceration on children. Parental incarceration can involve the loss of a positive parenting figure and cause a decrease in stable, quality parenting, such as child supervision and consistent discipline (Braman & Wood, 2003; Hagan & Dinovitzer, 1999). "Comin' back and forth to jail. . . . I'm never there. Like I'm in and out her life. . . . I never knew how to raise a child" (Siegel, 2011, p. 40). Poor supervision is one of the strongest predictors of children's own antisocial behavior (Loeber & Stouthamer-Loeber, 1986; C. A. Smith & Stern, 1997). Harsh and inconsistent discipline can contribute to antisocial behavior through a cycle of aversive reactions between caregivers and children (Patterson, 1995). Similar processes may be involved in the development of internalizing problems such as anxiety (Vasey & Ollendick, 2000). As such, the removal of a positive parenting figure by incarceration, and extra burdens on remaining caregivers, may reduce the quality of care that children receive and increase the likelihood of antisocial or mental health problems.

Another way in which social learning might explain undesirable child outcomes after parental incarceration is through children modeling their parent's antisocial or criminal behavior by observational learning (e.g., Sack, 1977). This might occur if children are made more aware of their parent's criminality when their parent is incarcerated. One mother with a son struggling to cope with his father's imprisonment said the following:

> When his father had been in prison for a few months, I went into my son's room to find that he had written, in big black marker pen on his wall, "bad dad" and next to it, in smaller writing his own name, prefixed also by the word "bad."

There have been no rigorous tests about modeling of parental antisocial behavior after parental incarceration, but it does seem likely that parental incarceration increases children's consciousness of parental criminality.

STIGMA AND LABELING THEORIES

Children's peers, teachers, and other community members may believe that "the apple doesn't fall far from the tree" (Phillips & Gates, 2011) and tend to view children of incarcerated parents as destined toward a life of crime (Braman, 2004). In his landmark work on stigma, Goffman (1963) stated that the stigma of incarceration might "be transmitted through lineages and equally contaminate all members of a family" (p. 14). Work since then has shown that experiencing stigma can contribute to the development of psychopathology (Hinshaw & Cicchetti, 2000) and is linked to social isolation; physical illness; academic underachievement; low social status; poverty; and reduced access to housing, education, and jobs among adults (Major & O'Brien, 2005). Parental incarceration might cause children to experience stigma, bullying, and teasing, which might cause an increase in their antisocial behavior or mental health problems (Boswell & Wedge, 2002; Braman, 2004; Braman & Wood, 2003; Sack, 1977; Sack et al., 1976; Zalba, 1964).

Children as young as 8 years old are aware of discrimination because of stereotypic beliefs (Brown & Bigler, 2005). In interviews with 127 caregivers of children with incarcerated fathers, some children "had to make new friends and now attend different school. They got verbal abuse from other children. . . . The pressure was so great that the children didn't want to go to school" (child's caregiver, quoted in Boswell & Wedge, 2002, p. 67). Although criminological research has clearly shown that intergenerational criminal behavior is only a probabilistic phenomenon, according to labeling theory, social expectations can produce self-fulfilling prophecies by cutting children off from conventional others and fostering a delinquent self-image (Becker, 1963; Farrington & Murray, 2014; Lemert, 1967). Sherman (1993) also theorized that criminal punishment that is perceived as unjust and stigmatizing leads to "defiance" and anger, which can result in increased antisocial behavior. Parental incarceration might cause children's antisocial behavior and mental health problems via stigma or defiance: "I hate cops to this day. Because I seen them take my dad away" (Giordano, 2010, p. 99).

It is also possible that there is official (police and court) bias against children of prisoners, making them more likely than other children to be arrested, prosecuted, or convicted for their crimes (Murray, Blokland, Theobald, & Farrington, 2014). One prediction derived from this is that parental incarceration might have stronger effects on official measures of offending (e.g., convictions) than on self-reported offending (which are not influenced by police or court bias).

SELECTION PERSPECTIVE

Despite the fact that families and children often experience multiple difficulties during a parent's incarceration, the incarceration itself might not cause long-term adverse outcomes for children. Even if parental incarceration does predict adverse outcomes for children, this might be because of preexisting disadvantage in children's lives, not because parental incarceration itself adds to that risk. Parental criminal behavior, parental mental illness, and other environmental influences before parental incarceration might explain children's outcomes, rather than the incarceration itself. Genetic transmission might also play an important role (Miller & Barnes, 2013; Rhee & Waldman, 2002). As one female prisoner in the study by Healey, Foley, and Walsh (2000, p. 23) said, "the damage was done before I came to prison" (see also DeHart & Altshuler, 2009).

Parental antisocial behavior is one of the strongest predictors of children's own offending (Lipsey & Derzon, 1998). Almost half (46%) of parents in state prisons reported that they were repeat offenders with either a current or past violent offense, and most (54%) were using drugs in the month prior to their offense (Mumola, 2000). Therefore, any association between parental incarceration and children's antisocial behavior might just reflect the effects of parental criminality and parental antisocial behavior on children. Prisoners are also much more likely to have mental health problems than the general population (James & Glaze, 2006; Singleton, Meltzer, Gatward, Coid, & Deasy, 1998). More than 20 studies have reported an association between parental mental illness and childhood anxiety (see the review by Klein & Pine, 2002, p. 497–499), and children of depressed parents have about three times the risk of developing major depression themselves compared with children of nondepressed parents (Weissman, Warner, Wickramaratne, Moreau, & Olfson, 1997; Weissman et al., 2006). Therefore, any association between parental incarceration and children's later mental health problems might just reflect the effects of parental mental ill health on children.

Prisoners are also much more likely than the general population to have experienced severe social and economic disadvantage. For example, in England and Wales, 52% of male prisoners and 71% of female prisoners had no educational qualifications, compared with 15% of the general population; 67% of prisoners were unemployed before incarceration, compared with 5% of the general population; and 72% of prisoners were on benefits before incarceration, compared with 14% of working-age people in the general population (Social Exclusion Unit, 2002).

In addition, many children of prisoners have already experienced separation from their parent before parental incarceration. As mentioned earlier, only 42% of fathers and 61% of mothers were living with their children before incarceration (Glaze & Maruschak, 2008). Wakefield and Wildeman (2014) carefully documented the numerous differences in family situations before fathers were incarcerated, highlighting domestic violence, drug and alcohol abuse, father absence, income, and social class backgrounds. As such, even if children of prisoners are at increased risk for adverse life outcomes, this might be the result of multiple, preexisting adversities (i.e., selection effects), rather than parental incarceration itself.

PROTECTIVE EFFECTS?

"If she wasn't locked up all the shit outta my house would have been sold to all these people round here [for drugs] and I'd end up fightin' and shootin' at 'em or, I don't know, shit would be a lot crazier" (Siegel, 2011, p. 143). Contrary to the idea that parental incarceration has adverse effects on children, or no effects at all above preexisting risk, another possibility is that it actually reduces children's exposure to risk and reduces children's own adjustment problems. Several researchers (Cunningham & Baker, 2003; Eddy & Reid, 2003; Hagan & Dinovitzer, 1999; Wildeman, 2010) have suggested that there might be beneficial effects of parental incarceration if parents have been particularly antisocial and disruptive in the home. Parental antisocial behavior is associated with increased risk of harsh discipline, parental conflict, child and spousal abuse, and substance misuse, which all predict adverse outcomes for children (Patterson, 1995; C. A. Smith & Farrington, 2004; Thornberry, Freeman-Gallant, Lizotte, Krohn, & Smith, 2003). Thus, incarceration of an antisocial parent could actually reduce chances of adverse outcomes for children by decreasing exposure to these adversities. As Hagan and Dinovitzer (1999, p. 123) stated, "There obviously are cases involving the incarceration of negligent, violent, and abusive parents where the incarceration of the parents benefits children by removing serious risks of current and future harm." For example, in a study of 469 English wives of prisoners in the early 1960s, Pauline Morris (1965) concluded that about 8.5% of the children showed improved behavior since their father's incarceration, including many victims of incest where the incarceration provided definite relief for the children.

Related evidence comes from a study of 1,100 English families with twins, in which a three-way relationship was investigated between paternal antisocial behavior, length of time living with the father, and children's conduct problems at age 5 years. Jaffee, Moffitt, Caspi, and Taylor (2003) found that when fathers were low to moderate in antisocial behavior, children had fewer conduct problems the longer they lived with their father. By contrast, when fathers were high in antisocial behavior, children had more conduct problems the longer they lived with their father. Thus, incarceration of an antisocial parent might sometimes reduce children's problem behavior.

ECOLOGICAL THEORY

Arditti (2005) usefully reviewed the importance of ecological theory for understanding how parental incarceration can impact on families and children (see also Poehlmann, Dallaire, Loper, & Shear, 2010). Ecological theory concerns how different levels of social context interact to affect development and is typically focused on four nested levels: microsystem, mesosystem, exosystem, and macrosystem (Bronfenbrenner, 1979). Briefly, the *microsystem* refers to the immediate context of the developing child, principally intimate family relationships and the critical role of parental functioning. The *mesosystem* involves interrelations between microsystems in which the child participates—for example, links between the home and school. The *exosystem* refers to other environmental settings in which the child may not participate, but which affect the functioning of the immediate microsystem—for example, institutional practices within the prison that affect the home life of the prisoners' family. Finally, the *macrosystem* refers to "institutional patterns and cultural prototypes such as economic, social, educational, legal, and political systems" (Arditti, 2005, p. 252). Critical to ecological theory, these contexts interact, and the developing human being can only be understood in relation to all levels and their interrelations.

In our cross-national comparisons in this book, we examine whether national contexts (macrosystems) affect how parental incarceration impacts children's life chances. As Bronfenbrenner (1979) argued, child development "can be enhanced by the adoption of public policies and practices that create additional settings and societal roles conducive to family life" (p. 7). Thus, variation in social and penal policies relevant to family and penal life may mean that the effects of parental incarceration differ between countries.

To summarize, various theoretical perspectives suggest different effects of parental incarceration on children, which might be harmful, nonexistent, protective, or highly dependent on context. We aim to contribute to understanding these issues in three principal ways in this book. First, we aim to separate as far as possible effects of incarceration itself from preexisting disadvantage in children's lives. Second, where harmful consequences are identified, we aim to test different possible mechanisms accounting for the effects. Third, we consider how the macrolevel context relates to the effects of parental incarceration on children in cross-national comparisons.

3

KEY QUESTIONS AND RESEARCH METHODS

Insights from several in-depth qualitative studies of the experiences of prisoners' families were discussed in Chapter 1. Our own research takes a different approach, being based on large-scale longitudinal surveys of hundreds and sometimes thousands of children. Ideally, in-depth qualitative and large-scale quantitative studies can complement each other to help understand mechanisms and long-term effects. Longitudinal surveys assess the same participants at multiple time points and can show how early life events shape and predict later life chances. In the studies in this book, children were assessed multiple times over several decades of life, from childhood to adulthood. Because our studies include both children with incarcerated parents and many hundreds of children whose parents were not incarcerated, by comparing them we can test whether parental incarceration predicts adverse outcomes for children in general population samples over several decades of life.

http://dx.doi.org/10.1037/14377-004
Effects of Parental Incarceration on Children: Cross-National Comparative Studies, by J. Murray,
C. C. J. H. Bijleveld, D. P. Farrington, and R. Loeber

We use a *risk factor* framework to organize the analyses in each study. The risk factor paradigm emerged in epidemiology and public health (Kazdin, Kraemer, Kessler, Kupfer, & Offord, 1997) and has now spread its way through psychiatry and developmental psychopathology (Cummings, Davies, & Campbell, 2000; Kazdin et al., 1997; Rutter & Sroufe, 2000) into criminology (Farrington, 1997, 2000a). Kraemer, Lowe, and Kupfer (2005) provided an excellent review of what risk factors are and how they should be studied. The key aims in risk factor research are to (a) identify variables that are associated with an outcome, which are called *risk factors*; (b) identify which risk factors have causal effects, which are called *causal risk factors*; (c) investigate the mechanisms by which risk factor effects are produced, called *mediators*; and (d) specify the conditions under which the effects are stronger or weaker, called *moderators*. These are the broad aims of our research on parental incarceration—to assess whether it is a risk factor, whether it is causal, what mediates its effects, and what moderates its effects. Next, we discuss the meaning of these questions in more detail and describe some of the analytic techniques we use to address them. As this is not a methodological textbook, we do not provide an exhaustive discussion of risk factor methodology, but instead draw the reader's attention to some key issues to provide better understanding of the studies that follow. For several excellent book-length discussions of some of these methodological issues, see Kraemer et al. (2005); Shadish, Cook, and Campbell (2002); Morgan and Winship (2007); and Academy of Medical Sciences (2007).

IS PARENTAL INCARCERATION A RISK FACTOR?

A risk factor is "a characteristic, experience, or event that, if present, is associated with an increase in the probability (risk) of a particular outcome over the base rate of the outcome in the general (unexposed) population" (Kazdin et al., 1997, p. 377). In this book, we investigate whether parental incarceration is a risk factor for several different adverse outcomes for children: their own antisocial behavior and crime in adulthood, poor educational outcomes, poor mental health, drug use, and poor marital outcomes. We investigate whether parental incarceration is a risk factor by comparing the probability of these outcomes between children with incarcerated parents and "control" children without incarcerated parents. If the probability of an outcome is higher among the parental incarceration group, this means that parental incarceration is a risk factor for that outcome. Note that parental incarceration might be a risk factor for one outcome (e.g., arrest) but not another outcome (e.g., depression). It might be a risk factor for an outcome measured at one point in time (e.g., arrest in adolescence) but not the same outcome measured at a different point in time (e.g., in adulthood).

In each study in this book, we examine whether parental incarceration is a risk factor using a statistic called the *odds ratio* (*OR*). The *OR* measures the size of the association between a risk factor and an outcome—between parental incarceration and a child's own arrest, for example. The *OR* is derived by first calculating the odds of the outcome for children with incarcerated parents and then for children without incarcerated parents (i.e., the control group). The odds of the outcome is equal to the number of children with the outcome divided by the number of children without the outcome. For example, among 60 children with incarcerated parents, if 20 are arrested and 40 are not arrested, the odds of arrest is 20 divided by $40 = 0.5$. The *OR* is calculated by dividing the odds for children with incarcerated parents by the odds for the comparison group children. An *OR* less than 1.0 indicates that children with incarcerated parents are less likely to have the outcome than other children. An *OR* larger than 1.0 shows an increased probability of the outcome for children with incarcerated parents. An *OR* of 2.0 or larger indicates relatively strong prediction (Cohen, 1996).

As well as estimating ORs for the risk associated with parental incarceration, we calculate p values and confidence intervals (CIs) to indicate the level of confidence that our sample results can be generalized to the populations from which the samples were drawn. Many results reported in this book are statistically significant ($p < .05$), but some are not. This implies that we cannot always be sure that our results would replicate if further similar studies were conducted using other samples from the same populations. It is important to bear in mind that nonsignificant results do not mean zero effects (as is sometimes implied in academic writing); they just mean that inferences beyond the study sample to the wider population cannot be made with confidence.

IS PARENTAL INCARCERATION A CAUSAL RISK FACTOR?

Even if parental incarceration is a risk factor and predicts adverse outcomes for children, this does not mean that it causes those outcomes for children. In other words, association should not be confused with causation. This is critically important for theory and for practice. If parental incarceration does not actually cause problems for children, reducing incarceration rates or implementing programs to reduce its harmful effects will be futile. Only if parental incarceration actually causes changes in children's outcomes might such prevention efforts yield the desired effects.

As described in the previous chapter, the difficult yet crucial issue for causal inference is that children with incarcerated parents, compared with other children in the general population, are likely to be differently exposed to other risk factors, even before their parent is incarcerated. Therefore, parental incarceration is likely to be a "marker" of risk, and any adverse outcomes associated with parental incarceration might be explained by other influences in children's lives (genetic, biological, psychological, social), not necessarily parental incarceration itself.

How can researchers evaluate whether a statistical association reflects a causal process? Randomized experiments are the best way to test a causal hypothesis (Aronson, Phoebe, Carlsmith, & Gonzales, 1990; Cook & Campbell, 1979; Cook & Shadish, 1994; Farrington, 2003b; Rezmovic, 1979; Shadish et al., 2002). Randomized experiments are often used in medicine and are increasingly used in behavioral sciences, particularly in education and psychology (Petrosino, Boruch, Farrington, Sherman, & Weisburd, 2003). In an experiment, people are randomly assigned to either a treatment condition (e.g., a new drug) or a control condition (e.g., a placebo). This random assignment assures that, on average, the two groups are equal in all ways except for the treatment being received. Therefore, if any differences are observed after the treatment, one can infer that the difference was an effect caused by the treatment itself.

Our studies of parental incarceration are not experimental, and tight causal conclusions cannot be drawn from them. All four studies described in this book, and indeed all studies that have ever been done on the effects of parental incarceration on children, are *observational* studies—that is, studies examining what naturally takes place for children after their parent is incarcerated. Researchers have not determined whether children's parents are incarcerated, and no random assignment took place in our studies. As such, it is a great challenge to estimate the causal effects of parental incarceration in these studies—to try to separate out the effects of parental incarceration itself from influences of other risk factors that are associated with parental incarceration.

A variety of nonexperimental methods can be used to investigate whether a risk factor has causal effects. We use a blend of different strategies in this book. No method is perfect; each has strengths and weaknesses, but particularly in combination, they help evaluate the plausibility of whether there are causal effects. A basic method to estimate causal effects of an event like parental incarceration is to compare children with incarcerated parents with a control group of children whose parents are not incarcerated, but who are as similar as possible in other respects. Outcome differences found when comparisioning the matched groups might have been caused by parental incarceration. Of course, the critical issue is how similar the control group is to the parental incarceration group. One control group we compare with is children with convicted but not incarcerated parents. Parental criminality, regardless of incarceration status, is predictive of children's own future offending. Thus, comparing children with incarcerated parents with children with convicted but not incarcerated parents begins to isolate the specific influence of parental incarceration. However, such a basic comparison does not account for the seriousness of the crime for which parents are convicted. Incarceration is used for punishment of more serious crimes (except the death penalty, in the United States). Therefore, while helping rule out alternative explanations, tight causal conclusions still cannot be drawn about incarceration effects on the basis of comparisons with children of convicted but not incarcerated parents.

Propensity score matching is another method used to consider causal effects. This enables researchers to create a matched control group similar to children with incarcerated parents on many background variables at once. First, a predicted probability (a *propensity score*) of having a parent incarcerated is calculated for all children in the study, based on measured background characteristics. In a second step, children with incarcerated parents are matched to children without incarcerated parents on the propensity score. The result is that the two groups of children, on average, will be similar on all background characteristics used to create the propensity score. Finally, the two groups are compared on outcome variables to estimate the "effects" of the parental incarceration experience. We use this method in our analysis of data from the Pittsburgh Youth Study (Chapter 7).

Another common approach for estimating causal effects is to use statistical models to control for background risk factors. Regression models are used to estimate how study participants' outcomes vary as a function of multiple background characteristics measured in the study. In this way, *statistical controls* are used to compare predicted outcomes for children with incarcerated parents with other children, while holding constant other variables in the model, such as family income or child IQ. We use regression models, as well as matched control groups, extensively in this book.

A limitation to the methods of traditional matching methods, propensity score matching, and regression models is that they only take account of *measured* background characteristics that might provide alternative explanations for the association between parental incarceration and a child outcome. Thus, these methods are only as good as the measures in the study. We believe that parental criminality and antisocial behavior is a key background variable that should be accounted for when estimating parental incarceration effects. Therefore, we always try to account for this variable, through matching or modeling, in our estimations of the effects of parental incarceration on children. The rich variety of other measures available in our studies allows us to rule out many other background influences as alternative explanations for the observed associations. But what if something important has not been measured?

Another method used to evaluate the validity of causal inference that does account for some unmeasured background characteristics is analysis of within-individual change. When changes in children's outcomes through time are examined—from before to after parental incarceration—essentially the child acts as his or her own control. Before parental incarceration the child is in the unexposed control condition, and after parental incarceration the same child enters the *treatment condition*. The strength of analyzing within-individual change is that it controls for all time-constant characteristics of the child and his or her environment, whether they are measured or unmeasured in the study. We combine analysis of change with propensity score matching using a large set of background risk factors in the Pittsburgh Youth Study (Chapter 7), providing probably the strongest test of causal effects of parental incarceration to date. One must note, however, that even analysis of within-individual change has its limitations: Any unmeasured time-varying variable that is associated with parental incarceration will not be accounted for in these tests.

A limitation of all these techniques is that because parents were generally already released from prison when children's outcomes were assessed in the studies in this book, the effects of the incarceration itself cannot be separated from any effects of the parent's return home from custody. Studies starting before parental incarceration, with regular assessments during and after incarceration, would be highly desirable for future research.

WHY DOES PARENTAL INCARCERATION CAUSE PROBLEMS FOR CHILDREN?

"A major task of risk-factor research is to identify more precisely what components contribute to the outcome and through what mechanisms of influence" (Kazdin et al., 1997, p. 395). Identifying mechanisms linking risk factors and outcomes is important for two reasons. First, knowledge of mechanisms makes causal inferences more plausible (Kazdin et al., 1997; Rutter, 1995a, 2003). Second, mechanisms are critical to understanding and preventing the effects of causal risk factors. Mechanisms can be investigated through analysis of "mediating" factors. Mediators are variables that occur after the risk factor and before the outcome, correlate with the risk factor, and reduce the association between the risk factor and the outcome in statistical models, although they do not necessarily cause the outcome (Kraemer, Kazdin, Offord, & Kuper, 2001). According to this definition, all causal mechanisms are reflected in mediators, but not all mediators represent causal mechanisms. The main method of identifying explanatory mediators is in statistical modeling.

Mediating mechanisms can also be examined by using carefully chosen comparison groups or contrasts in outcomes. For example, in the English Study (Chapter 4), we consider whether separation from a parent is the key mechanism explaining boys' outcomes after parental incarceration by using as comparison groups boys who are exposed to other types of separation, but not parental incarceration. We also consider whether official bias (police and court prejudice against children of incarcerated parents) might explain effects of parental incarceration by contrasting its effects on officially measured outcomes (conviction records) and self-reported criminal behavior; one would expect stronger effects on conviction records if official bias were an important mechanism explaining effects of parental incarceration.

We also compare children whose parents were incarcerated during childhood with children whose parents were incarcerated only before the child's birth. The significance of this contrast is that one group of children is directly exposed to parental incarceration (when it occurs during childhood), and the other group is not exposed (when it happened before birth), but the two groups share important characteristics—for both, their parents have a criminal history (serious enough to warrant incarceration) and their family backgrounds may be quite comparable. This comparison helps identify effects of environmental exposure to parental incarceration during childhood, over and above long-term effects of incarceration occurring before children's births.

HOW DO THE EFFECTS OF PARENTAL INCARCERATION DIFFER BY CIRCUMSTANCE AND CONTEXT?

Risk factors do not affect all individuals in the same way. Variation in risk-factor effects can be studied by testing for *moderators*, which may indicate resilience or vulnerability to risk. A moderator "is a variable that affects the direction and/or strength of the relation between an independent or predictor variable and a dependent or criterion variable" (Baron & Kenny, 1986, p. 1174). For example, if boys are more affected by parental imprisonment than girls, then children's sex moderates the relationship between parental imprisonment and child outcomes. Kraemer and colleagues (2001) specified that moderators should also precede the risk factor. This is because moderators should be clearly distinguished from mediators that occur after the risk factor and might be caused by the risk factor. Moderators can be tested by conducting analyses separately for different groups of children (e.g., boys and girls) and comparing effects between them or by using interaction terms in statistical models. In our cross-national comparative work in this book, we are essentially considering whether national context "moderates" the effects of parental incarceration on children.

In each study in this book, the analyses are thus organized around four key research issues: whether parental incarceration is associated with child outcomes (whether it is a risk factor), whether it causes those outcomes (whether it is a causal risk factor), how it might cause children's outcomes (what are the mediators), and under what conditions effects are stronger or weaker (what are the moderators). In Chapter 8, we consider whether effects of parental incarceration vary according to national context by bringing together matched results from four different countries, with varying social and penal contexts.

II

RECENT CROSS-NATIONAL STUDIES

4

FINDINGS FROM ENGLAND

In this chapter, we examine the possible effects of parental incarceration on boys' life outcomes in an English study—the Cambridge Study in Delinquent Development, hereafter called the *Cambridge Study*. The Cambridge Study is a prospective longitudinal survey of 411 males born in 1953 and followed from ages 8 to 48. It is a landmark study in criminology, having carefully documented the natural development of criminal behavior through time, and identified key risk factors for crime from childhood onwards. This study has provided some of the most compelling evidence that crime tends to run in families (Farrington, Barnes, & Lambert, 1996; Farrington, Coid, & Murray, 2009); that is, compared with the general population, offspring with criminal parents are more likely to commit crime themselves as adults.

http://dx.doi.org/10.1037/14377-005
Effects of Parental Incarceration on Children: Cross-National Comparative Studies, by J. Murray,
C. C. J. H. Bijleveld, D. P. Farrington, and R. Loeber

STUDY AIMS

The key question for our new research in the Cambridge Study was whether incarceration of parents put boys at risk for their own future offending. We also examined whether parental incarceration predicted several other outcomes in adulthood—poor educational attainment, drug use, poor mental health, and overall poor life success. The Cambridge Study is the only large English longitudinal study to have investigated the effects of parental incarceration on children. We tested the following hypotheses:

1. *Assuming that parental incarceration is a risk factor:* Separation because of parental incarceration predicts boys' antisocial behavior and other adverse outcomes through the life course.
2. *Assuming that parental incarceration is a risk marker for other childhood adversities:* Parental incarceration is associated with other childhood risk factors for antisocial behavior.
3. *Assuming that the experience of parental incarceration is a causal risk factor:* Separation because of parental incarceration during childhood predicts worse outcomes for boys than parental incarceration before the boys' birth.
4. *Assuming that parental incarceration is a causal risk factor:* Parental incarceration predicts boys' antisocial outcomes even after controlling for parental criminality and other childhood risk factors.
5. *Assuming the trauma of separation explains the risk:* Parental incarceration predicts similar antisocial outcomes compared with parent–child separation for other reasons.
6. *Assuming that official bias (labeling mechanisms) explain the risk:* Separation because of parental incarceration predicts official measures of crime more strongly than self-reported measures of crime.

THE ENGLISH CONTEXT

England is part of the United Kingdom and had a population of 53.5 million in 2012 (Office for National Statistics, 2013). The United Kingdom consists of England and Wales, Scotland, and Northern Ireland and is a relatively prosperous industrialized democracy and a constitutional monarchy. It has a system of common law, based on precedent. The minimum age of criminal responsibility in England and Wales is 10; persons ages 10 to 17 are tried separately from adults in special Youth Courts. Although the English incarceration rate is not nearly as high as in the United States, England has, since the early 1990s, begun to emulate American criminal justice politics and policies (Newburn, 2002; Tonry, 2004). Incarceration rates had been rising in England and Wales since the Second World War, but a famous announcement in 1993 by Michael Howard, the home secretary, that "prison works" preceded a sharp acceleration and then doubling of the incarceration rate until 2012. Today, England and Wales have 130 prisons and an incarceration rate of 153 per 100,000 population—high by Western European standards (International Centre for Prison Studies, 2013).

When boys in the Cambridge Study were growing up in the 1950s and 1960s, crime rates were relatively low in England (Rutter, Giller, & Hagell, 1998), and divorce rates were low compared with recent generations. Families generally lived in traditional nuclear structures in which the husband was the family breadwinner; one-parent families comprised just 6% of all British families with dependent children in 1961 (Hess, 1995). The local context in which the boys in the study lived was described as follows: "Although the neighborhood seemed dreary by middle-class standards, it was a traditional English working-class community, and in no way a ghetto area, or at least no more so than any other large conglomeration of 'council' property" (West, 1969, p. 24). The incidence of illegitimate births, rate of infant mortality, deaths from respiratory tuberculosis, and the proportion of the population in receipt of national assistance were similar to surrounding areas (West, 1969). Most of the males (357 or 87%) were White and of British origin. Their residency was relatively stable; 6 years after the study began, three quarters of the sample were still in the immediate neighborhood, and half of the sample were still at the same address (West, 1969).

Three considerations suggest that when boys in the Cambridge Study were growing up, the English social and penal contexts might have left families particularly vulnerable to the effects of parental incarceration. First, because divorce rates were low, most families were intact, and children would likely be living with both parents prior to parental incarceration (unlike in more recent years). In fact, out of all 23 boys in the Cambridge Study whose parents were incarcerated between birth and age 10, none of them had been permanently separated from either parent beforehand. Second, most incarcerated parents were fathers, and fathers were the main breadwinners in English families. There was also less social or economic support for single parents than is available now. Thus, families would likely be harder hit economically by the incarceration of a father in the 1950s–1960s compared with families in more recent decades.

Third, prison policies were not family friendly compared with those of other European countries, such as Sweden and the Netherlands, which had relatively mild penal climates. In 1959, only 3% of the sentenced population was granted home leave in England and Wales (Kelemenis, 1999), and there was (and still is) no practice of conjugal or private visiting. According to prison rules, entitlement of prisoners to a visit was strictly one in every 2 months, but with discretion for the prison governor to allow monthly visits (Martin & Webster, 1971). Stigma associated with a parent's incarceration might also have been particularly strong in England. Unlike in Sweden, there was no protection of the identity of adult English offenders, and media accounts of trials and convictions were common (Walker, 1980). This resonates with findings from recent research with children of prisoners in the United Kingdom and Sweden that indicate the following:

> There was greater potential for adverse repercussions where offenses were widely reported during court trials and resulting sentences, as in the UK. By contrast, Sweden operates a strict privacy policy which protects the identity of Swedish offenders from being revealed in media accounts of trials up to the point of conviction. (Jones & Wainaina-Wozna, 2013, p. 535)

And in England, it remains the case today that "it is rare for any reduction of sentence to be accorded on the ground that the offender's family will suffer, because this is regarded as a normal concomitant of imprisonment" (Ashworth, 2000, p. 154).

DESCRIPTION OF THE CAMBRIDGE STUDY

The study was originally directed by Donald J. West, and it has been directed since 1982 by David P. Farrington, who has worked on it since 1969. Procedures, measures, and major findings of the Cambridge Study have been reported in six books (Farrington, Piquero, & Jennings, 2013; Piquero, Farrington, & Blumstein, 2007; West, 1969, 1982; West & Farrington, 1973, 1977) and in many publications. The original aims of the study were to describe the development of delinquent and criminal behavior in inner-city males; to investigate how far it could be predicted in advance; and to explain why juvenile delinquency began, why it did or did not continue into adult crime, and why adult crime often ended as men reached their 20s. The study was not designed to test one particular theory about delinquency. Hence, information was a wide variety of theoretical constructs at different ages, including biological (e.g., heart rate, height, weight), psychological (e.g., intelligence, impulsivity), family (e.g., parental supervision and discipline), and social (e.g., poor housing, socioeconomic status) factors. Fortunately for our new analyses, when the study started (and today) parental criminality was considered important for understanding delinquent development. Therefore, parental criminal records, including details of prison terms, were searched as well as the boys' own criminal records in the Cambridge Study.

Boys were recruited for the study over a 2-year period between 1961 and 1963 (2 academic years were included to allow home visits and psychological tests with all boys). The sample was chosen by taking all the boys who were then ages 8 to 9 and on the registers of six state primary schools within a 1-mile radius of a research office that had been established in South London. All boys in these two main cohorts were born between September 1, 1952, and August 31, 1954. Hence, the most common year of birth of study males was 1953. As well as the 399 boys from these six schools, 12 boys from a local school for the educationally subnormal were included in the sample in an attempt to make it more representative of the population of boys living in the area. Thus, the boys were not a probability sample drawn from a population, but rather a complete population of boys of that age in state schools in that area at that time. There were 14 pairs of brothers among the 411 boys in the study; therefore, there were 397 different families in the study.

The study males were first interviewed and tested in their schools when they were about 8–9, 10–11, and 14–15 years old, by male or female psychologists. The males were interviewed in the research office at about 16, 18, and 21 years, and in their homes at about 25, 32, and 48 years. In addition to interviews and tests with the study males, interviews with their parents were carried out by female psychiatric social workers who visited their homes. These took place about once a year from when the boy was about 8 until he was 14 to 15 years and was in his last year of compulsory education. The primary informant was the mother, although many fathers were also seen.

The teachers completed questionnaires when the boys were about 8, 10, 12, and 14 years. Ratings were also obtained from the boys' peers when they were in the primary schools. Searches were carried out in the central Criminal Record Office in London to try to locate findings of guilt of the males; of their biological mothers, fathers, brothers, and sisters; of their wives and female partners; and of people who offended with them (their co-offenders). Appendix A gives details of the measures in the Cambridge Study used in this book.

ANALYTIC PLAN

To examine the risks associated with parental incarceration, we compared five mutually exclusive groups of boys according to whether they were separated from a parent and according to whether their parent was incarcerated. The experimental group consisted of 23 boys who experienced parental incarceration in their first 10 years of life. The first control group consisted of 227 boys who did not experience parent–child separation in their first 10 years and whose parents were not incarcerated at any point before the boys' 18th birthday. The second control group consisted of 77 boys whose parents were not incarcerated, but who experienced separation from either parent in their first 10 years because of hospitalization (of the boy or parent) or parental death. The third control group consisted of 61 boys whose parents were not incarcerated, but who experienced separation from either parent in their first 10 years for other reasons than hospitalization or death. The fourth control group consisted of 17 boys of parents who were incarcerated before the boys' birth, but not again between the boys' birth and 18th birthday. Six cases were excluded from these analyses because the boys' parents were first incarcerated between the boys' 11th and 18th birthdays, and we wanted the explanatory variable to be genuinely predictive of outcomes.

Ten antisocial outcomes of boys were compared according to whether boys had experienced parental incarceration or parent–child separation for other reasons. Given the small number of cases of parental incarceration in the study, individual outcomes were less important than average effects on boys' antisocial–delinquent behavior across the life course. T-tests were used to investigate average effects of parental incarceration on boys' antisocial outcomes through the life course, as well as pooling results on antisocial behavior measured at different times in meta-analyses. Outcomes used in meta-analyses are derived from the same subjects in the study, and component measures of antisocial personality include some of the same outcomes that are measured separately. Therefore, the assumption of independence of measurements is not fully met in these meta-analyses.

In the final analyses, logistic regression models were used to examine the effects of parental incarceration on boys' outcomes, controlling for effects of parental criminality and other childhood risk factors previously found to predict boys' antisocial–delinquent outcomes in the study. Because logistic regression excludes missing data case wise and we wanted to maximize the number of cases, we only included control variables that independently predicted boys' antisocial–delinquent outcomes. To identify which of the risk factors were independent predictors (and not just correlates) of antisocial and delinquent outcomes, the 12 age-10 risk factors were entered in a forward stepwise logistic regression model for each outcome variable. Those variables retained in the final step using $p = .05$ as the cutoff point were selected as control variables for the analyses of parental incarceration.

RESULTS

Results from the Cambridge Study are presented here, with respect to parental incarceration as a possible risk factor, risk marker, and causal risk factor. These terms are defined in Chapter 3, referring to whether parental incarceration predicts adverse outcomes (risk factor), whether it indicates exposure to other risk factors (risk marker), and whether it actually causes increased risk for children (causal risk factor).

Parental Incarceration as a Risk Factor

Separation because of parental incarceration was a strong predictor of boys' antisocial and delinquent outcomes through the life course (see Table 4.1). For example, 71% of boys who were separated because of parental incarceration during childhood (ages 0–10) had antisocial personalities at age 32, compared with only 19% of boys who were not separated and whose parents never went to prison. This can be expressed as an odds ratio (OR) of 10.6 (95% CI = 3.9, 28.9). As described in Chapter 3, an OR of 1 indicates no prediction and ORs > 1 indicate increased risk of an outcome in the parental incarceration group. ORs were large (> 2) for all three self-reported delinquent and violent outcomes in the Cambridge Study, as well as all four officially measured criminal outcomes. For example, compared with no separation from parents, ORs associated with parental incarceration in the first 10 years of life were 3.4 for self-reported violence at age 18 (CI = 1.3, 8.7) and 3.5 for self-reported delinquency at age 18 (CI = 1.4, 8.7). This suggested that the risk associated with parental incarceration was not conferred on boys by official bias. Parental incarceration predicted self-reported crime with similar strength as official measures of crime.

We compared the average number of antisocial–delinquent outcomes between boys separated because of parental incarceration (0–10) and controls. The number of antisocial–delinquent outcomes out of 10 was summed for each boy, and the average (mean) number for each group is shown in the bottom row of Table 4.1.[1] Boys who were separated because of parental incarceration had, on average, more antisocial–delinquent outcomes than all four control groups. The differences were significant in comparison with boys who did not experience separation from a parent ($t = 5.13$, $df = 24$, $p < .001$); boys separated by hospitalization or death ($t = 5.01$, $df = 30$, $p < .001$); boys who were separated for other reasons ($t = 2.41$, $df = 38$, $p = .021$); and boys who whose parents had been to prison only before the boy was born ($t = 2.41$, $df = 38$, $p = .029$). The weighted mean ORs[2] comparing the boys separated because of parental incarceration and all four control groups were also large and significant in all four comparisons (also shown in bottom row of Table 4.1). Therefore, with respect to all four comparison groups, parental

---

[1]Where there were missing values, these were prorated for the total score out of 10. No boy was missing on over half of the antisocial–delinquent outcomes (> 5).
[2]Calculated using inverse variance weighting (Lipsey & Wilson, 2001).

TABLE 4.1
Parental Incarceration as a Risk Factor for Boys' Antisocial Outcomes in England

Sons' outcomes (age)	History of parental incarceration					ORs			
	No prison (A) no separation % (n = 227)	No prison (B) separated[a] % (n = 77)	No prison (C) separated[b] % (n = 61)	Prison (D) prebirth % (n = 17)	Prison (E) 0–10 % (n = 23)	E/A	E/B	E/C	E/D
Antisocial personality (14)	15.9	15.6	32.8	11.8	60.9	8.3*	8.4*	3.2*	11.7*
Antisocial personality (18)	17.1	15.7	23.3	46.7	71.4	12.2*	13.4*	8.2*	2.9
Antisocial personality (32)	19.1	16.4	29.6	40.0	71.4	10.6*	12.7*	5.9*	3.8
Self-reported violence (18)	18.0	15.7	25.0	20.0	42.9	3.4*	4.0*	2.3	3.0
Self-reported delinquency (18)	24.0	18.6	20.0	40.0	52.4	3.5*	4.8*	4.4*	1.7
Self-reported delinquency (32)	18.7	17.8	25.9	40.0	52.4	4.8*	5.1*	3.1*	1.7
Convicted juvenile (10–16)	15.9	16.9	26.2	29.4	47.8	4.9*	4.5*	2.6	2.2
Convicted young adult (17–25)	21.9	20.8	34.4	52.9	65.2	6.7*	7.1*	3.6*	1.7
Convicted adult (26–40)	14.1	18.2	24.6	31.3	47.8	5.6*	4.1*	2.8*	2.0
Incarcerated by 40	8.1	9.2	11.5	6.3	30.4	4.9*	4.3*	3.4*	6.6
Mean number of outcomes (SD)	1.7 (2.3)	1.6 (2.4)	2.5 (2.9)	3.0 (2.4)	5.2 (3.2)	5.8*	6.1*	3.6*	2.6*
					Weighted mean OR				

Note. Column percentages. Some numbers on individual outcomes are lower than the total n because of missing cases. OR = odds ratio. From "Parental Imprisonment: Effects on Boys' Antisocial Behaviour and Delinquency Through the Life-Course," by J. Murray and D. P. Farrington, 2005, Journal of Child Psychology and Psychiatry, 46, p. 1273. Copyright 2005 by Wiley. Adapted with permission.
[a]Parent–son separation within first 10 years of son's life because of death or hospitalization. [b]Parent–son separation within first 10 years of son's life for reasons other than death/ hospitalization/incarceration.
*95% confidence interval does not include 1.

incarceration was a risk factor for antisocial–delinquent outcomes. The fact that parental incarceration during childhood predicted worse outcomes than parental incarceration before birth suggests that environmental exposure was important. The fact that separation because of parental incarceration predicted worse outcomes than other forms of parent–child separation suggested that the trauma of parent–child separation was not the primary environmental mechanism explaining antisocial outcomes among prisoners' children.

Table 4.2 shows summary results for some of the other outcomes measured in the study. Boys separated because of parental incarceration had worse educational performance (no exams), more drug use, more mental health problems (anxiety and depression measured on the General Health Questionnaire), and higher rates of "poor life success" up to age 48 compared with other boys in the study, although individual outcome measures were not always significant, perhaps because of small numbers.

Parental Incarceration as a Risk Marker

If parental incarceration is a risk marker, then boys experiencing parental incarceration should have more individual, parenting, and family risk factors for delinquency than other boys. This was indeed the case. The total number of childhood risk factors out of 12 was summed for each boy,[3] and the average number of risk factors for each group of boys is shown in the bottom row of Table 4.3. Boys separated because of parental incarceration had, on average, more risk factors than all four control groups. The differences were significant in comparison with boys who were not separated from a parent ($t = 6.56$, $df = 241$, $p < .001$); boys separated by hospitalization or death ($t = 4.27$, $df = 94$, $p < .001$); and boys separated for other reasons ($t = 3.18$, $df = 76$, $p = .002$). Although boys separated because of parental incarceration had more risk factors than boys whose parents were only incarcerated before the boys' birth, the difference was not quite significant ($t = 1.86$, $df = 34$, $p = .072$). The weighted mean ORs for the 12 risk factors were significant in all four comparisons (also shown in the last row of Table 4.3). Therefore, parental incarceration was associated with multiple childhood risk factors in the Cambridge Study.

Unsurprisingly, the number of parents' criminal convictions (regardless of sentences following them) was also higher for boys separated by parental incarceration ($M = 5.2$, $SD = 4.1$) than for other boys in the Cambridge Study. The differences were significant in comparison with boys who were not separated from their parents ($M = 0.2$, $SD = 0.6$; $t = 5.64$, $df = 20$, $p < .001$); boys separated because of hospitalization or death ($M = 0.5$,

---

[3]Cases missing up to half (6) the total number of risk factors were prorated.

TABLE 4.2

Parental Incarceration as a Risk Factor for Boys' Other Outcomes in England

Sons' outcomes (age)	History of parental incarceration					ORs			
	No prison (A) no separation % (n = 227)	No prison (B) separated[a] % (n = 77)	No prison (C) separated[b] % (n = 61)	Prison (D) prebirth % (n = 17)	Prison (E) 0–10 % (n = 23)	E/A	E/B	E/C	E/D
Education (18)	45.2	50.7	56.7	66.7	76.2	3.9*	3.1*	2.4	1.6
Drug use (48)	17.4	13.9	17.6	0.0	43.5	3.6*	4.8*	3.6*	10.8*[c]
Mental health (48)	15.1	14.5	17.0	14.3	36.4	3.2*	3.4*	2.8	3.4
Poor life success (48)	9.5	6.9	17.6	7.1	34.8	5.1*	7.1*	2.5	6.9

Note. Column percentages. Some numbers on individual outcomes are lower than the total *n* because of missing cases. *OR* = odds ratio. Data from Murray and Farrington (2008a).
[a]Parent–son separation within first 10 years of son's life because of death or hospitalization. [b]Parent–son separation within first 10 years of son's life for reasons other than death/hospitalization/incarceration. [c]For prison prebirth, the zero was replaced by 1 to calculate the odds ratio.
*95% confidence interval does not include 1.

TABLE 4.3
Parental Incarceration and Other Childhood Adversities in England

Risk factors (age 10)	History of parental incarceration					ORs			
	No prison (A) no separation % (n = 227)	No prison (B) separated[a] % (n = 77)	No prison (C) separated[b] % (n = 61)	Prison (D) prebirth % (n = 17)	Prison (E) 0–10 % (n = 23)	E/A	E/B	E/C	E/D
Low junior attainment	21.7	14.5	17.0	40.0	54.5	4.3*	7.1*	5.9*	1.8
Low IQ	19.4	24.7	26.2	52.9	52.2	4.5*	3.3*	3.1*	1.0
High daring	27.0	24.7	36.7	41.2	45.5	2.3	2.5	1.4	1.2
Poor supervision	9.0	26.8	24.6	20.0	42.9	7.5*	2.1	2.3	3.0
Poor attitude father	16.9	14.9	31.9	28.6	42.1	3.6*	4.1*	1.6	1.8
Poor attitude mother	27.6	35.2	20.0	13.3	30.0	1.1	0.8	1.7	2.8
Neurotic father	17.8	30.9	16.3	14.3	33.3	3.5*	1.7	2.6	3.0
Neurotic mother	27.7	34.2	21.8	33.3	15.8	0.7	0.5	0.7	0.4
Poor marital relations	16.3	22.9	41.7	28.6	36.8	3.0*	2.0	0.8	1.5
Large family size	15.7	28.0	17.5	40.0	61.9	8.7*	4.2*	7.6*	2.4
Low family SES	14.3	18.7	24.6	13.3	47.6	5.4*	4.0*	2.8	5.9*
Low family income	12.6	22.7	33.3	20.0	61.9	11.3*	5.5*	3.3*	6.5*
Mean number of risks (SD)	2.3 (2.1)	3.0 (2.3)	3.4 (2.4)	3.8 (2.7)	5.4 (2.4)	3.8*	2.2*	2.1*	1.6*
					Weighted mean OR				

Note. Column percentages. Numbers on individual outcomes might be lower than the total *n* because of missing cases and deleted brothers. *OR* = odds ratio. From "Parental Imprisonment: Effects on Boys' Antisocial Behaviour and Delinquency Through the Life-Course," by J. Murray and D. P. Farrington, 2005, *Journal of Child Psychology and Psychiatry, 46*, p. 1273. Copyright 2005 by Wiley. Reprinted with permission. [a]Parent–son separation within first 10 years of son's life for reasons other than death/hospitalization/incarceration. [b]Parent–son separation within first 10 years of son's life because of death or hospitalization.
*95% confidence interval does not include 1.

$SD = 1.0$; $t = 5.32$, $df = 21$, $p < .001$); and boys separated for other reasons ($M = 0.5$, $SD = 0.9$; $t = 5.27$, $df = 21$, $p < .001$). The number of parental convictions was higher for boys separated because of parental incarceration than for boys whose parents were only incarcerated before the boy's birth ($M = 3.6$, $SD = 2.1$), but the difference was not significant ($t = 1.58$, $df = 32$, $p = .124$).

The fact that separation because of parental incarceration was associated with higher rates of childhood adversities compared with all four control groups was consistent with the hypothesis that parental incarceration represents a risk marker for children's antisocial–delinquent outcomes.

Parental Incarceration as a Possible Causal Risk Factor

The results previously presented show that separation because of parental incarceration (0–10) was a risk factor for boys' antisocial–delinquent outcomes, but it was also associated with a number of other risk factors, meaning that other influences might account for the association between parental incarceration and boys' outcomes. Therefore, next we estimated the effect of separation because of parental incarceration on antisocial outcomes, controlling for the effects of parents' convictions and other childhood risk factors, using logistic regression. Boys separated because of parental incarceration were compared with each control group in turn. Figures 4.1–4.4 show ORs for these comparisons for each outcome, first controlling just for parental convictions and then controlling for parental convictions and other childhood risk factors. The other independently predictive risk factors that were controlled for in these analyses were junior attainment, IQ, daring (for the outcome of antisocial personality age 14); IQ, daring, mother's attitude, neurotic mother, family size (antisocial personality age 18); IQ, daring, family size (antisocial personality age 32); daring, family size (self-report violence 18); daring (self-reported delinquency age 18); none (self-reported delinquency age 32); IQ, daring, family size (convicted ages 10–16); junior attainment, daring, parental supervision, family size (convicted ages 17–25); daring, family size (convicted 26–40); and junior attainment, daring, family size, family SES (incarcerated by 40).

Separation because of parental incarceration still predicted worse outcomes for boys compared with no separation and no incarceration, even after controlling for parental convictions (see Figure 4.1). All three ORs for antisocial personality were large and significant, and the weighted mean of all 10 ORs was large (2.8) and significant (CI = 1.8, 4.4). This suggests that parental incarceration was not just a marker of parental criminality, but also conferred specific risk on children. When independently predictive risk factors were also added to the model, all three ORs for antisocial personality were still large (although not all significant). The weighted mean of all

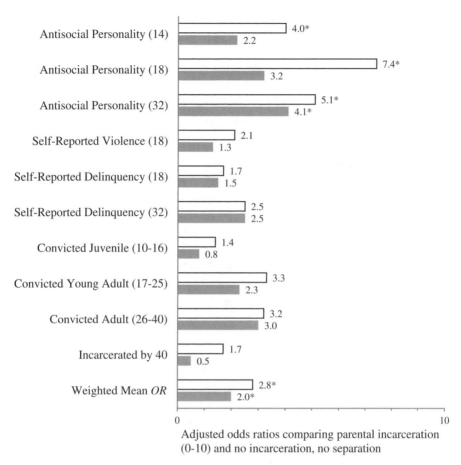

Figure 4.1. Effects of parental incarceration compared with no separation on boys' antisocial outcomes in England. *OR* = odds ratio. Data from Murray and Farrington (2009).
*95% confidence interval does not include 1.

10 ORs was large (2.0) and significant (CI = 1.2, 3.2). This suggests that parental incarceration might be a causal risk factor for boys in the Cambridge Study.

Parental incarceration also remained an independent predictor when compared with separation caused by hospitalization or death (see Figure 4.2). ORs for all outcomes in the study were large, even after controlling for parental convictions, and the weighted mean *OR* was large and significant (*OR* = 4.2; CI = 2.6, 6.5). Moreover, all three ORs for antisocial personality were still

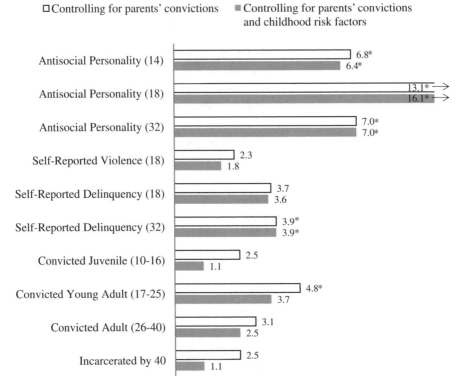

Antisocial Personality (14) — 6.8* / 6.4*
Antisocial Personality (18) — 13.1*→ / 16.1*→
Antisocial Personality (32) — 7.0* / 7.0*
Self-Reported Violence (18) — 2.3 / 1.8
Self-Reported Delinquency (18) — 3.7 / 3.6
Self-Reported Delinquency (32) — 3.9* / 3.9*
Convicted Juvenile (10-16) — 2.5 / 1.1
Convicted Young Adult (17-25) — 4.8* / 3.7
Convicted Adult (26-40) — 3.1 / 2.5
Incarcerated by 40 — 2.5 / 1.1
Weighted Mean *OR* — 4.2* / 3.3*

0   10
Adjusted odds ratios comparing parental incarceration
(0-10) with no incarceration, separation by
hospitalization or death

Figure 4.2. Effects of parental incarceration compared with separation through hospitalization or death on boys' antisocial outcomes in England. *OR* = odds ratio. Data from Murray and Farrington (2005).
*95% confidence interval does not include 1.

large after controlling for independently predictive risk factors, and the weighted mean *OR* was large (3.3) and significant (CI = 2.0, 5.4).

Boys separated because of parental incarceration also had worse outcomes than boys separated for other reasons (usually parental disharmony), even after controlling for parental convictions and other childhood risk factors (see Figure 4.3). After controlling for the number of parental convictions, all *OR*s for antisocial outcomes were large, and the weighted mean *OR*

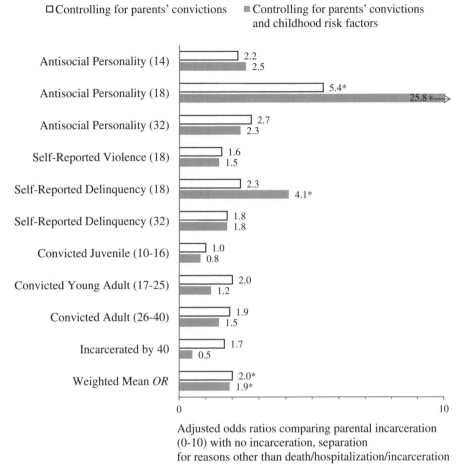

Legend:
☐ Controlling for parents' convictions   ■ Controlling for parents' convictions and childhood risk factors

Antisocial Personality (14)	2.2 / 2.5
Antisocial Personality (18)	5.4* / 25.8* →
Antisocial Personality (32)	2.7 / 2.3
Self-Reported Violence (18)	1.6 / 1.5
Self-Reported Delinquency (18)	2.3 / 4.1*
Self-Reported Delinquency (32)	1.8 / 1.8
Convicted Juvenile (10-16)	1.0 / 0.8
Convicted Young Adult (17-25)	2.0 / 1.2
Convicted Adult (26-40)	1.9 / 1.5
Incarcerated by 40	1.7 / 0.5
Weighted Mean OR	2.0* / 1.9*

Adjusted odds ratios comparing parental incarceration
(0-10) with no incarceration, separation
for reasons other than death/hospitalization/incarceration

Figure 4.3. Effects of parental incarceration compared with separation for other reasons on boys' antisocial outcomes in England. *OR* = odds ratio. Data from Murray and Farrington (2005).
*95% confidence interval does not include 1.

was large (2.0) and significant (CI = 1.1, 3.0). After adding independently predictive risk factors to the model, all three antisocial personality outcomes still had large ORs, and the weighted mean OR was fairly large (1.9) and just significant (CI = 1.1, 3.0). This increase in risk is impressive given that approximately half (48%) of boys separated for other reasons were in permanently disrupted homes at age 10, compared with only 13% of children who were separated because of parental incarceration.

Finally, boys who experienced parental incarceration during childhood were compared with boys whose parents only went to prison before the boys' birth (see Figure 4.4). Again, the timing of parental incarceration remained predictive, even after controlling for parental convictions. All three ORs for antisocial personality were large, and the weighted mean OR was large (2.6) and significant (CI = 1.6, 4.1). Moreover, after adding childhood risk factors to the model, the timing of parental incarceration remained strongly predictive (weighted mean OR = 2.6, CI = 1.5, 4.4). This shows that there was an effect of environmental exposure to parental incarceration over and above

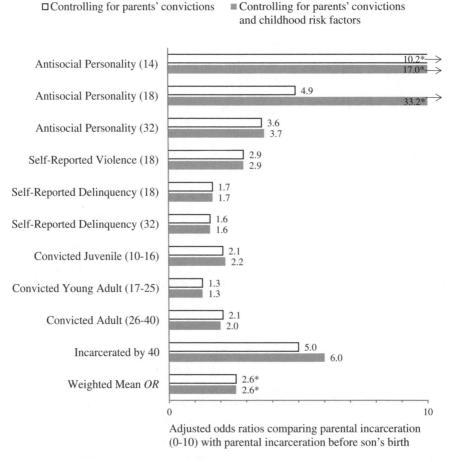

Figure 4.4. Effects of separation by parental incarceration compared with parental incarceration before birth on boys' antisocial outcomes in England. *OR* = odds ratio. Data from Murray and Farrington (2005).
*95% confidence interval does not include 1.

the influence of parental convictions, other childhood risk factors, and even parental incarceration before birth.

These results were consistent with the hypothesis that parental incarceration is a causal risk factor (although they do not prove that this is the case). One should note that the largest effect sizes tended to be for measures of antisocial personality in these analyses. Thus, the weighted mean effect sizes mainly reflect effects on antisocial personality measures.

In other analyses (Murray, Janson, & Farrington, 2007), we compared outcomes for boys whose parents were incarcerated for long periods (over 2 months when offspring were 0–19, $n = 17$, $M = 18.8$ months, $SD = 21.4$) and short periods (under 2 months, $n = 14$, $M = 1.1$ months, $SD = 0.36$) to test whether longer periods in custody had worse effects on sons. Of boys whose parents were in custody for less than 2 months, 7% became chronic offenders (7% of study males with the most number of convictions between 19 and 30), compared with 35% of boys whose parents were held in custody for over 2 months ($n = 31$, $\chi^2 = 3.48$, $df = 1$, $p = .062$). The trend was in the same direction for sons' young adult offending (50% and 77%, respectively, offended between ages 19 and 30), although the difference was not significant. However, the finding could be attributable to a selection effect, if longer sentence prisoners were more antisocial than shorter sentence prisoners.

DISCUSSION

In this chapter, data from the Cambridge Study were used to investigate the effects of parental incarceration on boys' antisocial behavior and other adverse outcomes through the life course in an English sample. Separation because of parental incarceration was a strong predictor of all outcomes in the study, even up to age 48. Therefore, separation because of parental incarceration represented a risk factor for those outcomes. We then investigated whether parental incarceration might also act as a risk marker. Separation because of parental incarceration was indeed associated with more childhood adversities than the four comparison conditions.

However, further analyses showed that parental incarceration was a possible causal risk factor for boys' antisocial outcomes. First, it was established that the timing of parental incarceration (whether it happened before or after the boy's birth) was predictive of sons' antisocial outcomes; therefore the actual experience of parental incarceration in childhood seemed to be important. Second, after statistically controlling for other associated childhood risks (including parental criminality), separation because of parental incarceration still predicted worse outcomes for boys. These results were consistent with the hypothesis that parental incarceration is a causal risk factor, although they did not prove that this is the case. Previously, we found similar patterns for mental health outcomes in the Cambridge Study, controlling for background risk factors (Murray & Farrington, 2008b).

Theory and qualitative research have suggested that parental incarceration might affect children because of separation, stigma, loss of family income, reduced quality of care, poor explanations given to children, and children modeling of their parents' behavior. The results in the Cambridge Study shed some light on these and other hypothesized mechanisms. Parental incarceration predicted worse outcomes for boys than separation for other reasons (usually disharmony). This shows that separation itself was not the key mechanism explaining boys' outcomes. Moreover, it seems unlikely that the additional effects of parental incarceration were explained by relationship breakdowns, changes in child care arrangements, or loss of family income, which also tend to follow parental separation and divorce (Rodgers & Pryor, 1998). The effects of parental incarceration could not be explained by legal bias toward prisoners' sons, because antisocial behaviors measured by self-reports, teachers' reports, and parents' reports were also predicted by parental incarceration. It was not possible to test the hypotheses that the effects of parental incarceration were mediated by stigma, modeling, or poor explanations given to the boys, and these possibilities warrant further research.

Several other possible interpretations of the results should be considered. First, with small numbers of boys with incarcerated parents, statistical conclusions are less reliable. Second, despite controlling for a wide range of individual, parenting, and family variables, it is still possible that prisoners' sons were deviant before their parents were incarcerated or that unmeasured environmental or genetic differences accounted for their outcomes. Third, the sequencing of parental incarceration and childhood risk factors was not known in this study. Therefore, it was not possible to test if risk factors were present before the incarceration or were acting as mediating factors after the incarceration. To the extent that parental incarceration actually caused these risk factors, the effects of parental incarceration were underestimated by controlling for childhood risk factors in this study.

Nevertheless, this is one of the first large prospective studies of the outcomes of children with incarcerated parents through the life course, and major strengths of the study are the high rate of retention among study males (94% of those still alive at age 32 were interviewed), the use of well-validated measures, and the control for a wide variety of possible confounds.

5

FINDINGS FROM SWEDEN

Chapter 4 showed that parental incarceration increased the risk for boys' antisocial behavior and crime in England. In this chapter, we examine whether parental incarceration has similar effects in a large Swedish study called *Project Metropolitan*. In many ways Project Metropolitan is well matched to the English study, including a large cohort of children born in 1953 (the same year of birth as the English boys) and followed in criminal records into adulthood. Parental criminal records were also collected in the Swedish study until children were age 19, permitting examination of children's own offending outcomes according to their parents' criminal and incarceration histories. Project Metropolitan differed from the English study in including girls as well as boys and in including an entire cohort of children living in the Stockholm area (thus not being focused on working-class families). This means that sex and class differences in the effects of parental incarceration on children could also be examined in Project Metropolitan.

http://dx.doi.org/10.1037/14377-006

STUDY AIMS

Four hypotheses about the effects of parental incarceration on children were tested in this Swedish study:

1. *Assuming that parental incarceration is a risk factor for children's crime:* Parental incarceration during childhood predicts children's crime in later life.
2. *Assuming that separation because of parental incarceration is a causal risk factor:* Parental incarceration during childhood predicts worse outcomes for children than parental incarceration only before children's births.
3. *Assuming that separation because of parental incarceration is a causal risk factor:* There is a dose–response relationship between the number of times a parent is incarcerated and the number of offenses committed by their children.
4. *Assuming that parental incarceration is a causal risk factor:* Parental incarceration during childhood predicts children's crime, even after controlling for parental criminality.

Additionally, three other questions were explored in this study:

1. Does parental incarceration during childhood have different effects on children depending on children's age at the time of parental incarceration (0–6 vs. 7–19)?
2. Does parental incarceration have different effects on boys and girls?
3. Does parental incarceration have different effects on children according to their family social class?

THE SWEDISH CONTEXT

Sweden is one of the Scandinavian countries in Northern Europe. Sweden is a constitutional monarchy with a parliamentary form of government—the monarch has only ceremonial functions. The population of Sweden was 9.5 million in 2012 (World Bank, 2013). Sweden has a system of civil law with a codified system. Its minimum age of criminal responsibility is 15 years, and only if there are special grounds can an offender below age 18 be sentenced to imprisonment. There are 82 prisons in Sweden (International Centre for Prison Studies, 2013). The incarceration rate is 55 per 100,000 people (Walmsley, 2011).

Particularly in the period after the Second World War, Sweden was one of the world's most egalitarian states, where "the basic needs of all Swedish citizens for a minimum income, job security, satisfactory health care, educational opportunities, adequate housing, good public transportation, and other social services have been met" (Ward, 1979, p. 152). Prison policies were also family friendly, emphasizing the importance of maintaining outside contacts via mail, phone calls, visits, and home leave (Friday, 1976):

> Unlike the United States, where visits are supervised and often physically inhibiting (e.g., wire mesh or glass separating visitor from inmate), Sweden has introduced unsupervised visits which means, in essence, conjugal visits for all categories of offenders from the beginning of the sentence. (Friday, 1976, p. 52)

Rates of pretrial incarceration in Sweden in the 1950s were very low. In 1957, 417 persons were remanded in custody in the whole of Sweden; of these, only 17 were still in custody at the end of the year (personal communication, Janson, 2005). Visiting the United States from Sweden, Gunnar Marnell (1972) noted that

> one system of holiday prisons [in Sweden], which make it possible for about 120 long-term prisoners a year to spend a month with their families in a village and in open cottages, seems to be quite unknown in this country and is always considered a bit shocking! (p. 756)

Incarceration might have been associated with less social stigma in Sweden because of the penal culture that was focused on reintegration and because many prisoners were incarcerated for drunk-driving offenses; consequently, middle-class people were more at risk of incarceration in Sweden.

Juvenile justice systems were very different in Sweden and England in the 1950s and 1960s. In Sweden, child welfare, rather than punishment, was the paramount concern in cases of child "delinquency" (Janson, 2004). Delinquency cases in Sweden were handled by an extensive system of Child Welfare Committees, each of which included a member of the poor-law board, a clergyman, a schoolteacher, and a physician. By contrast, in England until the late 1960s, juvenile delinquents were dealt with in courts that were similar to adult criminal courts (Bottoms, 2002).

STUDY DESCRIPTION

Project Metropolitan is a prospective, longitudinal study of 7,719 males and 7,398 females born in 1953 and registered as living in the Stockholm metropolitan area in November 1963. Of the 15,117 study members, 12,391 were registered as born in the Stockholm area and 2,726 as born elsewhere (about 400 were born abroad). Project Metropolitan has studied a wide range of social phenomena, including class structures, family socialization practices, educational achievement, mental disorders, and crime. Data were collected on the youths until 1985 from children's delivery records, the Swedish Child Welfare Committee (1953–1972), censuses in 1960 and 1963, school records, Draft Board data for boys, police records, and the criminal records of the heads of families. Project Metropolitan was directed by Carl-Gunnar Janson since its inception in 1964. Detailed descriptions of the data archive and major findings from Project Metropolitan have been published in over 40 research reports from the University of Stockholm, Department of Sociology (for overviews of Project Metropolitan, see Hodgins & Janson, 2002, Chapters 2 and 3; Janson, 2000). Appendix B provides details of the measures used in our analysis of parental incarceration in Project Metropolitan.

The Stockholm area in which Project Metropolitan is based was defined as Stockholm city and those surrounding municipalities that held more than 50% "agglomerated population," had less than one third of the population in agriculture, and had more than 15% of the economically active population commuting to the central city (Janson, 1984). The population of the study area was 1,130,000 in 1960.

Social registers, cross-referenced by ID numbers, were the primary source of data in Project Metropolitan. Official records in Sweden are extensive, old, and usefully coded by a unique identification (ID) number for each citizen. "For centuries parish records have been kept in Sweden on births, deaths, marriages, movings, and inhabitants" (Janson, 1984, p. 14). From 1947, nine-digit ID numbers constructed from birth dates have been allocated to all registered persons in Sweden, and most social registers have been organized according to these numbers. Children are allocated numbers when they are registered at the local population record office (which must be done by hospitals, midwives, or parents within 1 month of the child's birth). Immigrants and those who have not had numbers are also allocated ID numbers as required. Once a person is given a population registration number, she or he keeps it for life, unless it has to be corrected as a result of some error in numbering. The only information that can be inferred from the number alone is the date of birth and the sex of an individual.

Data gathering started in 1964 "with the listing of cohort members, their birth dates and addresses. Later, the family members, their birth dates, birth places, and assessed incomes were recorded" (Janson, 1984, p. 50). In November 1980, out of the original sample, 7,486 men and 7,126 women were still living in Sweden (or 97.0% and 96.3%, respectively; Janson, 1984). Following 1983, all data series were de-identified, and no further data were collected on cohort members.

Project Metropolitan represents a rare opportunity to study the effects of parental incarceration on children because criminal record data were collected on two generations and because the study is based on such a large sample, including several hundred prisoners' children.

ANALYTIC PLAN

First, we compared criminal outcomes of children according to whether their parents were incarcerated or convicted and received other sentences (e.g., fine, probation). Second, we investigated the effects of parental incarceration on different types of crime. Third, we tested whether a dose–response relationship existed between the extent of parental incarceration and the extent of children's offending. Fourth, we examined possible sex and class differences in the effects of parental incarceration. Fifth, using logistic regression, we examined the effects of parental incarceration on children's offending, controlling for parental criminality. Variables of parental criminality, parental incarceration, and child offending were mostly dichotomized for these analyses. As well as other advantages (Farrington & Loeber, 2000), using dichotomous variables in Project Metropolitan facilitated more direct comparison with results found in England.

RESULTS

Results from Project Metropolitan are presented here, addressing whether parental incarceration is a risk factor, its effects on different types of crime, possible variations by children's sex and social class, evidence for a dose–response relationship between parental incarceration and children's own criminal behavior, and results pertaining to whether parental incarceration is a causal risk factor.

Parental Incarceration as a Risk Factor for Children's Crime in Adulthood

During childhood (birth–age 19), 2% ($n = 283$) of the Project Metropolitan cohort had a parent incarcerated. Having a parent convicted predicted children's crime in Sweden (see Table 5.1). However, parental incarceration was generally a stronger predictor of children's crime than parental conviction without incarceration. For example, of children who had a parent incarcerated when they were ages 0 to 6, 25% offended between ages 19 and 30, compared with 18% of children who had a parent convicted (but not incarcerated). The odds ratios (ORs) for offending for these two groups were 2.4 (CI = 1.6, 3.5) for children of prisoners and 1.6 (CI = 1.1, 2.2) for children of

TABLE 5.1
Effects of Parental Criminality and Incarceration by Children's Age in Sweden

Children's offending	Before child was born			Child 0 to 6			Child 7 to 19		
	Parent not convicted	Parent convicted only	Parent convicted and incarcerated	Parent not convicted	Parent convicted only	Parent convicted and incarcerated	Parent not convicted	Parent convicted only	Parent convicted and incarcerated
N	14,217	590	310	14,757	223	137	14,516	393	208
Offended up to 19	7.1%	9.8%	12.3%	7.2%	11.7%	18.2%	xxx	xxx	xxx
Odds ratio (95% CI)	Reference group	1.4* (1.1, 1.9)	1.8* (1.3, 2.6)	Reference group	1.7* (1.1, 2.6)	2.9** (1.9, 4.5)			
Offended 19 to 30	11.9%	20.8%	19.4%	12.2%	17.9%	24.8%	12.0%	21.6%	26.0%
Odds ratio (95% CI)	Reference group	1.9** (1.6, 2.4)	1.8** (1.3, 2.4)	Reference group	1.6* (1.1, 2.2)	2.4** (1.6, 3.5)	Reference group	2.0** (1.6, 2.6)	2.6** (1.9, 3.5)
Chronic offender	5.2%	9.3%	9.4%	5.3%	9.4%	13.9%	5.0%	13.7%	14.9%
Odds ratio (95% CI)	Reference group	1.9** (1.4, 2.5)	1.9* (1.3, 2.8)	Reference group	1.9** (1.2, 2.9)	2.9** (1.8, 4.7)	Reference group	3.0** (2.2, 4.0)	3.3** (2.2, 4.9)

Note. Column percentages. Offended up to age 19 is not shown for parental convictions when children were ages 7 to 19 because we wanted explanatory variables to be genuinely predictive of outcomes. CI = confidence interval. From "Crime in Adult Offspring of Prisoners: A Cross-National Comparison of Two Longitudinal Samples," by J. Murray, C.-G. Janson, and D. P. Farrington, 2007, *Criminal Justice and Behavior, 34,* p. 139. Copyright 2007 by Sage. Reprinted with permission.
*p < .05. **p < .001.

convicted parents (using children of unconvicted parents as the comparison group), but the size of this difference is not statistically significant.[1] Parental incarceration (ages 0–6) also predicted higher rates of chronic offending than parental conviction (without incarceration). ORs for chronic offending were 2.9 (CI = 1.8, 4.7) for children of incarcerated parents and 1.9 (CI = 1.2, 2.9) for children of convicted parents (using children of unconvicted parents as the comparison group).

Parental incarceration during childhood was a slightly stronger predictor of children's offending than parental incarceration occurring before children's births. For example, the OR for children's offending (ages 19–30) was 2.4 (CI = 1.6, 3.5) for parental incarceration when children were ages 0 to 6, compared with 1.8 (CI = 1.3, 2.4) for parental incarceration only before children were born. However, the timing of parental incarceration during children's lives did not seem important. For children whose parents were incarcerated when they were ages 0 to 6, the OR for offending at ages 19 to 30 was 2.4 (CI = 1.6, 3.5), compared with 2.6 (CI = 1.9, 3.5) for children whose parents were incarcerated when they were ages 7 to 19. Because parental incarceration had similar effects in different periods during childhood, for the remainder of the analyses we examined the effects of parental incarceration occurring at any time during childhood (ages 0–19).

Parental Incarceration as a Risk Factor for Different Types of Crime

We explored whether parental incarceration (ages 0–19) predicted some types of crime better than others in Sweden. As Table 5.2 shows, parental incarceration predicted a range of crimes (from ages 19–30) with similar strength, reflecting the versatility of criminal careers (Farrington, 2004; D. J. Smith, 2002). For example, the OR associated with parental incarceration from 0 to 19 (compared with no parental incarceration) was 2.7 (CI = 1.7, 4.1) for violence and 3.0 (CI = 2.1, 4.2) for theft. This concurred with the findings from the Cambridge Study (in Chapter 4) that parental incarceration predicted self-reported general delinquency and violence with similar strength. ORs associated with parental incarceration for five other types of crime were 3.2 (CI = 2.1, 4.9) for fraud; 2.5 (CI = 1.7, 3.5) for traffic offenses; 2.7 (CI = 1.6, 4.6) for drug offenses; 1.6 (CI = 0.8, 3.2) for vandalism; and 2.3 (CI = 1.6, 3.4) for other offenses.

---

[1]We previously reported that this difference and some other differences between the size of ORs were significant in this study (Murray, Janson, & Farrington, 2007). Since then, we have learned of a better (and more conservative) test of the significance of differences between two ORs (Altman & Bland, 2003), which is the test we use throughout this book. This means that some previously reported "significant" differences are not significant. Nonetheless, the size of the differences in our samples—for example, here the difference OR of 2.6 compared with 1.6—is still accurate.

TABLE 5.2
Effects of Parental Incarceration on Different Types of Children's Crime in Sweden

	Parent never incarcerated	Parent incarcerated (when child was 0–19)
N	14,589	283
Violence	3.3%	8.5%
Odds ratio (95% CI)	2.7* (1.7, 4.1)	
Theft	5.7%	15.2%
Odds ratio (95% CI)	3.0* (2.1, 4.2)	
Fraud	2.9%	8.8%
Odds ratio (95% CI)	3.2* (2.1, 4.9)	
Vandalism	1.8%	2.8%
Odds ratio (95% CI)	1.6 (0.8, 3.2)	
Traffic	6.1%	13.8%
Odds ratio (95% CI)	2.5* (1.7, 3.5)	
Drugs	2.2%	5.7%
Odds ratio (95% CI)	2.7* (1.6, 4.6)	
Other	5.2%	11.3%
Odds ratio (95% CI)	2.3* (1.6, 3.4)	

Note. Column percentages. CI = confidence interval. Data from Murray, Janson, and Farrington (2007).
*$p < .001$.

Parental Incarceration and Children's Crime: A Dose–Response Relationship?

To investigate whether there was a dose–response relationship between parental incarceration and children's offending, we examined the mean number of offenses committed by children according to the number of times their parents had been incarcerated. In Sweden, the more times a child's parent was incarcerated (before children were age 19), the more offenses children were likely to commit between ages 19 to 30 (see Figure 5.1). The correlation coefficient between the number of times parents were incarcerated and the number of children's offenses was significant ($p < .001$) but small ($r = .06$). However, the different distributions of the two variables might have accounted for this low correlation coefficient (13,241 children had no criminal record, and 14,589 children had parents who had not been to prison). We calculated that the maximum possible r was .10 given these two distributions.[2] Dividing

---

[2]The maximum possible r was calculated by cross-tabulating the number of times parents were incarcerated and the number of offspring offenses. As many cases as possible (given the column and row totals) were placed on the diagonal of the table (0,0; 1,1; 2,2; etc.). Other cases were placed, unambiguously, as close to the diagonal as possible (given the remaining row and column totals). The maximum possible r was calculated from this distribution.

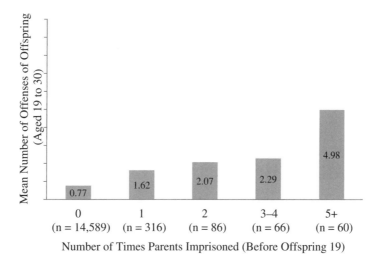

Figure 5.1. Dose–response relationship between parental incarceration and children's offending in Sweden. From "Crime in Adult Offspring of Prisoners: A Cross-National Comparison of Two Longitudinal Samples," by J. Murray, C.-G. Janson, and D. P. Farrington, 2007, *Criminal Justice and Behavior, 34*, p. 141. Copyright 2007 by Sage. Reprinted with permission.

the actual r (.06) by the maximum r (.10) gave an adjusted r value of .62, which perhaps better represents the nature of the dose–response relationship. Farrington and Loeber (1989) showed that in 2×2 tables, the actual r divided by the maximum possible r was mathematically identical to the widely accepted measure of strength of relationship termed *relative improvement over chance*.

Sex and Class Differences in the Effects of Parental Incarceration

We examined whether the effects of parental incarceration differed according to children's sex and social class in Sweden. In risk factor terms, children's sex and class might *moderate* the effects of parental incarceration. Parental incarceration predicted offending among females and males, and among working and middle- to upper-class children (see Figure 5.2). For the two social classes, the effects of incarceration were similar, and there was no significant difference between the relevant ORs. ORs for the effects of parental incarceration appeared somewhat larger for females than for males, although differences were not significant. It is possible that females appeared to be affected more by parental incarceration because of the low number of female offenders. Of females in Project Metropolitan, only 4% offended between ages 19 and 30, compared with 21% of males. Perhaps the few female offenders were more extreme cases and hence were more likely to

Offended 19 to 30

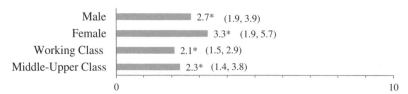

Odds ratios (95% CI) comparing children of incarcerated parents
(0-19) with children whose parents were never incarcerated

Chronic Offender

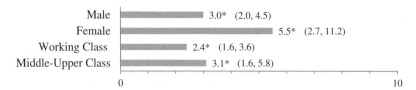

Odds ratios (95% CI) comparing children of incarcerated parents
(0-19) with children whose parents were never incarcerated

	Male	Female	Working Class	Middle-Upper Class
N parent incarcerated	136	147	180	103
N parent not incarcerated	7,459	7,130	5,806	8,783

Figure 5.2. Effects of parental incarceration by children's sex and class in Sweden.
CI = confidence interval. Data from Murray, Janson, and Farrington (2007).
*p < .001.

have deviant backgrounds (including incarcerated parents) than the more common male offenders—thereby producing a stronger association between parental incarceration and offending for females in this sample.

Parental Incarceration as a Possible Causal Risk Factor for Children's Adult Crime

Although parental incarceration predicted children's own offending, this might have been because incarcerated parents were highly criminal, not

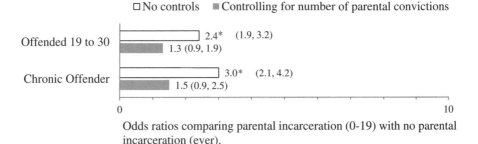

Odds ratios comparing parental incarceration (0-19) with no parental incarceration (ever).

Figure 5.3. Effects of parental incarceration before and after controlling for parental convictions in Sweden. Data from Murray, Janson, and Farrington (2007). *p < .001.

because incarceration had specific effects on children. We tested whether parental incarceration predicted children's offending independently of parents' convictions using logistic regression. The first model, including only parental incarceration (vs. no parental incarceration) as a predictor, showed a strong bivariate association with children's adult criminal behavior. ORs were large and highly significant (see Figure 5.3). However, once the number of parental convictions was controlled for as an indicator of the seriousness of parental criminality, the effects of parental incarceration reduced and became insignificant. These results suggest that parental incarceration was not a causal risk factor for children's offending. Rather, parental criminality explained the link between parental incarceration and children's offending in Sweden; parental incarceration did not contribute additional risk.[3]

Although the correlation between parental incarceration and parental convictions was high (r_{pb} = .68, p < .01), collinearity did not appear to bias these regression results. The maximum variance inflation factor value for the regression analyses presented in Figure 5.3 was 1.9 (well below the value of 10, which would be cause for concern). As we see in Chapter 8, analyzing these data on the basis of comparisons with a matched group of children whose parents were convicted but not incarcerated (instead of using regression models) produced similar conclusions.

___

[3]To examine the same issue, we also previously used step-wise logistic regression to examine whether parental incarceration or parental convictions, significantly improved model fit (Murray et al., 2007). In the first step, the number of parents' convictions was entered into the model, which significantly improved the prediction of children's offending. In the second step, the parental incarceration variable was entered into the model. Parental incarceration did *not* significantly improve the prediction of children's offending after parental convictions were controlled for. By contrast, when parental incarceration was entered into the model first, and then parental convictions, parental convictions significantly improved the prediction of children's offending.

DISCUSSION

In this study, the effects of parental incarceration on children's adult offending outcomes were examined using data on 15,117 children in Project Metropolitan in Sweden. The large numbers of prisoners' children in the sample ($n = 528$) was a great strength of this study and facilitated an examination of the effects of parental incarceration on different types of crime, sex and class differences in the effects of parental incarceration, and a dose–response relationship between parental incarceration and children's offending.

Parental incarceration was a risk factor for children's offending in Sweden. Moreover, there was a dose–response relationship between the number of times parents were incarcerated and the number of times children offended in adulthood. Parental incarceration predicted a range of different types of crime committed by children, reflecting the versatility of criminal careers. However, the most striking finding was that parental incarceration did not predict children's offending independently of parental criminality. This implied that parental incarceration was not a plausible causal risk factor in Sweden. Instead, the increased risk of offending among children with incarcerated parents in Sweden reflected only their parent's criminal behavior and associated factors—rather than effects of parental incarceration itself.

This conclusion was different from that drawn from analyses of the English study (Chapter 4). However, the samples had different compositions (only working-class males in England), and the timing of the predictor parental incarceration variable and the outcome crime variable for children was different between the two studies, which could have accounted for the different findings between the studies. Therefore, in previous work (Murray, Janson, & Farrington, 2007), we matched the English and Sweden studies as closely as possible by analyzing only working-class males in Sweden, comparing parental incarceration during childhood (0–18 years) to parental incarceration before birth and examining a similar outcome (any offense between 19 and 30 years) in both studies. These matched analyses also suggested that the effects of parental incarceration on a son's crime were stronger in England than in Sweden. Thus, there might be important differences in the effects of parental incarceration on children according to national context (see Chapter 8).

Although not based on quantified public surveys, visitors to Sweden in the 1960s were impressed by the sympathetic attitudes toward crime and punishment they found there. In 1966, Norval Morris (1966) noted that "the Swedish criminal or prisoner still remains a Swedish citizen meriting respect, continuing properly to enjoy a quite high standard of living and remaining part of the community" (p. 5; see also Friday, 1976; Janson & Wikström, 1995). As such, the weaker effects of parental incarceration in Sweden "may have been the result of shorter prison sentences in Sweden, more family-friendly prison policies, a welfare-oriented juvenile justice system, an extended social welfare system, and more sympathetic public attitudes towards crime and punishment" (Murray et al., 2007, p. 133).

6

FINDINGS FROM THE NETHERLANDS

This chapter examines the effects of parental incarceration on children in the Five Generation Study of Risk in the Netherlands,[1] which we refer to as *Transfive*. Transfive has traced five generations of Dutch families from around 1870 onwards in official criminal and social records. It is one of only two large longitudinal studies to have investigated the effects of parental incarceration on children in the Netherlands (see also van de Rakt, Murray, & Nieuwbeerta, 2012). Having found different effects of parental incarceration on children in England (see Chapter 4) and Sweden (Chapter 5), we were interested in how effects in the Netherlands would compare with these two countries. The Netherlands had a very mild penal climate in the mid-20th century and was well known for its culture of tolerance. In addition, we were interested in whether sex differences in effects of parental incarceration

[1]This chapter presents entirely new results from this study, and we are very grateful to Steve G. A. van de Weijer, Sytske Besemer, and Doreen Huschek for their help preparing these results.

http://dx.doi.org/10.1037/14377-007
Effects of Parental Incarceration on Children: Cross-National Comparative Studies, by J. Murray, C. C. J. H. Bijleveld, D. P. Farrington, and R. Loeber

would be found in Transfive, whether effects might differ between generations (as social and prison policies changed over time), and whether children's marital outcomes in adult life might be affected by childhood experiences of parental incarceration, as well as criminal behavior.

STUDY AIMS

Our investigation of the effects of parental incarceration on children in Transfive aimed to test the following key hypotheses:

1. *Assuming that parental incarceration is a risk factor:* Children of incarcerated parents are at greater risk of offending and poor marital outcomes than children of noncriminal parents.
2. *Assuming that parental incarceration is a causal risk factor:* Children of incarcerated parents are at greater risk of offending than children of criminal, but not incarcerated, parents.

Additionally, we investigated whether

1. findings differed for male and female children, and
2. findings differed by generation.

THE DUTCH CONTEXT

The Netherlands is a country in Western Europe with a population of 16.8 million in 2012 (World Bank, 2013). It is a constitutional monarchy and a parliamentary democracy, in which the monarch plays mainly a ceremonial role. The minimum age of criminal responsibility in the Netherlands is 12 years. After the Second World War, the incarceration rate dropped in the Netherlands and remained the lowest in Western Europe until the late 1980s, after which the Netherlands became increasingly punitive (Downes & van Swaaningen, 2007). Today, the Netherlands has 57 prisons (International Centre for Prison Studies, 2013) and an incarceration rate of 94 per 100,000 people (Walmsley, 2011). Between 1970 and 1996, the number of crimes recorded per 100,000 people ages 12 to 79 grew from 2,700 to 9,300 (Tak, 2001).

The Netherlands has been renowned for its "culture of tolerance," liberal social policies, and humane prison system and sentencing guidelines (Downes, 1988). For 3 to 4 decades after the Second World War, "Dutch penal policy became a byword for humane prison conditions and sparing use of custody" (Downes & van Swaaningen, 2007, p. 32), where resocialization was the primary goal. The 1953 Principles of Prison Administration Act reflected this aim: "While maintaining the nature of imprisonment, its implementation is to be subservient to the preparation of the prisoner for his return into free society" (Tak, 2001, sec. 26, p. 182). In the 1970s, "more than two-thirds of the Dutch (72 percent) agreed with the proposition that criminals should not be punished, but that they should be changed" (Buruma, 2007, p. 81). Possibilities for families to visit prisoners were more easily available in the Netherlands than in other countries (Downes, 1992a), and Dutch prisoners earned more money for their work in custody, which would have enabled increased contact with families. By contrast, England had much higher incarceration rates, longer sentences, and less humane prison conditions (Downes, 1992a).

Furthermore, the "generous welfare state" in the Netherlands assured "comprehensive social insurance over the life span" (Downes & van Swaaningen, 2007, p. 38), which might have resulted in more financial support for families of prisoners. Because of the focus on resocialization, social stigma for prisoners and their families might have been relatively low. However, by the early 1980s, an increase in the crime rate and some highly visible crimes led to a "heart of darkness" narrative in the mass media and "harsher punishment was reinvented as the only feasible means of social defence" (Downes & van Swaaningen, 2007, p. 44). As such, Dutch penal culture shifted to become much more similar to England than before, both countries being relatively punitive, recently having some of the highest incarceration rates in Western Europe (Downes, 1988; Tonry & Bijleveld, 2007). Thus, one might expect that effects of parental incarceration on children might have become stronger in more recent Dutch cohorts.

STUDY DESCRIPTION

Data collection in Transfive started with a group of 198 high-risk, working-class boys (Generation 2, referred to as G2) born around 1899 in the Netherlands. These adolescent males had all been sent to a reform school between 1911 and 1914. Some were sent there because they exhibited problem behavior or minor delinquency, most because their parents could not take proper care of them according to guardian organizations. Using genealogical and municipal records, all descendants of these men have been traced, with a retrieval rate of 100%. Figure 6.1 summarizes the generations included in the study. Conviction data were available for their children (G3), grandchildren (G4), and great-grandchildren (G5). All analyses in this chapter use data from generations G3–G5. On average, G3 were born in 1932, G4 in 1960, and G5 in 1986. At the point of data collection, the surviving G3 were approximately 76 years old, on average. The surviving G4 were about

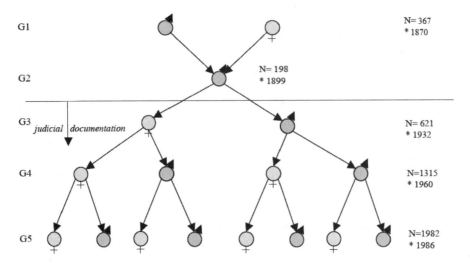

Figure 6.1. Five generations in the Transfive study, the Netherlands.
*average year of birth.

48 years old, and G5 were approximately 22 years old. Partners were also included in the dataset, which enabled analysis of transmission from both parents. Transfive is directed by Catrien Bijleveld. For more information, see Bijleveld and Wijkman (2009) and Bijleveld, Wijkman, and Stuifbergen (2007). The measures used in this study were taken from official criminal records and population registration systems (see Appendix C for details).

In Transfive, we do not know whether parents and children cohabited while children were growing up or when and to what extent children were separated from parents on parental divorce (which was relatively common) or on a court order by a civil judge ("ondertoezichtstelling" or OTS, which was likely less common).[2] This means that we are unable to compare effects of parental incarceration on children according to their prior living arrangements with their parents.

ANALYTIC PLAN

In this study we compared children with incarcerated parents with two comparison groups: children from similarly high-risk families but with non-offending parents (or parents who had only minor offenses) and children of

---

[2]Civil court orders occurred in cases where Child Welfare or Youth Care organizations deemed that parents were incapable of raising their children or the children had such problem behavior that either a guardian was appointed or they had to be raised outside the parental home.

seriously offending but not incarcerated parents. All analyses use data on children in generations G4 and G5. For children's offending outcomes, we include only children at least 18 years old at the last moment of data collection and investigate offending over their life course. For children's marital outcomes, we examine whether children ever got married and, if they did, whether they ever divorced, including only children at least 35 years old at the last point of data collection. For analyses of the outcome "never married" all children (≥ 35) were included in the analyses, but for analyses of divorce, we included only children who were ever married in the analyses.

We analyze our data using generalized estimating equations (GEE) in SPSS. For technical information on GEE, see Lipsitz, Laird, and Harrington (1991) and Zeger and Liang (1992). We use GEE because siblings in the study are clustered within families. With the clustering of siblings, conventional statistics are inappropriate because those do not take into account the dependencies between cluster members, that is, between siblings in the study. GEE, however, accounts for this within-cluster similarity. It weights each cluster of data according to its within-cluster correlation. When there is no correlation between family members, the cluster receives a weight of 1 and cluster members are treated as if they were independent subjects. Highly correlated siblings receive a lower weight. With these weights, GEE then analyzes the relationships between the variables. GEE can deal with a large number of small clusters and is therefore especially suited for our data with a large number of families, generally consisting of fewer than 10 members. In all our GEE analyses, we control for exposure time (the age of participants at time of data collection).

For comparing odds ratios (ORs) between cohorts or sexes, we use the ratio of odds ratios (ROR; Altman & Bland, 2003). The ROR shows the number of times greater or smaller the OR is for one group of children (e.g., boys) compared with another group (e.g., girls). The significance of the RORs we report here should, however, be taken as not more than indicative, as there is dependency between some of the samples compared; for example, those who appear as a son in one generation can also be a father in the next generation.

RESULTS

Among all children above age 18 in generations G4 and G5 in Transfive, 442 have at least one parent who was ever incarcerated. Among these children, 406 have a father who was ever incarcerated, 21 have a mother who was ever incarcerated, and 15 children have two parents who were ever incarcerated. About half (226 children) experienced parental incarceration between

TABLE 6.1

Mean Number of Offenses Committed by Children by Parental Criminality
and Incarceration in the Netherlands

	All offenses		Serious offenses		Violent offenses		Incarceration
	Mean	% convicted	Mean	% convicted	Mean	% convicted	% incarcerated
Classification of parents							
Noncriminal (n = 1,364)	1.25	27.6	0.65	13.9%	0.09	5.2	4.0
Criminal (n = 582)	2.55	38.8	1.38	23.5%	0.26	10.1	9.6
Incarcerated (n = 442)	3.99	47.1	2.18	32.4%	0.42	15.2	13.8

birth and their 18th birthday. Among these children, 211 experienced the incarceration of their father, 10 experienced incarceration of their mother, and five experienced the incarceration of both parents. Therefore, as in the English and Swedish studies (Chapters 4 and 5), parental incarceration was overwhelmingly a phenomenon of paternal incarceration in this Dutch study.

The sentences of the fathers in Transfive lasted, on average, 121.4 days, with a minimum of 1 day, a maximum of 2.7 years, and a median of 60.83 days. The sentences of the mothers lasted an average of 33.2 days, with a minimum of 2 days, a maximum of 212.9 days, and a median of 14 days. Sentences for men in the more recent cohort (i.e., the G4 fathers) were, on average, longer (126.7 days) than for the older cohort (the G3 fathers—107.6 days). The average sentences for women, on the other hand, were shorter for the more recent cohort (32.7 days) compared with the older cohort (37.5 days). These differences between generations were not statistically significant.

Parental Incarceration as a Risk Factor for Children's Adult Crime

To establish whether parental incarceration was a risk factor for crime in Transfive, we compared three groups of children: (a) children of "noncriminal parents," including parents who committed only minor offenses; (b) children of "criminal parents," those parents who committed serious offenses but were never incarcerated; and (c) children of incarcerated parents, those parents who were ever incarcerated.[3] Table 6.1 shows, for each of these groups of children, the percentage of children who committed any

---

[3]We also carried out the analyses by separating out the parents who never offended from those who committed minor offenses. As the findings were very similar, we combine these into one group.

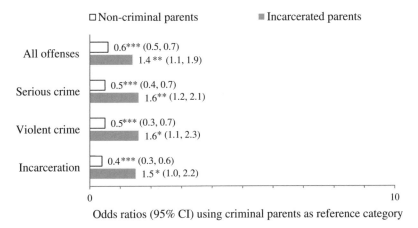

□ Non-criminal parents   ■ Incarcerated parents

All offenses   0.6*** (0.5, 0.7)
                   1.4** (1.1, 1.9)

Serious crime   0.5*** (0.4, 0.7)
                   1.6** (1.2, 2.1)

Violent crime   0.5*** (0.3, 0.7)
                   1.6* (1.1, 2.3)

Incarceration   0.4*** (0.3, 0.6)
                   1.5* (1.0, 2.2)

0   10

Odds ratios (95% CI) using criminal parents as reference category

Figure 6.2. GEE models of children's offending behavior by parental criminality and incarceration in the Netherlands. *N* = 2,388. GEE = generalized estimating equations. CI = confidence interval.
*p < .05. **p < .01. ***p < .001.

crime, serious crime, and violent crime, as well as the percentage of children who were incarcerated themselves.

Table 6.1 shows that children of incarcerated parents committed more offenses (including serious and violent offenses), were convicted more frequently, and were more often incarcerated than both children of noncriminal parents and children of criminal but not incarcerated parents. We ran GEE models to examine the significance of the increased risk of being convicted or incarcerated for children with a criminal parent compared with children of incarcerated parents and children with noncriminal parents. The ORs showing the increased risk estimated in these GEE models appear in Figure 6.2. As this figure shows, children of incarcerated parents were at increased risk of being convicted for any crime, serious crime, and violent crime, as well as being incarcerated themselves, compared with children of criminal parents.[4] Children of criminal parents were, in turn, at higher risk than children of noncriminal parents (indicated by ORs below 1 with children of criminal parents as the reference category).

---

[4]Table 6.1 and Figure 6.2 refer to parental crime and incarceration that could have taken place any time in the past, and some parents may have offended or been incarcerated before their children's birth, in which case these children were never exposed to the criminal behavior or the penitentiary sanction. We therefore also reran the analyses contrasting the following groups: (a) children whose parent(s) were incarcerated between the child's birth and 18th birthday, (b) children whose parents offended (but were not incarcerated) after the child's birth, and (c) children whose parents were neither convicted nor detained between when children were born and age 18. The findings comparing these groups were similar to those in Table 6.1 and Figure 6.2, except that the effects on violent offending were not significant, possibly because of smaller numbers in the analyses.

TABLE 6.2
Marital Outcomes of Children by Parental Criminality
and Incarceration in the Netherlands

	% never married	% divorced
Classification of parents		
Noncriminal (*n* = 724)	17.5	28.5
Criminal (*n* = 337)	19.3	35.3
Incarcerated (*n* = 286)	28.3	36.1

Parental Incarceration as a Risk Factor for Poor Marriage Outcomes

Table 6.2 compares children of noncriminal, criminal, and incarcerated parents on marital outcomes. Children with incarcerated parents were least likely to marry. However, when they did marry, both children of incarcerated parents and children of criminal parents were more likely than children with noncriminal parents to have a marriage ending in divorce. Again, these basic comparisons do not account for clustering within families. Therefore, next we also inspected ORs in GEE models, investigating whether children of incarcerated parents had poor marital outcomes. As shown in Figure 6.3, these GEE analyses show similar patterns to the crude results.

Sex Differences in the Effects of Parental Incarceration

Next, we investigated whether effects of parental incarceration were different for girls and boys. A constraining issue was that very few daughters offended compared with sons, and too few to examine how criminal outcomes for girls varied according to parental incarceration status. We

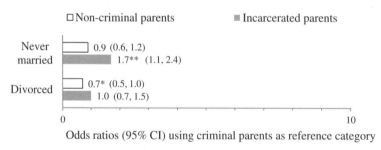

Odds ratios (95% CI) using criminal parents as reference category

Figure 6.3. GEE models of marital outcomes of children by parental criminality and incarceration in the Netherlands. *N* = 1,347. GEE = generalized estimating equations; CI = confidence interval.
*p < .05. ***p* < .01.

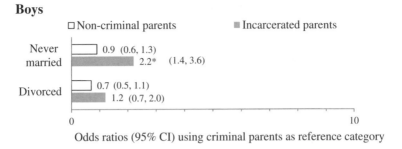

Boys

☐ Non-criminal parents   ■ Incarcerated parents

Never married
0.9 (0.6, 1.3)
2.2* (1.4, 3.6)

Divorced
0.7 (0.5, 1.1)
1.2 (0.7, 2.0)

0   10

Odds ratios (95% CI) using criminal parents as reference category

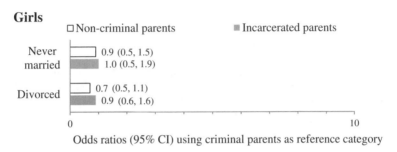

Girls

☐ Non-criminal parents   ■ Incarcerated parents

Never married
0.9 (0.5, 1.5)
1.0 (0.5, 1.9)

Divorced
0.7 (0.5, 1.1)
0.9 (0.6, 1.6)

0   10

Odds ratios (95% CI) using criminal parents as reference category

Figure 6.4. GEE models of marital outcomes of boys and girls by parental criminality and incarceration in the Netherlands. $N = 693$ boys; $N = 654$ girls. GEE = generalized estimating equations; CI = confidence interval. *$p < .01$.

therefore restricted our analyses of sex differences to marital outcomes. Figure 6.4 compares children's marital outcomes according to whether parents were noncriminal, criminal, or incarcerated, first for sons and then for daughters.

Sons of incarcerated parents married significantly less often than sons of criminal parents, although there were no significant differences in the chances of their marriages ending in divorce (Figure 6.4). These conclusions also held when restricting analyses to parental offending and incarceration taking place during the sons' childhood. For daughters, the findings appeared somewhat different. Daughters of incarcerated parents married at similar rates to daughters of criminal and noncriminal parents, and there was no significant difference in divorce rates among daughters according to parental incarceration status. The same patterns held if examining only parental offending and incarceration that occurred during their daughters' childhood. Although these results suggest that parental incarceration (compared with parental crime) had stronger effects on sons' chances of marrying than daughters' chances, this difference was not quite significant ($ROR_{never\ married} = 2.2$, CI = 1.0–5.0; $ROR_{divorce} = 1.2$, CI = 0.6–2.6).

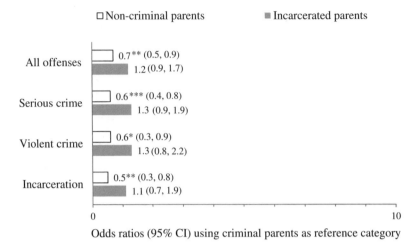

All offenses   0.7 ** (0.5, 0.9)
                1.2 (0.9, 1.7)

Serious crime   0.6 *** (0.4, 0.8)
                1.3 (0.9, 1.9)

Violent crime   0.6* (0.3, 0.9)
                1.3 (0.8, 2.2)

Incarceration   0.5** (0.3, 0.8)
                1.1 (0.7, 1.9)

0   10

Odds ratios (95% CI) using criminal parents as reference category

Figure 6.5. GEE models of G4 children's offending behavior by G3 parental criminality and incarceration in the Netherlands. *N* = 1,242. GEE = generalized estimating equations; CI = confidence interval.
*p < .05. **p < .01. ***p < .001.

Generational Differences in the Effects of Parental Incarceration

Last, we investigated whether the effects of parental incarceration differed across generations. We did this by separately analyzing effects of incarceration of G3 parents on G4 children and next the impact of incarceration of G4 parents on G5 children. This was done for offending outcomes and then for marriage outcomes. Again we present findings for parents who were ever incarcerated (although findings for children of parents who were incarcerated during their childhood were roughly similar, they had smaller numbers, which reduced statistical power).

Figure 6.5 and Figure 6.6 show how the effects of parental incarceration on children's own criminal offending differed across generations. G4 children of incarcerated G3 parents were not at significantly increased risk of offending or their own incarceration, compared with children of criminal parents (Figure 6.5). By contrast, G5 children of incarcerated G4 parents were at significantly increased risk for any offending, serious offending, violent offending, and their own incarceration (Figure 6.6). The ORs for these effects on G5 are around 2.0 or above, which indicates a substantial increase in risk. Using the ROR statistic, the size of the parental incarceration effects in G4–G5 were substantially greater than in G3–G4, but not statistically significantly different ($ROR_{\text{all offending}}$ = 1.4, CI = 0.8–2.3; $ROR_{\text{serious offending}}$ = 1.5, CI = 0.8–2.6; $ROR_{\text{violent offending}}$ = 1.5, CI = 0.7–3.1; $ROR_{\text{incarceration}}$ = 2.0, CI = 0.9–4.3).

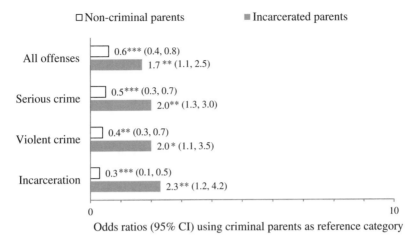

□ Non-criminal parents   ■ Incarcerated parents

All offenses
0.6*** (0.4, 0.8)
1.7** (1.1, 2.5)

Serious crime
0.5*** (0.3, 0.7)
2.0** (1.3, 3.0)

Violent crime
0.4** (0.3, 0.7)
2.0* (1.1, 3.5)

Incarceration
0.3*** (0.1, 0.5)
2.3** (1.2, 4.2)

0   10
Odds ratios (95% CI) using criminal parents as reference category

Figure 6.6. GEE models of G5 children's offending behavior by G4 parental criminality and incarceration in the Netherlands. *N* = 1,146. GEE = generalized estimating equations; CI = confidence interval.
*p < .05. ***p* < .01.

Figure 6.7 and Figure 6.8 show the relationships between parental incarceration and marital outcomes for different generations (G3–G4 and G4–G5). G4 children of incarcerated G3 parents were not at increased risk of poor marital outcomes compared with children of criminal parents (Figure 6.7). Although G5 children of incarcerated G4 parents had raised odds for never marrying and for divorcing, these results were not statistically significant (Figure 6.8). This lack of statistical significance may be because of small numbers[5] or because marriage became less common in more recent generations, or an event more frequently postponed until after age 35. Comparing effects of parental incarceration on marital outcomes between the generations, we again find that although there were differences in these samples ($ROR_{never\ married}$ = 1.5, CI = 0.5–4.3; $ROR_{divorce}$ = 1.9, CI = 0.5–6.6), the differences were not statistically significant.

DISCUSSION

Having found that parental incarceration was a strong risk factor for adverse outcomes in England (Chapter 4) but not a cause of children's offending in Sweden (Chapter 5), this study set out to examine the relationship

---

[5]Only 200 G5 children who had reached the age of 35 are analyzed in Figure 6.8. Among those, only 49 of the parents were ever incarcerated, and only 36 parents were criminal but not incarcerated. Moreover, the GEE models for divorce only include those 200 G5 children over 35 years old who were married (137 with noncriminal parents, 27 with criminal parents, 28 with incarcerated parents).

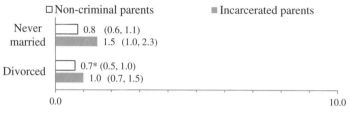

Figure 6.7. GEE models of G4 children's marital outcomes by G3 parental criminality and incarceration in the Netherlands. *N* = 1,147. GEE = generalized estimating equations; CI = confidence interval.
*p < .05.

between parental incarceration and children's outcomes in the Netherlands, focusing on children's own adult offending behavior and marital outcomes. In the Dutch study, children of incarcerated parents were at increased risk of adverse outcomes, regardless of whether they "experienced" parental incarceration during childhood or it occurred prior to their birth. They were more likely to commit crime and to be incarcerated themselves than were children of seriously criminal but not incarcerated parents. Children of incarcerated parents were also less likely to marry.

Our findings from England and Sweden can be most directly compared with the results from the G3–G4 generations in this Dutch study. The G4 Dutch children were born on average in 1960, a time when the Netherlands had a strong system of welfare support, extremely low incarceration rates, and a humane prison system focused on rehabilitation and resocialization, with good provision for prisoner–family contact. In this period, parental incarceration was not significantly associated with increased risk (in G4) for any offending, serious offending, violent offending, or children's own incarceration in the Netherlands. This was different from our findings in

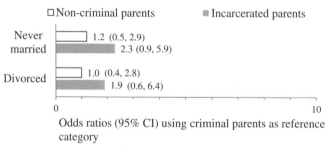

Figure 6.8. GEE models of G5 children's marital outcomes by G4 parental criminality and incarceration in the Netherlands. *N* = 200. GEE = generalized estimating equations; CI = confidence interval.

England but comparable to those in Sweden. In Chapter 8 we revisit these comparisons, bringing together results from each study in England, Sweden, the Netherlands, as well as the United States.

We were intrigued by results suggesting possible cohort differences in the effects of incarceration on children in the Netherlands. Although there were no effects of parental incarceration on offending in the older generation (G4), there were large and significant effects in the younger generation (G5). It should be noted that this difference between generations was not itself statistically significant, but our samples were nonetheless suggestive of increased impact of parental incarceration on children over time. One possible explanation is the general increase in punitivism from the late 1970s, reflected in longer prison sentences, higher rates of incarceration, and a change in penal focus from welfare and rehabilitation to a managerial climate focused on control (Downes & van Swaaningen, 2007).

Whereas the discourse in the 1970s talked of shielding lawbreakers from the state, perhaps reflecting a general Dutch "culture of tolerance" (Downes & Mitchel, 1982), by the 1990s this had changed to focusing on protection of victims from criminals (Boutellier, 2008). As Downes and van Swaaningen (2007) reported, between 1975 and 1985 "this ten-year period was to prove a decisive phase of transition from a liberal penal climate favoring decarceration to a more managerial penal climate oriented towards the expansion of imprisonment" (p. 43). In 1976, skepticism about the ability of prisons to reform prisoners led to a Prison Memorandum that "expressed the idea that the requirement to rehabilitate should be less ambitious than formerly was the case. The idea that the prisoner can be made into a better person does not seem very realistic" (Tweede Kamer, as cited in Tak, 2001, p. 259). Thus, in older cohorts, crime and incarceration might have been regarded as caused by wider social problems, but in an increasingly meritocratic society, with more upward (and downward) mobility, the culture may have become more individualistic and blameworthy, and parental incarceration may have come to carry greater stigma.

A second possible explanation for the weaker association between parental incarceration and adverse child outcomes in the older cohort is that detention of fathers was imposed for shorter periods and often for less serious offenses than in more recent cohorts in the Netherlands. Shorter sentences might have had fewer consequences for families and children, and incarceration might not have indicated such serious deviance in the older cohort. Until the beginning of the 1970s, a large proportion of the people who were incarcerated were sentenced for drunk driving and received relatively short sentences (Besemer, van der Geest, Murray, Bijleveld, & Farrington, 2011). The average sentence length in days increased from 61 in 1975 to 96 in 1980, 133 in 1985, and 152 in 1990 (Tak, 2001). Between 1978 and 1984, the number of long-term prison sentences of 1 year or more nearly doubled from 731 to 1440, an increase which was substantially related to increases in sentence length for drug offenses (de Haan, 1986). Previously, shorter sentences might have had fewer consequences for families and children. Another possible explanation is that because official crime rates, convictions, and incarceration rates increased substantially over the period of study, children in more recent cohorts may have been more likely to be convicted for their crimes and incarcerated following conviction—making our measures of official conviction and incarceration better indicators of criminal behavior in more recent periods.

7

FINDINGS FROM THE UNITED STATES

In previous chapters, we found that parental incarceration had adverse effects on children's outcomes in England but not in Sweden and only in later generations in the Netherlands. In this chapter, we examine the effects of parental incarceration on boys in the United States, in the *Pittsburgh Youth Study*. The Pittsburgh Youth Study is a longitudinal survey including two cohorts of some 1,000 boys in Pittsburgh, Pennsylvania recruited in the late 1980s. The study has a number of highly desirable features for investigating the effects of parental incarceration. Most notably, rich data have been collected every single year on the boys in the study and their social environments during adolescence. This provides a highly unusual uninterrupted time series with which to trace the development of youth problem behavior from before to after incidents of parental incarceration. Whereas preceding chapters have examined individual outcomes at particular points in time, in this chapter we use the annual repeated measures in the Pittsburgh Youth

http://dx.doi.org/10.1037/14377-008
Effects of Parental Incarceration on Children: Cross-National Comparative Studies, by J. Murray,
C. C. J. H. Bijleveld, D. P. Farrington, and R. Loeber

Study to examine changes in behavior through time, from before to after parents are incarcerated. The study also includes many high-risk youth, such that parental criminal justice contact is quite common in the study, and it includes a large number of both Black boys and White boys so that effects of parental incarceration can be compared across races.

STUDY AIMS

Our analyses of the effects of parental incarceration on boys in the Pittsburgh Youth Study aimed to test the following three main hypotheses in relation to boys' theft, marijuana use, depression, and academic performance:

1. *Assuming parental criminal justice contact and incarceration are risk factors:* Parental arrest, conviction, and incarceration all predict the development of youth problem behavior during adolescence.
2. *Assuming that parental incarceration is a causal risk factor:* Controlling for prior youth behavior, parental antisocial behavior, and other family and peer risk factors, parental incarceration still predicts increases in problem behavior.
3. *Assuming that the effects of parental incarceration are explained by changes in family and peer dynamics:* Effects of parental incarceration are reduced when controlling for family and peer processes after parental incarceration.

Additionally, we investigated the following two questions:

1. Does parental incarceration predict youth theft, marijuana use, depression, or academic performance differently?
2. Does prediction vary according to the age of the boy when the parent is incarcerated, the boy's race, which parent is incarcerated, whether the boy was living with the incarcerated parent, and levels of parental antisocial behavior?

THE UNITED STATES CONTEXT

The population of the United States was 313.9 million in 2012 (World Bank, 2013). There are 4,575 jails and prisons in the United States (International Centre for Prison Studies, 2013). As described in Chapter 1, the United States stands out as having both the largest prison population in the world and the highest rate of imprisonment (Walmsley, 2011). After half a century of fairly stable imprisonment rates (of about 110 per 100,000 population), from the late 1970s there was a dramatic rise (of about 6% annually), leading to an imprisonment rate of about 500 per 100,000 by 2010 (Blumstein, 2011). Including people held in local jails, the incarceration rate is about 750 per 100,000 (Blumstein, 2011). The main criminal justice changes behind these enormous increases in incarceration from the mid-1970s were both longer sentence lengths and more people being committed to prison. Most notably, there was a tenfold increase in the rate at which drug offenders were committed to custody between 1980 and 2001 (Blumstein & Beck, 2005). Currently, drug offenders account for more than 20% of state prisoners and 50% of federal prisoners (Blumstein, 2011). Increases in the incarceration rate were substantially greater for women than for men and for minorities compared with non-Hispanic Whites (Blumstein & Beck, 1999).

Considering prisons in the United States, Robert Johnson (2005) stated the following:

> In America, more people are sentenced to more time in more prisons under more anachronistic conditions than at any time in recent memory. Prisons dot the American landscape, often opened and operated at the expense of schools, roads and social services. Most of these prisons are overcrowded, underfunded and located in remote areas, far from the urban centres from which most prisoners originate. The sheer number of prisons and prisoners is remarkable, creating what amounts to a parallel penal universe, a world surrounded by fortress walls or barbed-wire barriers that hold offenders at bay, away from the world, locked in a grim suspended animation. (p. 258)

There are enormous racial disparities in incarceration rates in the United States. About 20% of Black people compared with about 3% of White people in their early 30s had ever spent time in prison in 1999 (Pettit & Western, 2004). Among Black men without a high school education, about 60% had been incarcerated (Pettit & Western, 2004). Incarceration is also highly concentrated in impoverished neighborhoods, which may reduce social cohesion, erode economic opportunities, increase stigma of particular neighborhoods, and possibly contribute to higher crime rates (Clear, 2007).

Public welfare support is decidedly weaker in the United States than in the European countries featured in this book, and from this perspective one might expect a larger impact of parental incarceration on families and children in the United States than in Europe. However, it is important to bear in mind that more children in the contemporary United States are raised by single parents, usually mothers, than children in the European studies in this book. Therefore, children in the United States are less likely to have been living with their father before paternal incarceration than in the European studies. Indeed, recent national prison surveys have shown that under half (42%) of fathers incarcerated in U.S. state prisons were living with at least one of their children immediately before incarceration (Glaze & Maruschak, 2008). Nonetheless, although most incarcerated fathers lived apart from their children prior to incarceration, the majority maintained contact through coresidence or visitation (Geller, 2013). As demonstrated in the Fragile Families and Child Wellbeing Study, coresidence and visitation in America have decreased as a consequence of paternal incarceration (Geller, 2013).

The distinction between jails and prisons is an important issue regarding incarceration effects in the United States (Massoglia & Warner, 2011). Local jails house people who are not necessarily convicted of a crime, and many individuals spend only a single night in jail, whereas prisons house people with a felony conviction who have considerably longer stays. Moreover, although there are jails in most counties in the United States, and people are often jailed relatively close to their families, prisons are often much farther from home. Although inmates disproportionately come from poor urban areas, prisons are typically located in rural areas, making visitation difficult (Massoglia & Warner, 2011). As such, effects of incarceration in jails and prisons, both on inmates and their families, may be quite different. In the current study, data were not available to distinguish between incarceration periods in prison and jail, which is a limitation.

STUDY DESCRIPTION

We used data on the youngest and oldest samples of the Pittsburgh Youth Study. For full details of the study—participant selection, methods, measures, and descriptive statistics—see Appendix D in this book, as well as Loeber, Farrington, Stouthamer-Loeber, and van Kammen (1998) and Loeber, Farrington, Stouthamer-Loeber, and White (2008). Briefly, boys attending the first and seventh grades in the public school system in inner-city Pittsburgh (about 1,000 in each grade) were randomly selected from schools across the city in 1987–1988. Among those families contacted, 85% of the boys and their parents agreed to participate. An initial screening assessment identified about 250 participants with disruptive behavior scores in the upper 30% of the distribution on the basis of caretaker, teacher, and self-reports. These and a roughly equivalent-sized random subset of the remaining 70% of boys were drawn at each grade level to form a complete follow-up sample. This selection process yielded 503 boys in the youngest sample and 506 in the oldest sample, roughly half high risk and half low risk. Of these 1,009 boys, 56% were Black and 41% were White (the remainder were Asian, of mixed race, or American Indian). Each sample was followed regularly, every 6 months initially (nine assessments for the youngest sample and six assessments for the oldest sample), and every year thereafter. They were assessed on a variety of measures quantifying the correlates, causes, and consequences of antisocial behavior. The youngest sample has been followed from ages 7 to 19, and the oldest sample has been followed from ages 13 to 25, and data collection is ongoing. In 18 follow-up assessments of the youngest cohort, participant retention rates have never fallen below 82% of the original cohort. By age 25, 83% of the oldest cohort was still participating. No consistent pattern of selective attrition of participants has been found in terms of initial risk status, race, substance use, or serious offending (Loeber et al., 2008).

ANALYTIC METHODS

The analyses of the effects of parental incarceration on boys in the Pittsburgh Youth Study were conducted in four stages. First, we examined the development of boys' behaviors according to whether their parents were arrested, convicted, or incarcerated at any time between the boy's birth and age 18. We examined separately youth theft, marijuana use, depression, and academic performance as outcomes. We did not include youth violence as an outcome because comprehensive data collection on youth violence did not start until some years after the start of the study for the youngest cohort.

Second, we tested whether the association between parental incarceration and youth theft varied according to the age of the boy at the time of parental incarceration, the race of the boy, which parent was incarcerated, whether the boy had been living with the parent, and the level of parental antisocial behavior. Third, we examined rates of youth theft in the years immediately after incidents of parental incarceration while controlling for preexisting risk factors and prior youth behavior. Fourth, we investigated parenting and peer factors as possible mediators of the effects of parental incarceration. All analyses were pooled across the youngest and oldest samples to increase statistical power. Because the oldest sample was studied from age 13, depiction of youth behaviors before age 13 come from the youngest sample only.

To represent the repeated annual data in the study, we graphically depict developmental trajectories of youth behavior and family and peer functioning in relation to parental criminal justice involvement. The plots are based on 3-year moving averages that smooth over random fluctuations in measurement response, except for the plots depicting changes from before to after parental incarceration, because yearly timing is more important for these results.

Generalized estimating equations (GEE; Liang & Zeger, 1986) were used in all tests of differences in youth behavior according to parental criminal justice system involvement. The repeated measures in the study result in observations that are clustered within individuals. As described in Chapter 6, GEE enables analyses of all such clustered observations simultaneously, weighting each subject's data according to within-subject correlations in the observations. We used a first-order autoregressive correlation structure in these analyses—assuming that observations nearer in time have higher correlations than observations further apart in time. GEE is a flexible modeling technique that can be used with count and skewed data as well as normally distributed data. We model theft, marijuana use, and depression using a negative binomial distribution because of their skewed and overdispersed distributions, and academic performance scores using a normal distribution.

A major challenge was to estimate effects of parental incarceration on youth behavior net of social selection processes. We used propensity score matching (Rosenbaum & Rubin, 1983) to select a control group of boys with similar behaviors and family and peer environments before parental incarceration occurred during the study. A *propensity score* is the probability, conditional on measured covariates, that an individual will be exposed to a "treatment," which in this case is parental incarceration. By matching treatment-exposed and unexposed individuals on propensity scores, two groups are created that should be "balanced" (similar) on all covariates included in the propensity score. Although propensity score matching is a powerful method, we must always be vigilant to the reality that, unlike randomization in an experiment, propensity score matching does not control for covariates that are not measured.

We used propensity score matching to estimate effects of parental incarceration occurring after the start of the study, from age 7 in the youngest sample and from age 13 in the oldest sample. If a boy experienced parental incarceration multiple times during the course of the study, the first incident was taken as the Index 1 for analysis. Note that these were not necessarily the first incidents of parental incarceration that the boy had ever experienced. About one quarter of boys whose parents were incarcerated during the study had parents who had also been incarcerated before the start of the study. Because we treated parental incarceration as an event, examining changes in behavior from before to after the index event, this is not too problematic. However, it does mean that our results pertain to effects of "any incident of parental incarceration" occurring during late childhood and adolescence and not specifically "first incidents" of parental incarceration (which might have stronger effects on children).

Given that boys experienced parental incarceration at different ages (between ages 7 and 18), we followed the methods of Nieuwbeerta, Nagin, and

Blokland (2009)[1] and used *risk set matching*, which is a form of propensity score matching appropriate for time varying treatments (Li, Propert, & Rosenbaum, 2001). Our aim in using risk set matching was to find, for each boy exposed to parental incarceration, controls with similar propensity scores in the year before parental incarceration. To achieve this, we first computed a propensity score for each year, for each boy, using a logistic hazard model based on both time-varying and time-constant covariates as described by Nieuwbeerta et al. (2009).[2] Then we matched each boy exposed to parental incarceration (e.g., a boy whose parent was incarcerated at age 12) to controls with similar propensity scores in the previous year (i.e., at age 11 in this example). We used nearest neighbor matching, without replacement, and with a caliper of .01 to identify three controls with propensity scores most similar to each boy with an incarcerated parent. Potential controls were all those in the sample who did not have a parent incarcerated between the start of the study and age 18. The calculation of propensity scores and matching algorithms were run separately on the youngest and oldest samples so that boys with incarcerated parents were always matched to controls in the same sample.

RESULTS

We start by describing the development of youth behavior in relation to parental arrest, conviction, and incarceration occurring any time from the boy's birth to age 18. Parental criminal justice system involvement was quite common in the Pittsburgh Youth Study: Between birth and age 18, 122 boys had a parent incarcerated, 84 had a parent convicted without incarceration, and 41 had a parent arrested without conviction or incarceration.

Parental Incarceration as a Risk Factor

Figure 7.1 shows the development of youth theft, marijuana use, depression, and academic performance according to whether parents were arrested, convicted, or incarcerated between the boy's birth and age 18.[3] A rise and fall in youth theft occurred during adolescence for all groups of boys in the study.

---

[1]We are grateful to these colleagues for sharing their SPSS syntax, which we used to run the matching procedures.

[2]Because propensity scores can only be computed with complete data on all covariates, if a boy was missing data on a covariate in one year, his score from an adjacent year was used in these analyses.

[3]Slightly more years of outcome data are analyzed for youth theft than for marijuana use and depression because data on drug use and depression stopped being collected at age 19 for the youngest sample, whereas criminal record data on youth theft continued to be collected. Academic performance was not assessed for most participants after the end of compulsory school attendance, so fewer years are analyzed for this outcome.

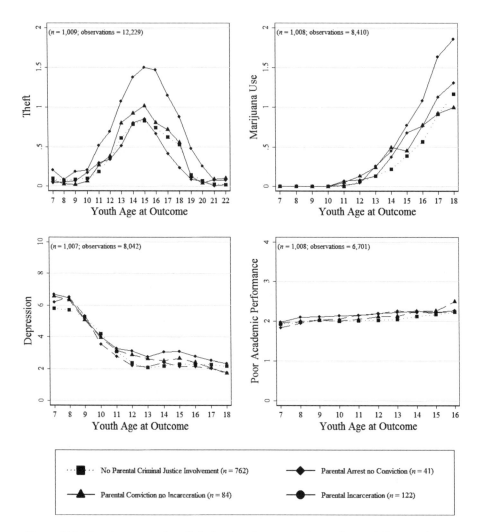

Figure 7.1. Development of youth behaviors by parental arrest, conviction, and incarceration during childhood (0–18 years) in the United States. From "Parental Involvement in the Criminal Justice System and the Development of Youth Theft, Depression, Marijuana Use, and Poor Academic Performance," by J. Murray, R. Loeber, and D. Pardini, 2012, *Criminology, 50*, p. 273. Copyright 2012 by Wiley. Reprinted with permission.

However, boys with incarcerated parents show higher levels of theft compared with their peers at almost every age. Similarly, marijuana use increased through adolescence for all groups of boys, but appears to have done so more rapidly for boys with incarcerated parents. Notably, the course of depression and poor academic performance appears almost identical regardless of whether boys' parents were arrested, convicted, or incarcerated.

To examine whether deeper penetration of parents into the criminal justice system has stronger effects on youth, we compared youth behavior scores (across the whole study period) between the following groups: (a) youth with arrested parents versus youth with no parental criminal justice contact, (b) youth with convicted parents versus youth with arrested parents, and (c) youth with incarcerated parents versus youth with convicted parents. The only significant difference was between parental incarceration and parental conviction. Youth with incarcerated parents had higher mean theft scores than youths with convicted parents ($M = 0.73$ and 0.47, respectively, $p < .05$). Youth with incarcerated parents also had higher mean marijuana use scores than boys of convicted parents, but the difference was not quite significant ($M = 0.70$ and 0.44, $p = .07$). We conclude that parental arrest and conviction are not associated with youth problem behaviors, but that parental incarceration is significantly associated with youth theft and nearly significantly associated with marijuana use.

Differences in the Effects of Parental Incarceration

We investigated whether the association between parental incarceration and youth theft (the strongest association) differed according to the timing of parental incarceration, the youth's race, which parent was incarcerated, whether the youth was living with a parent in the year before the incarceration, and levels of parental antisocial behavior.

Figure 7.2 plots the development of youth theft according to the timing of parental incarceration: before the boy's birth and at ages 0–6, 7–12, and 13–18 years. The groups depicted in the graph are mutually exclusive (41 boys whose parents were incarcerated in multiple time periods are not included). Boys whose parents were incarcerated before the boy's birth had similar mean theft scores (0.45) to boys whose parents were never incarcerated (0.42, $p = .81$). The graph shows that their trajectories of theft are almost identical. Boys whose parents were incarcerated during the boy's lifetime (birth to age 18) had significantly higher theft scores (0.78) than boys whose parents were incarcerated before the boy's birth (0.45, $p = .04$). However, theft scores did not differ significantly according to the timing of parental incarceration during the boy's childhood to age 18 (at ages 0–6, 7–12, and 13–18).

Seventy-seven Black youth and 42 White youth had a parent incarcerated between birth and age 18 (three youth of other races had incarcerated parents but are excluded from this specific analysis). Figure 7.3 plots the frequency of theft for Black youth and White youth separately, according to whether they had parents incarcerated. Among youth who did not have a parent incarcerated, there was almost no difference in mean theft scores between Black youth (0.44) and White youth (0.41, $p = .56$). However, among youth

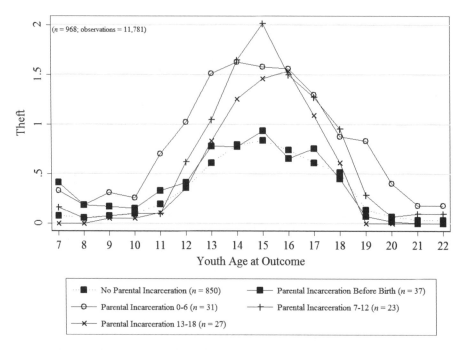

Figure 7.2. Development of youth theft by timing of parental incarceration in the United States. From "Parental Involvement in the Criminal Justice System and the Development of Youth Theft, Depression, Marijuana Use, and Poor Academic Performance," by J. Murray, R. Loeber, and D. Pardini, 2012, *Criminology, 50*, p. 275. Copyright 2012 by Wiley. Reprinted with permission.

with incarcerated parents, White youth had higher theft scores (.96) than Black youth (.59, $p = .05$). An interaction term representing this difference in the effects of parental incarceration by race was almost significant ($p = .09$).

Researchers have speculated that children may be affected differently by parental incarceration according to whether the mother or father is incarcerated (Cunningham & Baker, 2003; Murray & Farrington, 2008a; Parke & Clarke-Stewart, 2003), parent–child living circumstances (Parke & Clarke-Stewart, 2003), and the extent to which incarcerated parents have previously been violent or antisocial in the home (Eddy & Reid, 2003; Geller, Cooper, Garfinkel, Schwartz-Soicher, & Mincy, 2012; Jaffee, Moffitt, Caspi, & Taylor, 2003; Wildeman, 2010). In the current study, 20 boys had a biological mother incarcerated, 76 boys had a biological father incarcerated, and 16 boys had a stepfather incarcerated (another 10 boys had multiple parents incarcerated, but we excluded them from this specific analysis). Fifty-six percent of boys with incarcerated parents were living with their parent in the year before incarceration (which is very similar to national estimates; Glaze & Maruschak, 2008). However, we found no significant differences in mean

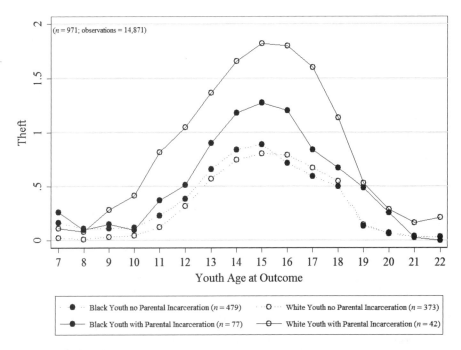

Figure 7.3. Development of youth theft by race and parental incarceration in the United States. From "Parental Involvement in the Criminal Justice System and the Development of Youth Theft, Depression, Marijuana Use, and Poor Academic Performance," by J. Murray, R. Loeber, and D. Pardini, 2012, *Criminology, 50*, p. 276. Copyright 2012 by Wiley. Reprinted with permission.

theft scores according to which parent was incarcerated, whether the boy lived with his parent before incarceration, and whether parents had high or low antisocial behavior scores (dichotomized at a similar point of 85% plus within the whole sample, as per the study by Jaffee et al., 2003).

Parental Incarceration as a Possible Causal Risk Factor

We investigated whether parental incarceration still predicted youth problem behaviors after controlling for family and peer influences and youth behaviors measured prior to parental incarceration. To do this, boys who experienced parental incarceration during the study were matched to boys whose parents were not incarcerated during the study on 14 background covariates using propensity scores. These 14 covariates (shown in Table 7.1) were chosen as four indicators of parental antisocial behavior and previous criminal justice system involvement, six important proximal (family and peer) influences on youth behavior, and four measures of youth behaviors before parental incarceration. Out of 57 boys who had parents incarcerated

TABLE 7.1
Mean Risk Factors and Youth Behaviors for Boys With Incarcerated Parents
and Matched Controls in the Year Before Incarceration in the United States

	Matched controls	Boys with incarcerated parents	Standardized mean difference (d)
Parent lifetime antisocial behavior	1.06	1.11	0.03
Parent lifetime substance use problem	0.03	0.04	0.05
Parental arrests/convictions[a]	0.79	0.94	0.11
Previous parental incarceration	0.27	0.27	0.00
Caretaker stress	24.45	24.48	0.01
Poor parent–child communication	37.93	36.61	−0.09
Poor supervision	12.49	12.24	−0.10
Boy not involved with family	14.93	15.11	0.05
Poor relationships with peers	2.09	2.28	0.16
Peer delinquency	3.52	3.63	0.02
Youth theft	0.39	0.31	−0.06
Youth marijuana use	0.13	0.08	−0.06
Youth depression	3.52	4.04	0.13
Youth poor academic performance	2.09	2.07	−0.04
N	156	52	

Note. All tests of mean differences between boys of incarcerated parents and matched controls are non-significant. From "Parental Involvement in the Criminal Justice System and the Development of Youth Theft, Depression, Marijuana Use, and Poor Academic Performance," by J. Murray, R. Loeber, and D. Pardini, 2012, *Criminology, 50,* p. 277. Copyright 2012 by Wiley. Reprinted with permission.
[a]Cumulative count up to the year before parental incarceration.

during the course of the study and had data on these covariates before parental incarceration, 52 were matched to three control boys each.[4] After matching, the parental incarceration group ($n = 52$) was very similar to the control group ($n = 156$) on all 14 covariates in the year before the index incident of parental incarceration (Table 7.1). There was no significant difference between the parental incarceration group and the matched control group on any of the 14 covariates. The success of propensity score matching is often judged by whether standardized difference scores (d) between groups exceed 0.20. For all covariates, d was smaller than 0.20, and mostly it was substantially smaller, showing that good "balance" was achieved between the parental incarceration group and the matched control group.

We also considered whether exposure to multiple risk factors differed between the matched groups. To do this we calculated a cumulative risk score for each boy in the year before parental incarceration took place. This risk score was based on the four indicators of parental antisocial behavior and

---

[4]Five boys could not be matched because there were not enough controls with similar propensity scores. Among the 52 boys with matched controls, 13 had incarcerated biological mothers, 28 had incarcerated biological fathers, and 11 had incarcerated stepfathers.

previous criminal justice system involvement and the six family and peer risk factors that went into the propensity score. Each risk factor was dichotomized so that as close as possible to 25% of boys were classified as high risk, and then the number of risk factors present for each boy was summed to create a cumulative risk score. The distribution of cumulative risk scores was almost identical between the two matched groups (parental incarceration group, $M = 2.7$, $SD = 1.6$; matched control group, $M = 2.5$, $SD = 1.6$; $p = .29$). Therefore, if differences emerge between the two groups after parental incarceration, we can be confident that these differences are not attributable to prior individual risk factors in the study or to multiple risk exposure.

Figure 7.4 plots youth behaviors from before to after parental incarceration for boys with incarcerated parents and in similar years for their matched controls. The dotted line of the matched controls represents the estimated counterfactual situation of what would have happened to the boys experiencing incarcerated parents if their parents had not been incarcerated. The graphs suggest that parental incarceration is associated with increases in youth theft but not with marijuana use, depression, or poor academic performance. The statistical analyses confirm this (Table 7.2). In the years after parental incarceration, youth with incarcerated parents had significantly higher theft scores than their matched controls (0.80 vs. 0.44, $p < .05$), but there were no significant differences in marijuana use, depression, or academic performance scores. Remember that youth with incarcerated parents were matched to controls on behavior scores before parental incarceration (as well as another 10 covariates). Therefore, comparing the matched groups after parental incarceration provides (indirectly) an estimate of change in youth behavior caused by the incarceration. The increase in youth theft after parental incarceration appears to peak a few years after the event and then declines toward similar levels as the matched controls.

The results based on propensity score matching suggest that parental incarceration might cause increases in frequency of youth theft. To examine the robustness of this finding, we used a fixed effects model to directly examine within-individual change from before to after parental incarceration. Fixed effects models have the advantage of controlling for both observed and unobserved time-constant variables. To maximize power in these analyses, we used all cases of parental incarceration from the start of the study to age 18 (even if a case was not included in the propensity score analyses), and we used theft data from ages 7 to 22. Parental incarceration was coded as a time-varying variable, scored 0 in years before the incarceration and 1 in years afterward. Two time-varying covariates were also included in the model: youth age (in years) and youth age squared. The fixed effects model showed a significant increase in youth theft from before to after parental incarceration ($B = .45$, $p = .04$, $n = 68$, observations = 859), consistent with the propensity score results.

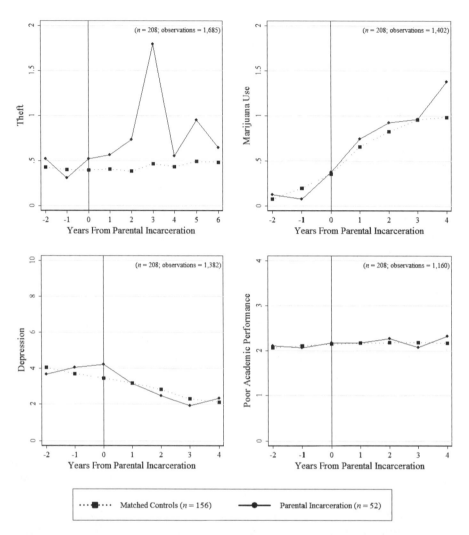

Figure 7.4. Changes in youth behaviors from before to after parental incarceration in the United States. From "Parental Involvement in the Criminal Justice System and the Development of Youth Theft, Depression, Marijuana Use, and Poor Academic Performance," by J. Murray, R. Loeber, and D. Pardini, 2012, *Criminology, 50*, p. 278. Copyright 2012 by Wiley. Reprinted with permission.

Possible Mediators of Effects of Parental Incarceration

Finally, we investigated possible mediating mechanisms linking parental incarceration and youth theft. Figure 7.5 plots changes in parenting and peer processes from before to after parental incarceration for youth with incarcerated parents and in similar years for their matched controls. The graphs show only very modest increases in some parenting problems from

TABLE 7.2

Mean Youth Behaviors After Parental Incarceration Compared With
Matched Controls in the United States

	Matched controls	Boys with incarcerated parents	B (SE)	n	Observations
Theft	0.44	0.80	.59* (.28)	208	1,286
Marijuana use	0.72	0.88	.20 (.34)	208	1,008
Depression	2.63	2.89	.10 (.16)	208	994
Poor academic performance	2.20	2.24	.05 (.08)	204	764

Note. More years of data were collected for theft than for marijuana use and depression, and fewer years of data were collected for academic performance. From "Parental Involvement in the Criminal Justice System and the Development of Youth Theft, Depression, Marijuana Use, and Poor Academic Performance," by J. Murray, R. Loeber, and D. Pardini, 2012, *Criminology, 50,* p. 279. Copyright 2012 by Wiley. Reprinted with permission.
*$p < .05$.

before to after parental incarceration. There appears to be a substantial rise in peer delinquency around the time of parental incarceration and maybe small changes in parent–child communication or supervision. However, there are no statistically significant differences in individual parenting or peer variables after parental incarceration compared with matched controls.

Although parental incarceration did not have significant effects on individual parenting or peer processes, it is possible that, in combination, these variables mediate some of the effects of parental incarceration on youth theft. To investigate this, we examined whether the effects of parental incarceration on youth theft were reduced after accounting for multiple parenting and peer variables measured after incarceration. Table 7.3 shows the results. Model 1 shows the significant association between parental incarceration and youth theft controlling only for preincarceration variables (by comparison of the propensity matched groups: $B = 0.59, p = .03$). Model 2 introduces a measure of caretaker stress after parental incarceration as a proxy for the various emotional and social strains that incarceration might cause for families. Controlling for caretaker stress after parental incarceration, effects of parental incarceration on youth theft were only slightly reduced ($B = 0.53, p = .09$).[5] Model 3 shows that, after controlling for three other parenting variables, effects of parental incarceration were moderately reduced and became insignificant ($B = 0.37$, $p = .21$). Controlling for peer variables alone (Model 4), effects of parental incarceration were only moderately reduced ($B = 0.51, p = .07$). However, when all six mediating variables measured after parental incarceration were

[5]Note that the fact that caretaker stress is significant in this model does not mean that parental incarceration had a significant effect on this variable; rather it means that caretaker stress is significantly associated with youth theft scores. The same applies to other covariates in Models 2–5.

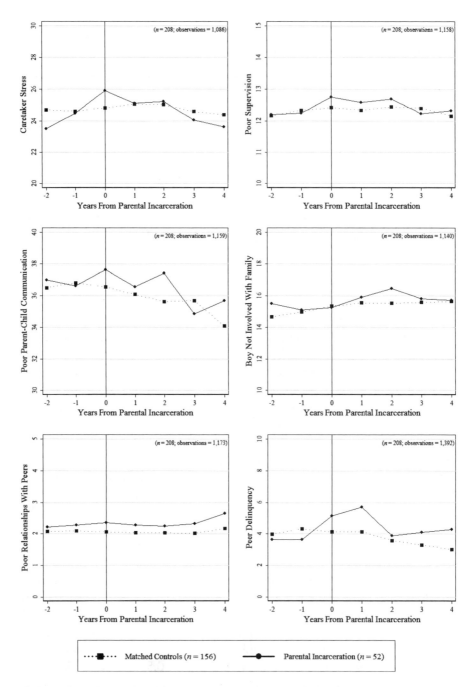

Figure 7.5. Changes in parenting and peer relationships from before to after parental incarceration in the United States. From "Parental Involvement in the Criminal Justice System and the Development of Youth Theft, Depression, Marijuana Use, and Poor Academic Performance," by J. Murray, R. Loeber, and D. Pardini, 2012, *Criminology, 50*, p. 281. Copyright 2012 by Wiley. Reprinted with permission.

TABLE 7.3
Effects of Parental Incarceration on Youth Theft Controlling for Mediators Measured After Parental Incarceration in the United States

	Model 1	Model 2	Model 3	Model 4	Model 5
	B (SE)	B (SE)	B (SE)	B (SE)	B (SE)
Parental incarceration vs. matched controls	.59* (.28)	.53 (.31)	.37 (.30)	.51 (.28)	.32 (.32)
Parenting and peer variables measured after parental incarceration					
Caretaker stress		.08** (.02)			.06* (.03)
Poor supervision			.11 (.06)		.07 (.05)
Poor communication			.01 (.01)		-.01 (.01)
Boy not involved in family			.12** (.05)		.13** (.04)
Poor peer relations				-.15 (.09)	-.18 (.10)
Peer delinquency				.13** (.01)	.13** (.01)
n	208	184	200	205	183
Observations	1,286	832	884	908	810

Note. From "Parental Involvement in the Criminal Justice System and the Development of Youth Theft, Depression, Marijuana Use, and Poor Academic Performance," by J. Murray, R. Loeber, and D. Pardini, 2012, *Criminology, 50*, p. 282. Copyright 2012 by Wiley. Reprinted with permission.
*p < .05. **p < .01.

controlled for simultaneously (Model 5), the association between parental incarceration and youth theft reduced to $B = 0.32$ ($p = .32$). Therefore, parenting and peer relations after parental incarceration explained about half (0.32/0.59) of the effects of parental incarceration on youth theft.

DISCUSSION

We investigated boys' problem behaviors after parental arrest, conviction, and incarceration in the Pittsburgh Youth Study in the United States, a large longitudinal study with an oversample of high-risk boys in which parental incarceration was relatively common. In this study, parental arrest and conviction without incarceration did not predict the development of problem behavior. Parental incarceration was associated with increases in youth theft but did not predict drug use, depression, or academic performance after controlling for other childhood risk factors and youth behavior before the incarceration. Parental incarceration was associated with youth theft more strongly for White youth than Black youth. Parenting and peer processes after parental incarceration explained about half of its effects on youth theft. A major strength of the current study was the collection of uninterrupted annual data on boys and their social environments throughout adolescence. Thus, for the first time, trajectories of youth behaviors, family processes, and peer relationships were examined using yearly data from before to after incidents of parental incarceration.

Parental incarceration did not predict increases in marijuana use, depression, or academic performance in the current study after controlling for preexisting risks. This is consistent with results from other studies that have analyzed changes in related outcomes from before to after parental incarceration in the United States (Cho, 2009; Geller et al., 2012; Wakefield & Wildeman, 2011). American studies that did find associations between paternal incarceration and poor educational outcomes (Foster & Hagan, 2009) and drug use (Roettger, Swisher, Kuhl, & Chavez, 2011); did not analyze within-individual change; and assessed paternal incarceration in youth questionnaires, which may contribute to stronger associations because youths might be more likely to remember events that affected their behavior.

The lack of effects of parental incarceration on drug use, depression, and academic performance in the current study could indicate that parental incarceration has little consequence for these outcomes in the context of other risk experiences (Giordano, 2010). However, it is important to emphasize that just because we found no effects on these outcomes in the medium term does not mean that parental criminal justice involvement did not cause significant difficulties for families and boys in the short term. Nesmith and Ruhland (2008) suggested that despite there being considerable social challenges and stress associated with parental incarceration, affected youth can show remarkable resiliency by seeking support from other adults and engaging in activities such as sports, theater, and church, which offer a focus beyond tensions at home.

Parental incarceration predicted increases in youth theft in the current study, consistent with findings from other American longitudinal studies of antisocial behavior among children and adolescents with incarcerated parents (Geller et al., 2012; Huebner & Gustafson, 2007; R. Johnson, 2009; Kjellstrand & Eddy, 2011b; Wakefield & Wildeman, 2011; Wilbur et al., 2007; Wildeman, 2010). Three considerations suggest that our findings for theft may not be spurious. First, only parental incarceration that occurred after the boy's birth was predictive of youth theft, suggesting that environmental mechanisms are important. Second, the effect was robust to control for family and peer influences and youth behavior measured before incidents of parental incarceration. Third, when a fixed effects model was used to control for other, unobserved, time-constant variables, incidents of parental incarceration still predicted increases in youth theft.

The specificity in the effects of parental incarceration on youth theft could indicate that mechanisms of stigma or labeling are particularly important. Parenting and peer variables measured after parental incarceration accounted for about half of the effects on youth theft. Stigma and labeling mechanisms (which were not measured in the current study) might account for the remaining variance. Labeling processes after parental incarceration might contribute to youth delinquency (including theft) in particular, because social expectations about children with incarcerated parents might cause children to adopt a "delinquent identity."

Increases in youth theft appeared to peak a few years after parental incarceration. This could result from chance fluctuation in frequency of theft year on year. Another possibility is that it reflects increased stress associated with the homecoming of the incarcerated parent, an aspect of parental incarceration that has rarely been explored for children. Perhaps the return of an incarcerated parent can represent additional stress for the family and child after new routines and child-care arrangements have been established. However, patterns of caretaker stress after parental incarceration were not consistent with this explanation; there were no parallel increases in caretaker stress when youth theft reached its highest level.

An intriguing finding was that parental incarceration seemed to be associated with youth theft more strongly for White youth than for Black youth. This result was limited in its statistical significance (interaction term $p = .09$), and it will be important to see if it replicates in other samples. Nevertheless, differences in the effects of parental incarceration across racial groups are an important issue for research, especially given racial disparities in rates of incarceration.

Three different views on the interaction between race and effects of parental incarceration have been put forward. According to some researchers, undesirable effects of incarceration may be exacerbated for racial minorities because stigma associated with incarceration and racism has amplifying effects (Amira, 1992; Light, 1994; Pager, Western, & Sugie, 2009). Other studies have found that the difficulties experienced by families and children of prisoners are similar, regardless of race, and suggest no significant interaction between race and parental incarceration in predicting child outcomes (Baunach, 1985; Schneller, 1975). A third view is that because parental incarceration is less common for White children, it might be more stigmatizing for White youth and have more detrimental effects on their family ties (Swisher & Waller, 2008); this could explain the stronger association between parental incarceration and theft for White youth compared with Black youth in the current study. Other race–risk interactions have also been observed in U.S. samples; for example, harsh physical punishment among Black children is less predictive of antisocial behavior than among White children (Deater-Deckard, Dodge, Bates, & Pettit, 1996; Farrington, Loeber, & Stouthamer-Loeber, 2003).

We did not find differences in the relationship between parental incarceration and youth theft by prior living circumstances, which parent was incarcerated, or levels of parental antisocial behavior. The question of whether parental incarceration sometimes reduces child problem behavior when parents have been antisocial or violent in the home is important. It is possible that the current study did not find this type of interaction because the measure of parental antisocial behavior did not refer to violence specifically. Another possible explanation is that there was insufficient statistical power to identify such interactions, especially among subgroups such as younger boys, or boys living with their parent before the incarceration, for which this kind of interaction might be specific. Because of these considerations, we urge caution in interpreting the lack of differences in effects of parental incarceration by different child and parent characteristics in the current study.

A major strength of the current study was the examination of changes in boys' behaviors from before to after parental incarceration, providing insight into a possible causal lag in the effects of parental incarceration on youth offending. Another important strength of the current study was the use of a combined index of self-report, caretaker report, teacher report, and official records on offending. The finding of robust effects of parental incarceration on youth crime (theft) in this American study is most similar to findings from England and dissimilar to results from Sweden and Holland. However, the analyses were conducted rather differently in the Pittsburgh Youth Study to make maximum use of the longitudinal data and focused on outcomes in adolescence only. Hence, the next chapter turns to direct comparisons between countries and those in other countries to evaluate these contrasts more closely.

8

CROSS-NATIONAL COMPARISONS

Our studies in England, Sweden, the Netherlands, and the United States in Chapters 4 through 7 revealed different patterns of risk for children with incarcerated parents.[1] The main conclusion in England was that parental incarceration appeared to contribute to boys' poor life chances across a range of outcomes, including their own offending in adulthood. In similar generations in Sweden and in the Netherlands, parental incarceration itself did not increase the probability of children's crime. In the United States, parental incarceration predicted increases in boys' theft during adolescence, but it did not predict other adverse outcomes. These differences across studies may reflect variation in the social and penal contexts in which parental

---

[1]We previously compared results on parental incarceration between England and Sweden (Murray, Janson, & Farrington, 2007) and between England and the Netherlands (Besemer et al., 2011), but the results shown in this chapter are new, matching all four studies in England, Sweden, the Netherlands, and the United States as closely as possible.

http://dx.doi.org/10.1037/14377-009
Effects of Parental Incarceration on Children: Cross-National Comparative Studies, by J. Murray, C. C. J. H. Bijleveld, D. P. Farrington, and R. Loeber

incarceration took place, or they may reflect different research methods, because each study was analyzed to maximize its individual strengths. Therefore, in this chapter, we reanalyze each study, matching their methods as far as possible to provide an overall comparison of the effects of parental incarceration on children's criminal outcomes across the four settings. This comparative chapter focuses on the effects of parental incarceration occurring up to when boys are age 18 on sons' own chances of offending between ages 19 and 30.

METHODS

To compare the effects of parental incarceration on children across studies, each sample was matched as closely as possible, as follows. First, we included only boys in the analysis, given that both the Cambridge Study and the Pittsburgh Youth Study included only boys. Second, a similar outcome was examined in all four studies—whether or not sons were convicted themselves between ages 19 and 30 for nonminor crimes (excluding convictions for crimes such as traffic violations). Third, the timing of parental incarceration was specified as up to age 18 in all four studies. Fourth, similar comparison groups were used across the studies.

Three similar comparisons were made in each study. First, boys with incarcerated parents (up to age 18) were compared with boys whose parents were never convicted or incarcerated up to age 18. Second, boys with incarcerated parents were compared with boys whose parents were convicted but not incarcerated up to age 18 to help assess whether parental criminality was the main explanation for effects of parental incarceration. Third, to consider whether environmental exposure to parental incarceration was an important mechanism, we compared boys whose parents were incarcerated during childhood (from birth to age 18) with boys whose parents were incarcerated only before the boy was born. Effects of incarceration (indicated as odds ratios [ORs]) were compared between countries by calculating the ratio of odds ratios (RORs; Altman & Bland, 2003) between each pair of countries.

For the Netherlands, we examined effects of parental incarceration on boys born in two time periods separately: (a) boys born between 1946 and 1962, around the time in which boys in the English and Swedish studies were born[2]; and (b) boys born between 1963 and 1977. The last year in which criminal records up to age 30 could be identified for participants in the study

---

[2]This range centers on the birth year (1953) of the English and Swedish boys and is the same period previously analyzed by Besemer and colleagues (2011).

was 1977 (because records were searched in 2007). We refer to these two periods by the approximate decades in which the Dutch children grew up: 1950s–1960s for children born 1946–1962, and 1970s–1980s for children born 1963–1977. For the Pittsburgh Youth Study, analyses were conducted using recently collected FBI felony records indicating whether study males were convicted of nonminor crimes between ages 19 and 30.

RESULTS

Table 8.1 shows the percentage of boys who were convicted themselves as young adults (between ages 19 and 30) in each country according to whether their parents had been convicted or incarcerated up to age 18. Figure 8.1 shows the corresponding ORs, comparing boys with incarcerated parents to each of the two comparison groups. In all countries, boys who had an incarcerated parent were at increased risk for their own crime compared with boys whose parents were never convicted or incarcerated. The ORs for this comparison were significant and large (about 2.0 or greater) in all countries and in both time periods in the Netherlands. In other words, in all contexts, parental incarceration was a significant risk factor for sons' own young adult crime.

However, only in England ($OR = 2.7$, $p < .05$), in the Netherlands in the 1970s–1980s ($OR = 2.9$, $p < .05$), and in the United States ($OR = 2.0$, $p < .05$) were sons of incarcerated parents at increased risk compared with sons whose parents were convicted but not incarcerated. In Sweden, and in the Netherlands in the 1950s–1960s, ORs were small and nonsignificant. Therefore, parental incarceration did not seem to be a causal risk factor for sons' own adult crime in Sweden or in the Netherlands in the 1950s–1960s, but it remained a plausible causal risk factor in England, in the Netherlands in the 1970s–1980s, and in the United States. We examined the differences between these effects using the ROR statistic. The effects of parental incarceration compared with parental conviction were significantly ($p < .05$) larger in England compared with both Sweden ($ROR = 2.5$) and the Netherlands in the 1950s–1960s ($ROR = 3.9$). Effects were significantly larger in the Netherlands in the 1970s–1980s than in both Sweden ($ROR = 2.7$) and the Netherlands in the 1950s–1960s ($ROR = 4.1$). And effects were significantly larger in the United States than in the Netherlands in the 1950s–1960s ($ROR = 2.9$).

Within each country and time period, we also examined sons' probability of their own conviction according to whether parental incarceration occurred before the boy's birth or during the boy's childhood (between birth and age 18). Table 8.2 shows the percentage of boys convicted themselves

TABLE 8.1

Percentage of Sons Convicted In Adulthood (Between Ages 19 and 30) After Parental Conviction and Incarceration in Four Countries

	England	Sweden	The Netherlands (1950s–1960s)	The Netherlands (1970s–1980s)	United States
Parent not convicted or incarcerated	18.1% (*n* = 51/282)	25.3% (*n* = 737/2,912)	14.5% (*n* = 34/235)	12.3% (*n* = 32/261)	43.3% (*n* = 322/743)
Parent convicted but not incarcerated	32.5% (*n* = 27/83)	37.8% (*n* = 71/188)	32.9% (*n* = 23/70)	21.3% (*n* = 16/75)	52.2% (*n* = 47/90)
Parent incarcerated	56.5% (*n* = 26/46)	39.6% (*n* = 36/91)	25.3% (*n* = 19/75)	43.8% (*n* = 42/96)	68.8% (*n* = 121/176)

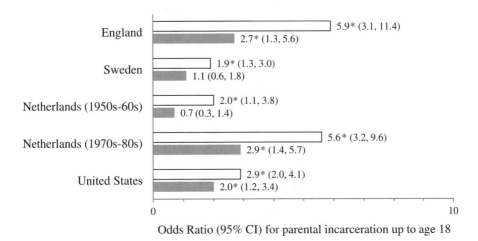

□ Compared to parent not convicted or incarcerated

■ Compared to parent convicted but not incarcerated

England — 5.9* (3.1, 11.4) / 2.7* (1.3, 5.6)

Sweden — 1.9* (1.3, 3.0) / 1.1 (0.6, 1.8)

Netherlands (1950s-60s) — 2.0* (1.1, 3.8) / 0.7 (0.3, 1.4)

Netherlands (1970s-80s) — 5.6* (3.2, 9.6) / 2.9* (1.4, 5.7)

United States — 2.9* (2.0, 4.1) / 2.0* (1.2, 3.4)

0   10

Odds Ratio (95% CI) for parental incarceration up to age 18

Figure 8.1. Effects of parental incarceration on sons' own conviction in adulthood in four countries. CI = confidence interval.
*p < .05.

according to this distinction, and Figure 8.2 shows the corresponding ORs. Only in England ($OR = 4.1$, $p < .05$) and in the Netherlands in the 1970s–1980s ($OR = 2.8$, $p < .05$) did parental incarceration during childhood predict sons' own conviction more strongly than parental incarceration before the boy's birth. However, we tested whether any difference between the countries and time periods was different using the *ROR* statistic, and no difference was significant (all $p > .05$). Therefore, environmental exposure to parental incarceration only had effects over and above enduring influences of parental incarceration before birth in England and the Netherlands in the 1970s–1980s, but differences between countries in this regard are not statistically significant.

DISCUSSION: EXPLAINING CROSS-NATIONAL DIFFERENCES

We investigated whether the effects of parental incarceration on sons' own young adult crime varied according to national context, using similar research methods in four different countries and in two time periods in the Netherlands. The effects of parental incarceration on sons' own offending appeared strong in England in the 1950s–1960s, in the Netherlands in the

TABLE 8.2

Percentage of Sons Convicted in Adulthood (Between Ages 19 and 30) Following Parental Incarceration Before or After Sons' Births

	England	Sweden	The Netherlands (1950s–1960s)	The Netherlands (1970s–1980s)	United States
Parent incarcerated before boy's birth	35.3% ($n = 6/17$)	37.5% ($n = 27/72$)	22.0% ($n = 9/41$)	31.3% ($n = 15/48$)	62.2% ($n = 23/37$)
Parent incarcerated in childhood (between birth and age 18)	69% ($n = 20/29$)	44.6% ($n = 41/92$)	29.4% ($n = 10/34$)	56.3% ($n = 27/48$)	67.2% ($n = 82/122$)

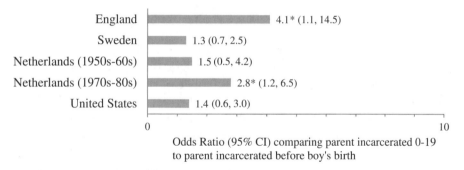

England   4.1* (1.1, 14.5)

Sweden   1.3 (0.7, 2.5)

Netherlands (1950s-60s) 1.5 (0.5, 4.2)

Netherlands (1970s-80s) 2.8* (1.2, 6.5)

United States   1.4 (0.6, 3.0)

0   10

Odds Ratio (95% CI) comparing parent incarcerated 0-19
to parent incarcerated before boy's birth

Figure 8.2. Effects of parental incarceration before and after sons' births on conviction in adulthood in four countries. CI = confidence interval.
*p < .05.

1970s–1980s, and in the United States in the 1980s–1990s, but weak in both Sweden and the Netherlands in the 1950s–1960s.

Before discussing these results, we emphasize three points of caution. First, we cannot be sure that the "effects" of parental incarceration identified here are causal and that other unmeasured influences do not explain the results. For the purposes of these cross-national comparisons, we used a rather basic matching strategy (comparing children of incarcerated parents with children of convicted but not incarcerated parents to maximize similarity in the studies). However, the pattern of results in this chapter are consistent with those from more nuanced analyses of each individual study, as reported in previous chapters, increasing confidence about the broad conclusions. A second point of caution is that the results in this chapter pertain to only one possible effect of parental incarceration on sons—on their own offending, measured as being convicted between ages 19 and 30. There may be different effects of parental incarceration on other outcomes and different effects for girls. Given both of these issues, we also considered results from other long-term longitudinal studies in each country, wherever possible.

Alert to important caveats about the results in this chapter, we considered possible substantive explanations for them—why effects of parental incarceration might have been larger in England, the Netherlands in 1970s–1980s, and the United States, and smaller or nonexistent in Sweden and the Netherlands in the 1950s–1960s.

We find it plausible that parental incarceration really did have harmful effects on boys in England in the 1950s–1960s, because parental incarceration seems likely to have caused major family, social, and economic disruptions in that context. As discussed in Chapter 4, divorce rates were extremely low in England in the 1950s–1960s, and none of the boys in our study whose parents were incarcerated during childhood were permanently separated from their parents before the incarceration—hence parental incarceration involved removal of a parent from the home. Moreover, it was usually the father who was incarcerated and, in the 1950s–1960s, fathers were the main family-income providers. Also, welfare support was less extensive in the 1950s–1960s, and English prisoners earned less money compared with those in countries like the Netherlands (Downes, 1992b). Therefore, it seems plausible that paternal incarceration often had a significant impact on families' economic situations, particularly in the working-class context of inner-city South London where the boys in the Cambridge Study grew up. Thane (2011) illustrated the challenges encountered by unmarried mothers in regard to child care and housing in England at that time, which might also have been experienced by families with imprisoned fathers. In her detailed study of prisoners' wives in England and Wales in the early 1960s, Pauline Morris (1965) found that reduction in income and financial hardship were significant burdens on the women, alongside child misbehavior: "although most children were too young to be officially termed delinquent; we regard this as one of the most striking findings of the research and one meriting further systematic investigation" (p. 292).

Furthermore, the penal climate in England after the Second World War was less liberal than in countries like Sweden and the Netherlands, and prison policies were less family friendly on issues such as visits and home leave (Downes, 1992b; Ward, 1979). Prison sentences were longer in England (Downes, 1988), and longer periods of parental incarceration predicted worse outcomes for sons in the Cambridge Study (see Chapter 4, this volume). Thus, it seems credible that parental incarceration was particularly difficult for families and harmful for children in England in the 1950s–1960s. Unfortunately, there are no other English longitudinal studies with which to compare our results in the Cambridge Study on this topic. One other investigation of the effects of parental incarceration on sons' offending was done using conviction data for the siblings of the main Cambridge Study males (see Besemer, van der Geest, Murray, Bijleveld, & Farrington, 2011). For male siblings, there were also possible harmful effects of parental incarceration on young adult offending, although the effect was observed most clearly when looking at counts of convictions rather than a dichotomous outcome measure (convicted vs. not convicted).

The contrast between the social and penal contexts of Sweden and England in the 1950s–1960s also suggests reasons why effects of parental incarceration on children were mitigated in Sweden. Sweden was striking for its egalitarian principles and humane treatment of prisoners. In the 1950s, the lower end of the income distribution was almost truncated, and families with children received a general child allowance and housing allowance (Janson & Wikström, 1995; Olsson, 1993). Pratt (2008) described Sweden as having had an exceptionally humane and inclusive penal culture following reforms in 1945:

> [inmates became] as it were, "orphans of the Swedish people's home" . . . the task of the criminal justice system now being to restore them to full membership of it—not by stigmatic punishment and exclusion, but by correctional treatment and inclusion. (p. 130)

In the 1960s, approximately one third of Swedish prisoners were held in open prisons; prisoners had a right to home leave every 3 or 4 months after serving a fixed proportion of their sentence. They had the opportunity to communicate with their family by telephone and uncensored mail, and although the institution of conjugal visits was not officially prescribed, private visits commonly occurred in Swedish prisons (N. Morris, 1966; Ward, 1979). Of those who were received into Swedish penal institutions in 1970, 57% were admitted for less than 2 months (Ward, 1972).

Unlike in England, the identity of Swedish offenders was almost never revealed in media accounts of trials and convictions (Walker, 1980). Moreover, by 1972 prisoners had the right to vote in general elections, unlike in England and the United States (Marnell, 1972). Thus, harmful effects of parental incarceration on children in England caused by stigma, loss of contact, and family economic hardship may have been mitigated in Sweden by egalitarian social policies and a penal culture focused on rehabilitation.

Turning to the Netherlands, its penal context closely resembled Sweden's in the 1950s–1960s in terms of short sentences, low incarceration rates, humane prison conditions, family-friendly prison policies, and strong social welfare policies (Downes, 1988, 1992b; Downes & van Swaaningen, 2007). Our results suggest that parental incarceration had negligible effects on sons' own offending in the Netherlands in this period, as in Sweden. However, intriguingly, by the 1970s–1980s the Netherlands had become more similar to England in terms of parental incarceration predicting increased risk for sons' own adult crime. As discussed in Chapter 5, the penal climate in the Netherlands turned toward harsher and deeper punishment from the 1970s–1980s following rising crime rates (Downes & van Swaaningen, 2007), and this may explain more harmful effects of parental incarceration in later periods.

> While in the 1960s and 1970s the most important sentencing objective was the rehabilitation of the offender—and judges were expected to consider "the personality of the offender," as well as mitigating and aggravating circumstances of the act committed—this approach lost credibility and neo-classical or retributive principles were rediscovered. . . . These changes resulted in a harsher sentencing policy and a growing prison population. (Junger-Tas, 1995, p. 293; Tak, 2001)

Thus, as Dutch attitudes and penal policies became less similar to Sweden and more similar to England in the second half of the 20th century, parental incarceration may have become more harmful for children in the Netherlands. The only other large Dutch longitudinal study that we know of to have examined parental incarceration and offspring crime is the Criminal Careers and Life Course Study, which traced all men who were convicted in the Netherlands in 1977 and their children who were mostly born in the 1970s and 1980s. In that study, van de Rakt, Murray, and Nieuwbeerta (2012) found a significant (albeit weak) effect of paternal incarceration on children's own adult offending (ages 18–30), even after controlling for fathers' criminal histories (measured using developmental trajectories of criminal convictions); paternal incarceration was most harmful when it occurred when children were ages 0 to 12 years. Corroborated by this additional evidence of harmful effects of parental incarceration on children born more recently in the Netherlands, we find it plausible that there were changes for the worse as the Netherlands become less liberal from the 1970s onward.

An important possible alternative explanation for the patterns of results discussed so far is that imprisonment was used for different crimes in England, Sweden, and the Netherlands in the mid-20th century. In Sweden and the Netherlands, imprisonment for relatively minor crimes (such as drunk driving, even for first-time offenders) was more common than in England. As such, selection into imprisonment was different across these three national contexts. The stronger "effects" of parental incarceration observed in England compared with Sweden or the Netherlands therefore might reflect selection differences, rather than varied consequences of incarceration itself. Although we have controlled for selection effects as much as we can in these studies, we cannot rule them out as an alternative explanation for the results.

Given that a liberal penal climate and extensive welfare support might reduce harmful consequences of incarceration for families and children, it is not surprising that such protective effects were not found in the United States in the 1980s–1990s. Clear (2007) described the prison problem in America as largely driven by "an unexamined commitment to the punitive theory of criminal justice" (p. 177). This has created a "'justice juggernaut' . . . 'being tough' on crime, regardless of evidence or experience in the matter" (Clear, 2007, p. 179). Our findings in the Pittsburgh Youth Study confirmed expectations that parental incarceration increases sons' chances of their own conviction in adulthood in the United States context.

There are several key aspects of prisons in the United States that may account for such long-term negative effects of parental incarceration on American children. The criminal justice system in the United States involves a "deep break" policy, in which prisoners are deliberately and extensively isolated from families and communities as a punishment strategy (Arditti, 2005;

Nurse, 2002). As one parolee described, "You broke the law, you bad. You broke the law, bang—you're not a part of us anymore" (Uggen, Manza, & Behrens, 2004, p. 273). Prison sentence lengths in the United States are several times higher than in several European countries for the same types of crime (Farrington, Langan, & Tonry, 2004). The United States is virtually the only nation to permanently disenfranchise ex-prisoners as a class (Uggen & Manza, 2002). The stigma of incarceration and lost-training opportunities are particularly problematic for ex-prisoner employment prospects in the United States, where criminal conviction history is widely available to prospective employers (Raphael, 2014). Moreover, social welfare support is considerably weaker in the United States than in many European countries (Kenworthy, 1999). In this toxic mix of profound social exclusion caused by incarceration in the United States, harmful consequences for the next generation seem entirely plausible. Given that parental incarceration both before and after a son's birth were equally predictive of sons' adult offending in the United States, long-term exclusionary processes, rather than more immediate problems resulting from separation, may be the most salient mechanisms explaining effects of parental incarceration on sons' own crime in the United States.

Notably, results from two other major studies of long-term outcomes of parental incarceration in the United States are consistent with our findings in the Pittsburgh Youth Study. Huebner and Gustafson (2007) investigated the effects of maternal incarceration on children's criminal outcomes in the National Longitudinal Survey of Youth. This is a nationally representative longitudinal study of men and women in the United States ages 14 to 22 in 1979 and the women's children ages 18 to 24 in 2000. Huebner and Gustafson compared adult offending behavior of 31 children whose mothers were incarcerated between 1979 and 2000, and 1,666 children whose mothers were not incarcerated. Twenty-six percent of children with incarcerated mothers were convicted as an adult (1994–2000), compared with 10% of comparison children. This translates into an OR of 3.1 (95% CI = 1.4–7.1), showing that maternal incarceration strongly predicted children's own convictions. Even after controlling for several other risk factors (child delinquency and education; maternal absence; maternal delinquency; maternal education; maternal smoking during pregnancy; adolescent mother; parental supervision; home environment; peer pressure; and the age, sex, and race of the child), there were still strong and significant effects of maternal incarceration on children's adult conviction (OR = 3.0; CI = 1.4–6.4).

Roettger and Swisher (Roettger, 2008; Roettger & Swisher, 2011; Swisher & Roettger, 2012) compared rates of serious and violent delinquency between 784 males whose fathers had ever been incarcerated and 5,344 males whose fathers had never been incarcerated in the National Longitudinal

Study of Adolescent Health (Add Health). This is a study of about 20,000 adolescents who were in Grades 7 through 12 in 1994–1995, including follow-up interviews with about 7,500 males at ages 18 to 24. Self-reported serious and violent delinquency was measured using 15 questionnaire items. Paternal incarceration predicted serious and violent delinquency with an OR of 1.8 (CI = 1.3–2.7). Paternal incarceration still predicted increased risk of serious and violent delinquency (OR = 1.6; CI = 1.2–2.2), even after controlling for several risk factors: the participant's race, drink/substance abuse, family structure, parental strictness, father involvement, physical abuse, care by social services, school attachment, high school dropout, employment, marriage, cohabitation, poverty, and the racial and educational characteristics of the neighborhood. Thus, our findings in the Pittsburgh Youth Study and those from other large American longitudinal studies combine to suggest that effects of parental incarceration in the United States are not limited to childhood, but rather extend to children's own offending in their early adult years. Note that all three of these studies were based on questionnaire reports about parental incarceration, rather than on official records. The lower reliability of questionnaire reports may mean that effects of parental incarceration have been underestimated in U.S. studies.

In conclusion, findings from our research and other studies suggest that effects of parental incarceration on sons' own offending were strong in England in the 1950s–1960s, in the Netherlands in the 1970s–1980s, and in the United States in the 1980s–1990s and weak or nonexistent in Sweden and the Netherlands in the 1950s–1960s. Different patterns of welfare support, penal climate, prison sentences, and incarceration rates may explain these variations.

III

RESEARCH SYNTHESIS
AND CONCLUSIONS

9

SYSTEMATIC REVIEW

In Chapters 4 through 8, we presented findings on the effects of parental incarceration on children in four different countries. Although individual studies can give important leads, replication is key to scientific progress, and synthesis of all the available evidence is critical to informed decision making. Therefore, in addition to our primary research, we conducted a systematic review and meta-analysis to summarize the evidence on the effects of parental incarceration on children's antisocial behavior, mental health, drug use, and educational performance. Systematic reviews use rigorous and transparent search methods to try to locate all available evidence on a research question. Meta-analyses use statistical methods to pool the results from the primary studies.

http://dx.doi.org/10.1037/14377-010

Effects of Parental Incarceration on Children: Cross-National Comparative Studies, by J. Murray, C. C. J. H. Bijleveld, D. P. Farrington, and R. Loeber

OBJECTIVES OF THE SYSTEMATIC REVIEW

The following questions were addressed in this systematic review and meta-analysis:

1. To what extent is parental incarceration associated with children's later antisocial behavior, mental health problems, drug use, and poor educational performance?
2. Do these associations vary across different types of sample (children in the community compared with children in clinics and courts)?
3. Does parental incarceration predict worse outcomes for children than other forms of parent–child separation?
4. Are associations between parental incarceration and children's outcomes moderated by the child's sex, maternal versus paternal incarceration, child's age at parental incarceration and age at outcome, type of outcome assessed, and country of study?[1]
5. Do results vary according to study methodologies?

METHODS

The key methods of the systematic review are presented here, involving how we searched for studies, the criteria we used to decide whether to include them in the review, the screening process, the coding of studies, and the meta-analysis.

Search for Studies

We systematically searched for relevant studies until February 2011. We started with an initial set of about 150 reports on children with incarcerated parents collected in our previous research on this topic. Four methods were used to search for additional studies. First, keywords were entered into 23 electronic databases and Internet search engines.[2] Second, bibliographies of prior

---

[1] Ideally, we would have also investigated other moderators, such as living circumstances and quality of relationships before incarceration, what children are told about the event, length of parental incarceration, levels of social support, and type of prison in which parents were held. However, it was extremely rare for studies to report such information, making it impossible to study these variables as moderators.
[2] The keywords entered were [Prison* OR Jail* OR Penitentiary OR Imprison* OR Incarcerat* OR Detention] AND [Child* OR Son* OR Daughter* OR Parent* OR Mother* OR Father*] AND [Antisocial* OR Delinquen* OR Crim* OR Offend* OR Violen* OR Aggressi* OR Mental Health OR Mental Illness OR Internaliz* OR Depress* OR Anxiety OR Anxious OR Psychological* OR Drug* OR Alcohol* OR Drink* OR Tobacco OR Smok* OR Substance OR Education* OR School OR Grade* OR Achievement].

reviews were examined (Dallaire, 2007; S. Gabel, 2003; Hagan & Dinovitzer, 1999; Johnston, 1995; Murray, 2005; Murray & Farrington, 2008a; Myers, Smarsh, Amlund-Hagen, & Kennon, 1999; Nijnatten, 1998), as well as edited books on children of incarcerated parents (Eddy & Poehlmann, 2010; K. Gabel & Johnston, 1995; O. Harris & Miller, 2002; Y. R. Harris, Graham, & Carpenter, 2010; Shaw, 1992b; Travis & Waul, 2003b). Third, experts in the field were contacted to request information about any other studies that we might not have located. The first group of experts contacted consisted of about 65 researchers and practitioners who we knew as professionals with an interest in children with incarcerated parents. The second group consisted of about 30 directors of major longitudinal studies in criminology (see Farrington & Welsh, 2007). We thought that longitudinal researchers might have important results that were eligible for this meta-analysis that had not been published or were hidden in articles that did not mention parental incarceration in titles, abstracts, or keywords. Finally, Jim Derzon and Aaron Alford kindly searched their extensive database of results on family factors and offending in longitudinal studies (see Derzon, 2010) to identify any other studies that we might not have located.

Inclusion Criteria

We used five criteria to determine which studies were eligible for inclusion in the review. Studies had to have numerical results and meet all five of the following criteria to be included:

1. The study includes children of incarcerated parents and at least one comparison group of children without incarcerated parents (i.e., children whose parents had not been incarcerated since the child's birth).
2. The study includes a measure of children's antisocial behavior, mental health, drug use, or educational performance.
3. Children's outcomes were measured after parental incarceration first occurred.
4. The study used the same outcome measure for children with incarcerated parents and the comparison group.
5. Numerical information: At least one effect size was reported, or there was enough numerical information to calculate at least one effect size.

All studies meeting these five criteria were included in the review. They could be published or unpublished. They may have been conducted in any country and may have been reported in English, German, Dutch, French, Spanish, Portuguese, Swedish, Danish, or Norwegian.

Screening for Eligible Studies

Our searches identified 14,690 references for further screening—to identify eligible studies. A flow chart of the screening process is shown in Figure 9.1. After examining the titles and abstracts of all the references and discarding obviously irrelevant ones, 454 reports were identified as potentially relevant to the review. Of these, 451 full-text documents were retrieved, and 188 described an empirical study of children of incarcerated parents with numerical results (and were not review articles or commentaries on previously reported research). Of these, 40 studies with 50 samples, reported in 74 documents, met all five eligibility criteria and were coded for the meta-analysis.

Four studies are briefly described here that were not included in the meta-analysis because an effect size could not be derived from the results. Friedman and Esselstyn (1965) compared 117 children with incarcerated fathers and 211 control children in the same schools on academic performance and other aspects of pupil adjustment. They reported that a higher proportion of children with incarcerated fathers scored "above average" on academic achievement than the controls, but exact proportions and significance tests were not reported. Guo, Roettger, and Cai (2008) tested for a gene–environment interaction between the DRD2*178/304 genotype and "dad jailed" in predicting delinquency in the sibling sample of the National Longitudinal Study of Adolescent Health (Add Health). The interaction was not significant. Further results for main effects were not available, and we were not able to include this study in the review (although we did include results on main study participants in Add Health on the basis of other analyses). Kampfner (1995) compared 36 children with incarcerated mothers and control children (n not reported) matched on age, race, sex, and social class. She reported that children with incarcerated mothers had significantly more posttraumatic stress symptoms than control children, but further information was not available to calculate an effect size (and it was not clear whether "significant" meant statistically significant or substantially different). Naudeau (2005) compared rates of depression, drug use, and delinquency between 18 youth with incarcerated parents and 36 matched controls who had never experienced parental absence in the 4-H Study of Positive Youth Development. It was reported that there were no significant differences between the groups on any of these outcomes, but further information was not available to calculate an effect size.

Coding of Studies

Studies included in the meta-analysis were coded for the following key features: reference information (e.g., title, authors, publication year); study location; sample characteristics (e.g., gender, age range); study design

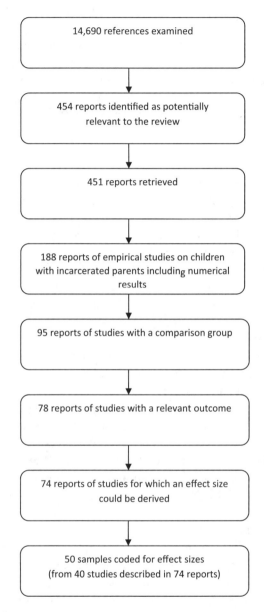

Figure 9.1. Flow chart of screening process in the systematic review. From "Children's Antisocial Behavior, Mental Health, Drug Use, and Educational Performance After Parental Incarceration: A Systematic Review and Meta-Analysis," by J. Murray, D. P. Farrington, and I. Sekol, 2012, *Psychological Bulletin, 138*, p. 181. Copyright 2012 by the American Psychological Association.

(prospective, retrospective, cross-sectional); details about the measure of parental incarceration; type(s) of comparison groups included; details of subsamples and multiple comparisons made; type(s) of outcomes measured and measurement details; statistical information used to derive an effect size; and methodological quality. If some statistical information was missing that was needed to calculate an effect size, study authors were contacted to try to obtain the relevant information. If other information was not available (e.g., details about the measurement of parental incarceration), this was coded as missing.

Meta-Analyses

To synthesize the findings from the studies included in the review, we conducted meta-analyses of their results. We used the results from each study that were most controlled (adjusted for the most covariates). The meta-analyses proceeded in three stages. In the first stage, results for each child outcome (antisocial behavior, mental health problems, drug use, and poor educational performance) were pooled for all studies and separately by type of sample (community samples and samples of children recruited from clinics and courts). Pooled results were also calculated separately for studies that compared children of incarcerated parents with children who were separated from parents for other reasons.

In the second stage of analysis, focusing on the outcome of child antisocial behavior (which was studied most frequently and showed the strongest association with parental incarceration, as well as the greatest variation in results), we examined possible moderating variables that might explain variation in effect sizes. In the third stage of analysis, we examined whether methodological characteristics of the studies were related to their findings.

Some studies were not included in some of the meta-analyses because they lacked relevant results. For example, some studies only provided results on children's antisocial behavior and no other outcome and so were only included in analyses of antisocial behavior. Thus, different numbers of studies are included in different analyses.

The meta-analyses were conducted using the inverse variance–weight approach recommended by Lipsey and Wilson (2001) and were performed in SPSS using the syntax available on David Wilson's website (http://mason.gmu.edu/~dwilsonb/ma.html). Effect sizes were first calculated in Microsoft Excel and then copied into SPSS to run the meta-analyses. Random effects models were used to pool results across studies because of significant heterogeneity in the results that we believed was not due to sampling error alone (given the diverse characteristics of the studies, as we describe in the Results section). Additional technical information on the methods used in this meta-analysis can be found in Appendix E.

SUMMARY OF STUDIES

Table 9.1 summarizes the characteristics of the 50 samples from the 40 studies included in the meta-analysis.[3] Details of the individual studies and their references can be found in Murray, Farrington, and Sekol (2012). In total, the 50 samples included 7,374 children with incarcerated parents and 37,325 comparison children without incarcerated parents. Research on the associations between parental incarceration and children's outcomes has been increasing. Since 2000, results on 39 samples have been reported, compared with 11 in previous years. The samples were recruited in seven different countries: the United States, the United Kingdom, the Netherlands, Denmark, Sweden, Australia, and New Zealand. Most samples of children were recruited in the community, rather than in juvenile courts or mental health clinics. Just fewer than half of the samples came from studies with a prospective design, which means that parental incarceration was measured at one point in time, and children's outcomes were assessed at a later point in time. Thirty-two samples included both children with incarcerated mothers and children with incarcerated fathers (but they were rarely analyzed separately). Children's parents had been incarcerated during childhood (ages 0–10) in 11 samples, during adolescence (ages 11–18) in two samples, and during both childhood and adolescence in 16 samples. In 12 samples, parental incarceration was measured in such a way that it might have occurred before children were born. In most samples, children's outcomes were assessed between birth and age 18, rather than in adulthood. A variety of informants (children themselves, caretakers, teachers, peers, clinical assessment, and clinical records) were used to assess children's outcomes. Only 10 samples of children were assessed using multiple informants.

Studies used several different types of comparison groups to assess the association between parental incarceration and children's outcomes. In nine samples, children with incarcerated parents were compared with children who were separated from parents for other reasons, such as parental divorce or parental death. These comparisons can help assess whether parent–child separation per se is the main factor explaining children's outcomes after parental incarceration. Several studies compared children with incarcerated parents with children whose parents were convicted but not incarcerated to try to parse out the effects of parental incarceration from the effects of parental criminality. Another method used to try to control for parental criminality was to compare

---

[3]Note that results from the Cambridge Study, Project Metropolitan, Transfive, and the Pittsburgh Youth study are not the same as those reported in other chapters in this book, because other results were calculated from these studies for the purpose of this meta-analysis (Murray, Farrington, & Sokol, 2012).

TABLE 9.1
Characteristics of Samples Included in the Meta-Analysis

Variable	Category	No. of samples (*k*)
Location	United States	36
	Europe (England, Sweden, Denmark, the Netherlands)	11
	Australia/New Zealand	3
Report date	1970s	3
	1980s	2
	1990s	6
	2000s	21
	2010s/unpublished with no date	18
Sampling frame	Children in the community	40
	Children in clinics/courts	10
Study design	Prospective	21
	Retrospective	17
	Cross-sectional	12
Child sex	Boys only	14
	Girls only	7
	Both boys and girls	29
Parent incarcerated	Mother figure only	6
	Father figure only	12
	Both mother and father figure	32
Age of children at time of parental incarceration	Childhood (0–10) only	10
	Adolescence (11–18) only	2
	Both childhood and adolescence	16
	Parent "ever incarcerated" (including before child's birth)	12
	Not known	10
Age at child outcome	Juvenile (0–17) only	28
	Adult (18+) only	12
	Both juvenile and adult	9
	Not known	1
Informant for child outcomes	Child only	12
	Caretaker only	9
	Teacher only	2
	Peers only	1
	Clinical assessment only	1
	Official records only	15
	Multiple informants	10
Comparison group	Children separated from parents for other reasons	7
	Children with parent convicted but not incarcerated	5
	Children with parent incarcerated only before child's birth	4
	Other children in same study, but not matched as above	27
	Multiple comparison groups	7

TABLE 9.1
Characteristics of Samples Included in the Meta-Analysis (*Continued*)

Variable	Category	No. of samples (*k*)
Number covariates controlled[a]	0	9
	1–4	20
	5–9	10
	10–14	8
	15+	3
Controlled for parental criminality	Yes	13
	No	37
Controlled for pretest of child outcome	Yes	4
	No	46

Note. From "Children's Antisocial Behavior, Mental Health, Drug Use, and Educational Performance After Parental Incarceration: A Systematic Review and Meta-Analysis," by J. Murray, D. P. Farrington, and I. Sekol, 2012, *Psychological Bulletin, 138,* p. 185. Copyright 2012 by the American Psychological Association.
[a]If different numbers of covariates were controlled for in different analyses, the maximum number was coded.

children whose parents were incarcerated after the child's birth to children whose parents were incarcerated only before the child's birth. The logic of this comparison is that the two groups should be quite similar in background characteristics, but only children whose parents are incarcerated after birth are actually exposed to the event, helping isolate its environmental effects.

Through matching and statistical modeling, most studies controlled for some covariates when estimating the association between parental incarceration and children's outcomes (only nine samples were analyzed without control for any covariates). Most samples ($k = 30$) were analyzed controlling for between 1 and 9 covariates. Only 13 samples were analyzed controlling for parental criminality, and only four samples were analyzed in terms of change in children's outcomes by controlling for a "pretest" of the child outcome, measured before parental incarceration took place.

RESULTS OF THE META-ANALYSES

Results of the systematic review are presented in four sections: main effects, possible moderators, differences in results by study methodology, and investigation of possible publication bias.

Main Effects

Table 9.2 shows weighted mean effect sizes for the associations between parental incarceration and children's antisocial behavior, poor mental health, drug use, and low educational performance in all samples with relevant results.

TABLE 9.2
Meta-Analysis of Associations Between Parental Incarceration and Children's Outcomes Across Different Types of Samples

	Antisocial behavior			Mental health problems			Drug use			Poor educational performance		
	OR (95% CI)	Q	k	OR (95% CI)	Q	k	OR (95% CI)	Q	k	OR (95% CI)	Q	k
Children in the community	1.7** (1.4–2.0)	112.9**	36	1.2* (1.0–1.4)	22.9	17	1.0 (0.9–1.1)	7.2	8	1.5** (1.1–2.1)	34.4**	11
Children in clinics/courts	1.4** (1.1–1.7)	8.3	9	0.9 (0.6–1.3)	9.7	6	1.0 (0.6–1.8)	20.3**	4	1.2 (0.8–1.8)	1.5	2
Comparison group separated for other reasons	1.4** (1.2–1.6)	7.6	9	0.9 (0.7–1.1)	10.6	8	0.8 (0.6–1.1)	4.7	5	1.3 (0.8–1.9)	4.2	4
All samples	1.6** (1.4–1.9)	121.3**	45	1.1 (1.0–1.3)	45.0**	23	1.1 (0.9–1.3)	27.6**	12	1.4** (1.1–1.8)	35.9**	13

Note. Samples with "comparison group separated for other reasons" are a subset of the "children in the community" and "children in clinics/courts" samples. Results from random effects models. OR = odds ratio; CI = confidence interval; Q = Q statistic for test of heterogeneity within samples; k = number of samples. From "Children's Antisocial Behavior, Mental Health, Drug Use, and Educational Performance After Parental Incarceration: A Systematic Review and Meta-Analysis," by J. Murray, D. P. Farrington, and I. Sekol, 2012, *Psychological Bulletin, 138,* p. 186. Copyright 2012 by the American Psychological Association.
*p < .05. **p < .01.

Across all samples, the pooled odds ratio (OR) for the association between parental incarceration and children's antisocial behavior was significant and quite large ($OR = 1.6$, CI = 1.4–1.9, $k = 45$). For poor mental health, the pooled OR was nonsignificant and showed almost zero association with parental incarceration ($OR = 1.1$, CI = 1.0–1.3, $k = 23$). Also, there was almost no association between parental incarceration and children's drug use ($OR = 1.1$, CI = 0.9–1.3, $k = 12$). Parental incarceration was significantly associated with poor educational performance ($OR = 1.4$, CI = 1.1–1.8, $k = 13$). For all four outcomes, the Q statistic was significant ($p < .01$), indicating heterogeneity in the results that could not be accounted for by sampling error alone.

Table 9.2 also shows the average effect sizes for different types of sample. We expected effect sizes to be larger among samples of children in the community than among samples of children recruited from clinics or courts (in which comparison children are also likely to be at risk for problem behavior). Within community samples, effect sizes were significant for antisocial behavior ($OR = 1.7$, CI = 1.4–2.0, $k = 36$), mental health ($OR = 1.2$, CI = 1.0–1.4; $k = 17$), and poor educational performance ($OR = 1.5$, CI = 1.1–2.1, $k = 11$), but not for drug use. By contrast, within court and clinic samples, parental incarceration was only significantly associated with increased risk for children's antisocial behavior ($OR = 1.4$, CI = 1.1–1.7, $k = 9$). However, these differences in effect sizes between community samples and clinic and court samples were not significant ($p > .05$ in QB tests of between-group heterogeneity, for all four outcomes). Table 9.2 also shows average results for the subset of samples that compared children with incarcerated parents to children separated from parents for other reasons. The average effect size for this comparison was positive and significant for children's antisocial behavior ($OR = 1.4$, CI = 1.2–1.6, $k = 9$), but not for the other outcomes.

Possible Moderators of Effects on Children's Antisocial Behavior

We investigated whether six possible moderators explained variation in the results for antisocial behavior. We chose to conduct these analyses for antisocial behavior because this outcome was examined most often ($k = 45$), had the largest mean effect size ($OR = 1.6$), and had the greatest heterogeneity in study results ($Q = 123.3$).[4] Figure 9.2 shows the distribution of individual effect sizes for all 45 samples in which antisocial behavior was measured. Forty effect sizes (89%) show a positive association between parental incarceration and children's antisocial behavior. Although not many individual effect sizes were statistically significant, as noted previously, pooled effect

---

[4]If we had conducted these six tests for all four outcomes, the probability of a Type I error (finding a significant result by chance) would have increased considerably.

Sample

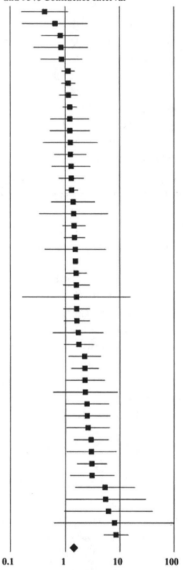

Besemer et al., 2011 (TRANSFIVE boys)
Carter & Dallaire, 2009
Poehlmann et al., 2008
Moerk, 1973
Dallaire et al., 2009
van der Rakt, Murray, & Nieuwbeerta, 2012 (boys)
Geller et al., 2012
Dannerbeck, 2003, 2005
Allegheny County DHS, 2008
Besemer et al., 2011 (CSDD siblings boys)
Kinner et al., 2007 (girls)
Besemer et al., 2011 (TRANSFIVE girls)
Kinner et al., 2007 (boys)
Giordano, 2010
Phillips et al., 2002
Cox, 2009
Murray, Janson, & Farrington, 2007 (PM girls)
Murray & Farrington, 2005, 2008a
Evens & Stoep, 1997
Murray, Loeber, & Pardini, 2012
Aaron & Dallaire, 2010 (siblings)
Swisher & Roettger, 2011
Wakefield & Wildeman, 2011 (PHDCN)
van der Rakt, Murray, & Nieuwbeerta, 2012 (girls)
Gabel & Shindledecker, 1993 (girls)
Siegel & Marano, 2008
Murray, Janson, & Farrington, 2007 (PM boys)
Besemer et al., 2011 (CSDD siblings girls)
Drabkin et al., n.d.
Tasca et al., 2011
Kjellstrand, 2009
Wilbur et al., 2007
Stanton, 1980
Bryant & Rivard, 1995
Aaron & Dallaire, 2010
Gordon, 2009
Huebner & Gustafson, 2007
Trice & Brewster, 2004
Dallaire & Zeman, n.d.
Johnson, 2009
Pakiz et al., 1997
Gabel & Shindledecker, 1993 (boys)
Johanson, 1974
Crowe, 1974
Kandel et al., 1988

Weighted Mean Odds Ratio

Odds Ratio for Antisocial Behavior and 95% Confidence Interval

0.01   0.1   1   10   100

Figure 9.2. Distribution of effect sizes for antisocial behavior in the meta-analysis. Only one finding per sample is represented in this figure, which may not correspond with other findings reported elsewhere. From "Children's Antisocial Behavior, Mental Health, Drug Use, and Educational Performance After Parental Incarceration: A Systematic Review and Meta-Analysis," by J. Murray, D. P. Farrington, and I. Sekol, 2012, *Psychological Bulletin, 138,* p. 187. Copyright 2012 by the American Psychological Association.

TABLE 9.3

Meta-Analysis of Possible Moderators of the Association Between
Parental Incarceration and Antisocial Behavior

Variable	Category	OR (95% CI)	k	QB
Child sex	Girls	1.4 (0.9–2.4)	7	0.5
	Boys	1.8** (1.3–2.6)	13	
Mother/father incarcerated	Mother	1.6* (1.0–2.6)	8	0.0
	Father	1.7** (1.2–2.5)	11	
Child age at parental incarceration	Childhood (0–10)	1.5* (1.1–2.3)	9	2.4
	Adolescence (11–17)	2.0* (1.2–3.5)	5	
	Parent "ever" incarcerated	2.4** (1.6–3.6)	9	
Child age at outcome	Juvenile (0–17)	1.6** (1.3–1.9)	26	1.1
	Adult (18+)	1.9** (1.4–2.6)	15	
Type of outcome	Antisocial	1.6** (1.2–2.1)	17	0.0
	Crime	1.6** (1.3–2.0)	28	
In the United States	U.S.	1.6** (1.3–1.9)	31	0.0
	Not U.S.	1.7** (1.2–2.2)	14	

Note. Results from mixed effects models. OR = odds ratio; CI = confidence interval; k = number of samples; QB = QB statistic for test of heterogeneity between categories, distributed as chi-square with c-1 degrees of freedom, where c is the number of categories in the moderator variable. From "Children's Antisocial Behavior, Mental Health, Drug Use, and Educational Performance After Parental Incarceration: A Systematic Review and Meta-Analysis," by J. Murray, D. P. Farrington, and I. Sekol, 2012, *Psychological Bulletin, 138*, p. 188. Copyright 2012 by the American Psychological Association.
$*p < .05. **p < .01.$

sizes were significant for all samples, for community samples, and for clinic and court samples (as reported in Table 9.2).

Table 9.3 shows the results of the moderator analyses. Slightly larger pooled ORs were found for boys (compared with girls), parental incarceration during adolescence and parental incarceration "ever" (compared with parental incarceration during childhood), and outcomes in adulthood (compared with outcomes in juvenile years). However, no moderator variable was statistically significant, and pooled effect sizes were almost identical for maternal compared with paternal incarceration, type of outcome measured (antisocial or crime), and whether studies were conducted in the United States.

We also examined whether effect sizes for U.S. studies varied according to the year in which parental incarceration took place, in a meta-regression analysis (which can examine variation in effect sizes by continuous-level predictors). We did this because the U.S. incarceration rate grew rapidly over several decades, and some researchers have hypothesized that as the event became more common, stigma associated with incarceration might have diminished, and harmful effects on children might have reduced. Figure 9.3 shows the distribution of the (logged) ORs by year of parental incarceration in U.S. samples. Although a very slight downward slope is observed in this graph, the regression analysis showed that the effects of parental incarceration on children's antisocial behavior were not significantly smaller among samples of children for whom parental incarceration occurred more recently ($B = -0.01, p = .52$).

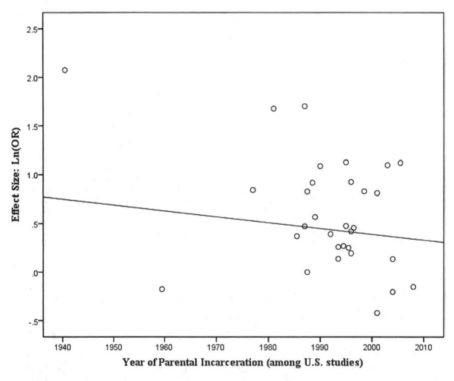

Figure 9.3. Meta-analysis of the association between parental incarceration and antisocial behavior through time in the United States. From "Children's Antisocial Behavior, Mental Health, Drug Use, and Educational Performance After Parental Incarceration: A Systematic Review and Meta-Analysis," by J. Murray, D. P. Farrington, and I. Sekol, 2012, *Psychological Bulletin, 138*, p. 183. Copyright 2012 by the American Psychological Association.

TABLE 9.4
Meta-Analysis of Variation in Effect Sizes for Antisocial Behavior by Study
Design and Control for Covariates

Variable	Category	OR (95% CI)	k	QB
Study design	Prospective	1.9** (1.5–2.4)	21	4.7
	Retrospective	1.4* (1.1–1.9)	13	
	Cross-sectional	1.3 (1.0–1.8)	11	
Covariates controlled	Zero covariates controlled	3.0** (2.1–4.2)	9	13.9**
	Any covariates controlled	1.4** (1.2–1.6)	36	

Note. Results from mixed effects models. OR = odds ratio; CI = confidence interval; k = number of samples; QB = QB statistic for test of heterogeneity between categories, distributed as chi-square with c-1 degrees of freedom, where c is the number of categories in the moderator variable. From "Children's Antisocial Behavior, Mental Health, Drug Use, and Educational Performance After Parental Incarceration: A Systematic Review and Meta-Analysis," by J. Murray, D. P. Farrington, and I. Sekol, 2012, *Psychological Bulletin, 138*, p. 190. Copyright 2012 by the American Psychological Association.
*$p < .05$. **$p < .01$.

Differences in Results by Study Methodology

We investigated whether study methodology explained variation in effect sizes for antisocial behavior. Table 9.4 shows average effect sizes for different study designs and whether studies controlled for covariates. Prospective studies had the largest average effect size, followed by retrospective and then cross-sectional studies, but these differences were not quite significant ($QB = 4.7$, $p = .10$). Where there existed a clear and significant difference was between studies that controlled for covariates ($OR = 1.4$) and studies that did not ($OR = 3.0$; $QB = 13.9$, $p < .01$). Given the importance of covariates for these results on antisocial behavior, we also examined whether effect sizes for educational performance (which were also positive and significant on average for all samples; see Table 9.2) differed according to whether studies controlled for covariates. Again, there was a significant difference. Studies that controlled for covariates had, on average, a significantly ($QB = 3.8$, $p < .05$) smaller association between parental incarceration and poor educational performance ($OR = 1.1$, CI = 1.0–1.3, $k = 8$) than studies that did not control for covariates ($OR = 1.5$, CI = 1.2–1.9, $k = 5$). In fact, the average effect size for educational performance when covariates were controlled ($OR = 1.1$) shows almost zero association with parental incarceration.

We expected that the type of covariates controlled might also make a difference to study results. We expected that studies that controlled for parental criminality or children's antisocial behavior before parental incarceration would have smaller effect sizes than other studies. In 13 samples, the association between parental incarceration and children's antisocial behavior was estimated while controlling for parental criminality, using three different methods: (a) by comparing children who experienced parental incarceration during childhood with children whose parents were incarcerated only before the child was born, (b) by comparing children whose parents were incarcerated with children whose parents were convicted but received noncustodial sentences, and (c) by comparing children whose parents were incarcerated with other children while statistically controlling for a measure of parental criminality (e.g., controlling for the number of parental convictions in regression analyses). In these 13 samples, the pooled association between parental incarceration and children's antisocial behavior was $OR = 1.4$ $(CI = 1.2–1.7, k = 13)$.

In three samples, the association between parental incarceration and children's later antisocial behavior was estimated while controlling for children's antisocial behavior before parental incarceration.[5] The pooled effect size in these samples was $OR = 1.3$ $(CI = 1.0–1.7, k = 3)$. Combining all 14 studies that controlled either for parental criminality or for children's antisocial behavior before parental incarceration, the pooled OR was 1.4 $(CI = 1.1–1.6, k = 14)$. This association was similar to that among other studies that controlled for some covariates but not for these two particular covariates $(OR = 1.4, CI = 1.2–1.6, k = 22; QB = .02, p = .89)$. Thus, the two covariates that we thought would be most important to take into account (parental criminality and previous child antisocial behavior) did not significantly influence the meta-analytic results.

We also considered whether effect sizes for antisocial behavior might have been biased by the omission of additional covariates. To do this, we examined the association between study results and the total number of covariates controlled in each study, both graphically and in meta-regression. Figure 9.4 shows the distribution of effect sizes according to the number of covariates controlled (excluding one outlier, which controlled for 32 covariates). As can be seen, there is greater variability in the results for samples in which fewer covariates were controlled (toward the left hand side of the graph). However, the regression line is almost flat, and meta-regression showed that, as the number of covariates controlled increased, effect sizes did not significantly decrease $(B = –.01, p = .46)$. Similar results were obtained

---

[5]Note that four samples included results controlling for children's antisocial behavior before parental incarceration. However, two samples (boys and girls in the study by Geller et al., 2012) were analyzed together here because otherwise only results for paternal incarceration (rather than both maternal and paternal incarceration) could be included.

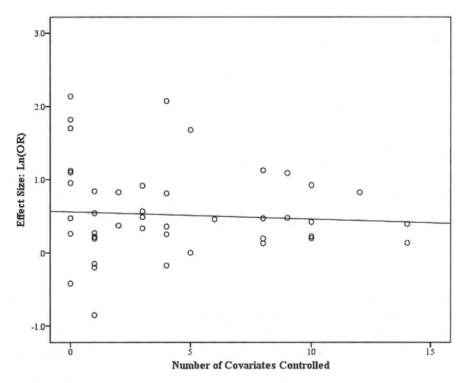

Figure 9.4. The association between parental incarceration and antisocial behavior by number of covariates controlled. From "Children's Antisocial Behavior, Mental Health, Drug Use, and Educational Performance After Parental Incarceration: A Systematic Review and Meta-Analysis," by J. Murray, D. P. Farrington, and I. Sekol, 2012, *Psychological Bulletin*, *138*, p. 190. Copyright 2012 by the American Psychological Association.

when including the outlier ($B = -.01$, $p = .24$). Therefore, there is no evidence that if studies had controlled for more covariates, the average association between parental incarceration and child antisocial behavior would have been smaller.

Finally, we examined if the five methodological quality characteristics of the studies, as coded on the Cambridge Quality Checklists, were related to effect size. None of the items examined (sampling methods, response rates, sample size, measure of parental incarceration, measure of outcome) were significantly associated with study results on antisocial behavior.

Investigating Possible Publication Bias

We investigated whether our meta-analytic results on antisocial behavior might be affected by publication bias—bias caused by unpublished studies having smaller effect sizes and being underrepresented in the review. The weighted mean OR for antisocial behavior among published studies was 1.8, and among unpublished studies it was 1.4, but the difference was not significant ($QB = 2.1$, $p = .14$). A funnel plot showed a roughly symmetrical dispersion of effect sizes by standard error that indicated a lack of publication bias. To consider possible effects of publication bias further, missing studies were imputed using the trim-and-fill method. When imputed missing studies were included in the analysis, the weighted mean OR for the association between parental incarceration and children's antisocial behavior changed only slightly from 1.6 (CI = 1.4–1.9) to 1.5 (CI = 1.2, 1.7), suggesting that the results of this meta-analysis are quite robust to possible missing studies.

DISCUSSION

A meta-analysis of the most rigorous empirical evidence, based on 50 samples in 40 published and unpublished studies, showed that parental incarceration predicts increased risk for children's antisocial behavior. However, we found no association between parental incarceration and children's mental health, drug use, or educational performance among the most rigorous studies.

One previous meta-analysis of eight samples demonstrated a large bivariate association between parental incarceration and children's mental health problems, and a smaller covariate-adjusted association (Murray, Farrington, Sekol, & Olsen, 2009). The fact that no association was detected in the current meta-analysis may be because it is based on a larger number of primary studies than the previous analysis, and it only includes studies that clearly measured mental health (e.g., results on "self-concept" were excluded from the current review, but they were included in the previous review). The different results might also be explained by the fact that the earlier review excluded certain types of studies that were included in the current review (e.g., studies that sampled children in clinics or courts). However, when we restricted the current meta-analysis to community samples only, the association between parental incarceration and poor mental health was only just significant, and the effect size was small ($OR = 1.2$). Thus, on the basis of the current review, summarizing the most rigorous evidence to date, we must revise previous findings and conclude that there are zero or only weak associations between parental incarceration and children's poor mental health, drug use, and educational performance.

The results from 45 samples confirm that, on average, children with incarcerated parents are at significantly higher risk for antisocial behavior compared with their peers. We conclude that although some individual studies and prior reviews have suggested that there are multiple types of adverse effects of parental incarceration on children, taking all evidence into account, the only outcome that remains associated with parental incarceration after adjustment for covariates is children's antisocial behavior. Among the most rigorous studies to date, the average effect size for antisocial behavior was $OR = 1.4$. This can be transformed into a percentage difference in antisocial behavior between children with incarcerated parents and children without incarcerated parents (Lipsey & Wilson, 2001). When this is done, the difference in antisocial behavior between children of incarcerated parents and comparison children is approximately 10%.

It must be emphasized again that although existing studies point toward the possibility that parental incarceration increases the risk for children's antisocial behavior, firm causal conclusions cannot be drawn. No randomized experiment has been conducted on this topic and the nonexperimental studies that have been conducted to date might be systematically biased. There was some evidence that even if studies included more covariates, effect sizes would not reduce much further: Meta-regression showed no reduction in effect sizes with more covariates controlled. Nonetheless, it is very hard to rule out all alternative explanations for associations in nonexperimental studies.

There may be important similarities between children's experiences of parental incarceration and other forms of parent–child separation, such as parental divorce (see Chapter 2). However, our meta-analysis of studies comparing children of incarcerated parents with children separated from parents for other reasons showed significantly higher risk for antisocial behavior among the parental incarceration group. Therefore, it is clear that parent–child separation per se is not the main factor explaining children's outcomes after parental incarceration.

Given considerable variation in the study results, we investigated possible moderators of the association between parental incarceration and children's antisocial behavior. Although several possible moderators have been suggested in the literature, we found no significant differences in study results according to the following variables: the child's sex, which parent was incarcerated, the child's age at the time of parental incarceration, the child's age at the time of outcome, "crime" outcomes versus outcomes of "general antisocial behavior," and whether studies were conducted in the United States. Also, there was no evidence that the effects of parental incarceration have diminished through time in the United States, as some researchers have speculated.

Why did the current meta-analysis reveal no significant moderator effects for the association between parental incarceration and children's antisocial behavior? First, it is possible that the effects of parental incarceration are similar across a range of different family circumstances. For example, the reasons why it has been speculated that maternal incarceration has stronger effects on children than paternal incarceration have to do with mechanisms of separation, changes in child care, and difficulties staying in contact. However, if other mechanisms are more important and have relatively uniform effects, this could explain the lack of significant moderator variables. For example, levels of stigma resulting from maternal and paternal incarceration might be quite similar and have similar consequences for children.

A second possible explanation for the lack of significant moderator effects relates to confounding. Expected moderator effects assume a causal relationship between parental incarceration and children's outcomes. The hypothesis that maternal incarceration is more harmful for children than paternal incarceration assumes that parental incarceration really does have causal effects. If the association is in fact spurious, rather than caused by the incarceration experience, then the rationale for expecting a moderator effect will not apply.

A third possible reason for the lack of moderator effects is that the range of moderator variables we investigated was limited, and perhaps there are other, untested moderator variables that do have significant effects. For example, it is possible that significant moderators would have been found if we had tested other variables, such as whether or not parents and children were living together before the incarceration, the quality of prior and ongoing family relationships, what children are told about the event, the offense for which parents are incarcerated, the length of parental incarceration, types of incarceration (jail or prison, and types of prison), levels of social support, family income, and neighborhood context. We could not test these variables as moderators because not enough primary studies reported the relevant information. Finally, it should be remembered that the tests of possible moderators in the current analysis compared results across a diverse group of studies that also varied in sample characteristics, measures used, and methodologies. Therefore, it is possible that real moderator effects were obscured because of these differences.

10

CONCLUSIONS

If, as societies, we cannot . . . break down the divisions and oppositions easily created by a jaded or thoughtless approach to policy making and procedure, I believe we will lose these children: they will becomes hostile, unreachable and angry.
—Mother of son with a father in prison, England, 2013

A unique aspect of the studies presented in this book is the follow-up of thousands of children into adulthood across four different countries—England, Sweden, the Netherlands, and the United States. A critical finding of the research is that parental incarceration can carry more or less risk for children depending on the social and penal context in which it takes place. Cross-national variations highlight opportunities to minimize children's difficulties by examining contexts where risks are minimized—that is, where parental incarceration does not appear to cause the same long-term harm as in other places. There was no evidence that parental incarceration caused increases in children's own adult offending in Sweden or in the Netherlands in the 1950s–1960s, when liberal penal climates prevailed and the focus of imprisonment was on rehabilitation rather than retribution. This contrasted starkly with England, the United States, and in a later generation in the Netherlands, when Dutch penal culture became more punitive than

http://dx.doi.org/10.1037/14377-011
Effects of Parental Incarceration on Children: Cross-National Comparative Studies, by J. Murray, C. C. J. H. Bijleveld, D. P. Farrington, and R. Loeber

before. In these contexts, parental incarceration predicted increased risk for numerous life difficulties, including children's own adult criminal behavior. It may seem naïve to look back to the mid-20th century for solutions to such an enormous modern problem as mass incarceration, but this may provide insight into key principles for reform efforts today. In this chapter, we summarize the empirical findings of all four studies covered in this book and the systematic review of the literature and consider policy, practice, and research implications for the future.

SUMMARY OF FINDINGS

The summary of findings from our four studies and systematic review is organized around the key questions presented in Chapter 3: Is parental incarceration a risk factor? Is it a causal risk factor? Why does parental incarceration cause harm for children? How do the effects of parental incarceration differ by circumstance and context?

Is Parental Incarceration a Risk Factor?

There is no doubt that parental incarceration, in most contexts, represents a significant risk factor for children's antisocial behavior and adult offending. A *risk factor* is something that predicts increased risk for an outcome, even though it does not necessarily cause the outcome. In all four countries in which our research was based, we found that children with incarcerated parents had increased risk for their own crime in adulthood. In England, Sweden, and the Netherlands, parental incarceration predicted various sorts of offending behavior, including both property and violent crime. Additionally, children with incarcerated parents were at increased risk of educational problems, mental health problems, drug use, and overall poor life success in England and poor marital outcomes in the Netherlands. A systematic review of evidence from all available community-based surveys (including over 40,000 children in 40 studies) confirmed that parental incarceration is a risk factor for children's own antisocial behavior, but effects were not found for children's mental health, drug use, and educational performance. This suggests that parental incarceration might have specific effects on children's antisocial behavior.

Is Parental Incarceration a Causal Risk Factor?

It is very difficult to answer the critical question of whether parental incarceration causes increased risk for children's adverse outcomes because preexisting social and genetic risks associated with having a parent in prison might account for observed associations. Even though parental incarceration predicts children's own antisocial behavior and crime, this does not imply that parental incarceration causes these outcomes. Across the studies in this book, we used various strategies to try to rule out alternative explanations for why parental incarceration predicts adverse outcomes for children. In each study, children with incarcerated parents were compared with children whose parents were convicted but not incarcerated to help assess whether parental crime and conviction was the main explanation for children's outcomes, rather than parental incarceration itself. We also used matching techniques and statistical models to control for background differences between children with incarcerated parents and other children in the studies. Additionally, in the Pittsburgh Youth Study in the United States, we examined trajectories of boys' problem behaviors to investigate changes from before to after parental incarceration.

According to these studies, it appeared that parental incarceration might have causal effects on children's life chances in some contexts but not in others. Specifically, parental incarceration appeared to be a possible causal risk factor for antisocial–criminal behavior and mental health problems in England, for crime and poor marital outcomes in the Netherlands in the 1970s–1980s, and for crime in the United States in the 1980s–1990s. However, we concluded that in Sweden and in the Netherlands in the 1950s–1960s, parental incarceration did not causally increase sons' own criminal behavior. A systematic review of all the evidence suggested that there might be moderate increases in children's antisocial behavior caused by parental incarceration, but that conclusive evidence is lacking, given that no experiments have been done and very few studies have examined changes in children's behavior from before to after parental incarceration.

Why Does Parental Incarceration Cause Harm for Children?

In Chapters 2 and 3 we discussed the range and depth of practical and emotional difficulties often experienced by families and children of prisoners, and the various theoretical perspectives about how these might lead to long-lasting adverse outcomes for children. If parental incarceration does cause increased risk for adverse life outcomes, such as children's own criminal behavior, it is important to understand why. Ideally, theoretical mechanisms should be tested by examining changes in children's attachment relationships, peer relations, social learning environments, experiences of stigma, and family social and economic support from before to after parental incarceration. The Pittsburgh Youth Study in the United States included repeated measures of some of these influences: caretaker stress and various parenting practices and peer factors. Although none of these measures on their own changed significantly from before to after parental incarceration, their combined influence appeared to account for about half of the effects of parental incarceration on boys' theft. Noticeably, in the American study, the chances that sons were convicted themselves were not much larger for sons experiencing parental incarceration during childhood, as opposed to having a parent incarcerated before birth. This suggests that the long-term effects of parental incarceration on sons' own crime in the United States might be principally explained by persistent family difficulties after parental incarceration, such as weakened relationships, reduced ex-prisoner employment opportunities, or enduring stigma.

In England, and in the Netherlands in the 1970s–1980s, parental incarceration after a son's birth predicted the boy's own criminal behavior more strongly than parental incarceration before birth. This suggests that environmental mechanisms in the immediate aftermath of incarceration were salient in these contexts. However, in England, comparisons between boys separated from parents because of parental incarceration and boys separated from parents for other reasons showed that the effects of parental incarceration were not explained by separation per se. A similar conclusion was drawn in the systematic review of the literature in Chapter 9. Thus, it may be the particular meanings attributed to parental incarceration and the social stigma that they evoke that are most significant for children's experiences after parental incarceration and their later life outcomes. However, official bias (police and courts being prejudiced toward children of incarcerated parents) did not seem an important explanatory factor for boys' crime in the English study because boys with incarcerated parents were at increased risk of both self-reported crime as well as officially recorded crime. More research is required on the precise processes of stigma that might link parental incarceration and adverse life chances for children.

The results from our systematic review of 40 studies on the topic showed robust associations between parental incarceration and children's antisocial behavior, but not children's mental health problems, drug use, or poor educational performance; this was also observed in our U.S. study. The specificity of this effect on antisocial behavior suggests particular mechanisms might be important. Note that, although antisocial behavior is commonly associated with other kinds of youth problems (such as drug use and mood disorders) explanatory factors are not necessarily the same (Loeber, Farrington, Stouthamer-Loeber, & van Kammen, 1998). There are three main possible explanations for the specific association of parental incarceration with children's antisocial behavior.

A first possible explanation for the specific effect of parental incarceration on antisocial behavior is an interaction between the stressful experiences caused by parental incarceration and children's pre-existing propensity for antisocial behavior. Social modeling processes might be implicated here. If children grow up seeing their parents respond to stressful life events with antisocial behavior, they may be socialized into having particularly antisocial reactions to disruptive events, such as parental incarceration. This "double whammy" of prior exposure to models of antisocial behavior and strains caused by parental incarceration might interact to increase the probability of children developing their own antisocial behavior, without necessarily affecting other outcomes. Another potentially important interaction is between the genetic risk transmitted by antisocial parents and the social impacts of parental incarceration. Thus, a gene-environment interaction or correlation may be implicated in the increased risk for antisocial behavior among children of incarcerated parents.

A second possible explanation for the specific association between parental incarceration and children's antisocial behavior is that the stigma of parental incarceration has particular effects on this outcome. Stigma can manifest itself in social bias toward children with incarcerated parents: peers, teachers, and other community members believing that "the apple doesn't fall far from the tree" (Phillips & Gates, 2011) or viewing children with incarcerated parents as destined toward a life of crime (Braman, 2004, pp. 173-174). Although criminological research clearly shows that intergenerational criminal behavior is only a probabilistic phenomenon, according to labeling theory, social expectations can produce self-fulfilling prophecies, by cutting children off from conventional others, fostering a delinquent self-image, and increasing the probability of antisocial and criminal behavior (Becker, 1963; Farrington & Murray, 2014; Lemert, 1967).

A third possible explanation for the specific effects of parental incarceration on children's antisocial behavior is that unmeasured confounding variables have stronger effects on this outcome: the observed association with antisocial behavior might be spurious. For example, pre-existing genetic and social influences that predispose children toward antisocial behavior might have been inadequately controlled in existing studies. If this were true, the association between parental incarceration and children's antisocial behavior would reflect the intergenerational transmission of antisocial behavior (via other mechanisms) rather than an impact of parental incarceration itself. To test this hypothesis, it would be highly desirable to employ genetically sensitive research designs, such as longitudinal twin studies, to tease apart the relevant environmental and genetic mechanisms involved (Moffitt & Caspi, 2006).

We conclude that, while immediate emotional, social, and financial stresses within the family may cause profound difficulties for children during parental incarceration, the enduring stigma of parental incarceration may be a critical mechanism accounting for long-term effects of parental incarceration on children's own antisocial behavior and crime. Future research should test this proposition.

How Do the Effects of Parental Incarceration Differ by Circumstance and Context?

We investigated whether the effects of parental incarceration varied for different groups of children, such as for boys and girls. In Sweden, effects of parental incarceration appeared roughly similar for girls and boys, and similar for children of different social classes, which might reflect buffering effects of an egalitarian social and welfare system in Sweden. In the Netherlands, parental incarceration seemed to affect sons more than daughters regarding their marital outcomes. In the English study, longer prison spells predicted increased probability of sons' own offending. In the Pittsburgh Youth Study in the United States, we tested whether effects of parental incarceration differed for children according to the boy's race, the timing of parental incarceration, which parent was incarcerated, whether the boy was living with his or her parent in the year before the incarceration, and levels of parental antisocial behavior. There was some evidence that parental incarceration predicted boys' theft more strongly for White youth than Black youth, but we found no evidence for other variations in effects. Our systematic review of the literature also showed no significant differences in effects of parental incarceration on children's antisocial behavior according to the child's sex, which parent was incarcerated, the child's age at the time of parental incarceration, the child's age at the time of outcome, "crime" outcomes versus outcomes of "general antisocial behavior," and whether studies were conducted in the United States. Although it has been pointed out that maternal incarceration can involve many more immediate difficulties for children, such as changes in child care, if other factors such as social stigma are more important for children's later life outcomes such as criminal behavior, this could explain why no differences were found in long-term effects of maternal and paternal incarceration on children.

Other researchers in the United States using data from the Fragile Families and Child Wellbeing Study found differences in the effects of paternal incarceration on children's aggressive behavior according to whether fathers lived with their child before the incarceration (stronger effects were observed when fathers were resident) and according to whether fathers were violent in the child's home (no effects were observed in the context of domestic violence; Geller, Cooper, Garfinkel, Schwartz-Soicher, & Mincy, 2012; Wildeman, 2010). More research is needed on these important issues. We may not have detected such interactions in our U.S. study because the sample was not large enough to reveal differences between subgroups of boys with incarcerated parents.

Our research comparing findings across four countries revealed that the effects of parental incarceration varied by national context. Effects on sons' own offending in young adulthood were stronger in England, the Netherlands in the 1970s–1980s, and the United States than in Sweden and the Netherlands in the 1950s–1960s. Although explanations for these cross-national differences have to remain speculative, we suggest that different social patterns, penal climates, and prison sentence lengths may explain the variation. Specifically, we hypothesize that harmful effects of parental incarceration in England were exacerbated by the fact that boys normally lived with both parents when parental incarceration did occur and relatively long prison sentences and less family-friendly prison conditions in England than other European countries. By contrast, Sweden and the Netherlands had particularly liberal penal cultures in the 1950s–1960s focused on rehabilitation, with relatively short prison sentences and good contact opportunities for prisoners and their families. However, the changing penal climate in the Netherlands, from the late 1970s onward, shifted closer to that of England, and this may have contributed to more harmful effects of parental incarceration in the Netherlands observed in the 1970s–1980s compared to in the 1950s–1960s. The main alternative interpretation of these differences is that they reflect variation in the population that was "selected" into prison in the different countries—less serious offenders in Sweden and the Netherlands in the mid-20th century than in England and later periods in the Netherlands.

The United States has had the highest incarceration rate and longest sentences out of all the countries examined in our research. In the context of such a punitive penal climate, long-term adverse consequences of parental incarceration seem entirely plausible and were evident in our research and in several other large American studies. Because U.S. studies to date have all relied on suboptimal measures of parental incarceration (questionnaire reports, rather than official records—as in England, Sweden, and the Netherlands), adverse effects of parental incarceration on children in the United States may even be underestimated in these studies.

IMPLICATIONS FOR POLICY:
REDUCE THE INCARCERATION RATE

"Research on collateral effects of imprisonment suggests that policy-makers have been flying blind, making decisions costing billions of dollars and affecting millions of lives without adequate knowledge of the nature and costs of unintended side effects" (Tonry & Petersilia, 1999a, p. 7). The main policy issue raised by the present research is that, under certain conditions, incarcerating parents might harm children and contribute to crime in the next generation. As we have emphasized throughout this book, knowledge of these causal effects is not beyond doubt, because unmeasured influences might explain the association between parental incarceration and adverse outcomes for children. However, the evidence does point toward parental incarceration causing increased risk for adverse adult outcomes, such as criminal behavior, particularly in harsh penal climates and less integrative social environments. As such, policymakers must consider reforms to reduce these harmful effects.

The most obvious strategy to prevent harmful effects of parental incarceration on children is to send fewer parents to prison. As Todd Clear (2007) cogently argued, "There is no discernible, principled foundation for U.S. prison policy"—"too many people go to prison, and too many of them stay there too long" (p. 176). The incarceration rate could be reduced by greater use of alternative forms of criminal punishment, such as probation, intensive supervision, house arrest, electronic monitoring, community service, and day fines. Given that the incarceration rate is a function of both the number of people being sent to prison and the length of time they are incarcerated, reductions in sentence length would also reduce the incarceration rate. Given that children seem most likely to be harmed when their parents are incarcerated for long periods, reducing sentence lengths seems a particularly appropriate reform to consider. Sentencing reforms could be introduced with a presumption against the use of incarceration (in favor of intermediate sentences; Tonry, 1998) and guidelines introduced to reduce sentence lengths and increase the use of parole and prison amnesties (Tonry, 2003). Because women tend to be incarcerated for more minor offenses than men and that maternal incarceration is often highly disruptive for children, these reforms might be particularly urgent for women. However, the obstacles to such criminal justice reforms are complex (Tonry, 1996) and often political (Gottschalk, 2010; Tonry, 2004).

Policy issues about reducing the incarceration rate as a means to prevent harmful effects of parental incarceration were discussed in a series of recent articles in the journal *Criminology and Public Policy*. In an important empirical study that launched the debate, Wakefield and Wildeman (2011) reported evidence suggesting that (a) children's conduct problems and internalizing problems were increased by paternal incarceration in two American longitudinal studies; (b) these effects were not observed in the context of domestic violence or paternal incarceration for a violent crime; (c) as incarceration rates grew in the 1980s and 1990s, Black children became increasingly likely to experience paternal incarceration compared with White children; and (d) racial differences in childhood behavioral problems would have been substantially smaller if paternal incarceration had not become so common in the United States (see also Wakefield & Wildeman, 2014). On this basis,

Wakefield and Wildeman (2011) suggested that policy reform focus on keeping nonviolent and drug offenders out of jail. They also suggested that current financial constraints in the United States provide an opportunity to reconsider policy options and encourage policymakers to reduce the prison population and save money while averting harm to the next generation.

These are sound suggestions, but with difficult practical and theoretical issues to consider. As discussed by Kruttschnitt (2011), financial pressures can be of small concern to policymakers in the context of extreme punitive public attitudes. In California, even when fiscal concerns were at their paramount with a $24 million budget shortfall, a bill proposal to release some nonviolent offenders created a "political firestorm" (Gottschalk, 2010, p. 70; quoted by Kruttschnitt, 2011). A practical difficulty with targeting nonviolent or drug offenders for diversion away from prison is that it is not entirely clear how they should be identified operationally (Sampson, 2011). This is because the charge leading to conviction is often arbitrary and depends on issues of evidence, and because a person's current offense is a very poor predictor of the next offense, and "minor" offenders often commit "major" crimes in the future (Sampson, 2011).

Of course, for policymakers to make fully informed decisions, any potential costs of incarceration must be weighed against its possible benefits across the population (Sampson, 2011). This balancing act is enormously difficult—weighing the harms caused to prisoners, their families and children, and the community, as well as fiscal costs of prisons, against potential benefits in terms of crimes averted through incarceration. Evidence is equivocal on the effects of incarceration on both individual-level criminal behavior and overall crime rates, and several studies have suggested counterproductive, criminogenic effects of incarceration rather than preventive benefits (Nagin, Cullin, & Jonson, 2009; Rosenfeld & Messner, 2009; Tonry, 2001). Although there are no tight empirical estimates of the varied and subtle costs and benefits of incarceration, any policy decision must be made while trying to take all of them into account. The evidence to date suggests that the costs of incarceration to children with incarcerated parents are considerable and long lasting; these children must not be forgotten in the debate.

IMPLICATIONS FOR PRACTICE

Whether you are a policeman searching a family home or a probation officer drawing up a sentence plan, please show my son that you care about him. . . . Please don't be like the probation officer who, when he complained about being moved to a prison so far away as to make contact with his son impossible, told my son's father "We don't care about your family; we care about your sentence plan." (Mother of boy with father in prison, England, 2013)

Given that the incarceration rate will never be reduced to zero, and indeed may not be reduced at all for political or other reasons, it is important to implement programs and reforms to reduce harmful effects of parental incarceration when it does occur (Parke & Clarke-Stewart, 2003). Children with incarcerated parents are a highly vulnerable group who are often exposed to multiple risk factors even prior to their parent's incarceration. As we have discussed throughout this book, under certain conditions, parental incarceration may exacerbate these problems and contribute to children's adjustment difficulties and later antisocial behavior. Corrections officials, schools, and social and health workers should be made aware of the difficulties faced by families and children with incarcerated parents to mitigate the effects. In considering possible interventions and reforms, any intervention aimed at preventing long-lasting harm for children with incarcerated parents must consider children's wider environment and their developmental context. It must be reemphasized that the difficulties observed for children after parental incarceration may not reflect effects of the incarceration itself; rather, they may reflect "side effects" of parents' antisocial behavior or other background risks in children's lives. Parental incarceration is likely to be only one event among many adversities that put children at risk during their development. However, distinct difficulties related to parental incarceration mean that correction reforms and targeted prevention programs are appropriate.

Interventions to reduce harmful effects during parental incarceration should be designed on the basis of evidence about the mechanisms linking parental incarceration and children's adverse outcomes (Murray & Farrington, 2006). Currently, the evidence base is too weak to draw strong conclusions about the types of interventions that would be most effective. However, we consider a number of interventions that might be useful, given the possible theoretical mechanisms at work.

If, during parental incarceration, children's difficulties arise because of the trauma of parent–child separation and threats to children's attachment relations, these effects might be mitigated using five strategies. Steps could be taken to ensure that children have stable care arrangements during parental incarceration, ideally with families or friends (Bernstein, 2005; Trice & Brewster, 2004). Children could be matched with mentors to provide consistent care through the period of parental incarceration and afterward (Shlafer, Poehlmann, Coffino, & Hanneman, 2009). Children's caregivers could be given professional advice about how to provide honest and developmentally appropriate explanations about parental absence to children (Poehlmann, 2005b). Counseling and therapeutic services could be offered to children of prisoners to help them cope with difficult emotions during separation (Hames & Pedreira, 2003; Parke & Clarke-Stewart, 2003; Sack, Seidler, & Thomas, 1976). Children's opportunities to maintain good-quality contact with their incarcerated parent could be increased, in particular by providing child-friendly visiting arrangements in prisons, housing prisoners closer to home, and extending visiting hours (Bernstein, 2005; Council of Europe, 1997; Parke & Clarke-Stewart, 2003; Trice & Brewster, 2004). In the Swedish and Dutch contexts where parental imprisonment did not cause adverse outcomes for children, more provision was available for prisoners to maintain contact with their families, including home leave and special family visits to prison. It is important to investigate the types of contact that are most beneficial for children and under which conditions contact is more distressing (Nickel, Garland, & Kane, 2009; Richards et al., 1994).

Children of prisoners could also be helped during parental incarceration by supporting their caregivers via a series of practical measures. Significant difficulties for prisoners' families include finding out what has happened to their relative, where they are, how they can be contacted, confusion about the prison system, and how to manage issues such as benefit claims while relatives are in custody. Therefore, basic information about where incarcerated relatives are located, rules governing family communication with prisoners, visiting procedures, and benefits rights could be provided to prisoners' families through telephone help lines, leaflets, handbooks, and public websites (Hairston, 2003). Caretakers consistently report financial difficulties in visiting remote prisons, and volunteer organizations can provide significant support in practical issues such as transport of children to detention facilities (Hissel, Bijleveld, & Kruttschnitt, 2011). Extremely simple and uncostly interventions (e.g., an answering machine for prison telephone lines or e-mail) could alleviate problems and facilitate contact (Hissel et al., 2011).

If parental incarceration affects children via parenting difficulties during the incarceration, parenting programs for incarcerated parents and their families might be used to reduce these difficulties. The provision of parenting programs in U.S. prisons is sporadic, and programs tend to have little scientific basis. However, there are ongoing efforts to develop and rigorously evaluate prison parenting programs that address the unique needs of incarcerated parents and their families (Eddy et al., 2008; Menting, 2012). Four well-tested parenting programs might be used and adapted to prevent undesirable effects on children (Eddy & Reid, 2003). Nurse home-visiting programs could be used to support mothers in high-risk circumstances and improve prenatal care and maternal health (Olds et al., 1998). Parent-management training programs could be used to enhance parenting skills and parents' handling of children's misbehavior (Sanders, Markie-Dadds, Tully, & Bor, 2000; Scott, Spender, Doolan, Jacobs, & Aspland, 2001; Webster-Stratton, 1998). Because children with incarcerated parents are often exposed to environments with multiple problems, multimodal therapies—probably involving all family members—may be required. Multisystemic therapy could be used to target parent–child interactions as well as wider social problems of youth (Eddy et al., 2008; Henggeler, Schoenwald, Borduin, Rowland, & Cunningham, 1998). Multidimensional treatment foster care could be used to provide therapeutic care for youngsters removed from their homes and to encourage reintegration and support of children with their natural family (Chamberlain & Reid, 1998). Obviously, programs designed for use in the community would need careful adaptation if they were used in prisons (Eddy et al., 2008; Loper & Tuerk, 2006). Coparenting presents particular challenges as the detained parent—who is generally in a position of dependence—has to negotiate with the children's caretaker for access to and contact with the children. Menting (2012) found some promising results regarding a training program for detained mothers evaluated in a randomized experiment: The Incredible Years intervention program was found to improve parenting behavior (consistency of discipline practices) and reduce disruptive behavior of children ages 2 to 10 years in the short term.

The high levels of social and economic disadvantage often associated with parental incarceration imply that clinical intervention might be rendered ineffective unless there is simultaneous provision of social and economic support to families. If parental incarceration harms children via family economic strain, three kinds of financial support might be provided to families of prisoners. Emergency funds could be given to help families of prisoners overcome the immediate financial difficulties after the incarceration (Council of Europe, 1997). Free transport or financial assistance to families could be provided for prison visits, and the costs of telephone calls between prison and home could be reduced or eliminated (Bernstein, 2005). Prisoners could be provided with more paid jobs while in custody, and more could be invested in work schemes to employ former prisoners (Clear, Rose, & Ryder, 2001; Council of Europe, 1997; Petersilia, 2003). In Sweden and the Netherlands, the strong social welfare system was well known in the periods when we found no effects of parental incarceration on children's own chances of offending. Social welfare reform thus might be able to reduce harmful effects of parental incarceration, as well as provide support to generally vulnerable populations.

On the basis of theories of stigma and labeling, three policies might be considered to reduce the stigma experienced by children of prisoners, as well as by prisoners themselves. The public identification of offenders could be prohibited, not only before conviction but also afterward (Petersilia, 2003; Walker, 1980). Offenders could be diverted away from courts to restorative justice conferences, which emphasize reconciliation between offenders, victims, family members, friends, and the community (Braithwaite, 1999; Braithwaite & Mugford, 1994; Sherman & Strang, 2007; Sherman et al., 2005). More community services could be used that emphasize the positive contributions that ex-offenders can make to the community, rather than their expected deficits—a "strengths-based approach" to reintegration (Clear et al., 2001; Maruna & LeBel, 2002, p. 167). According to Maruna and LeBel (2002), one of the most important aspects of strengths-based reintegration would involve "facilitation of active relationships and traditional parental responsibility among prisoners" (p. 172). Another way of increasing positive reintegration might be to give prisoners the right to vote:

> Giving back voting rights is another way to make a person feel part of that community. How can you feel that you're giving back to a community that you're a part of when you're exiled from it by not being able to vote and have a voice in it? (anonymous prisoner, quoted in Uggen, Manza, & Behrens, 2004, pp. 275–276)

For children themselves, Jones and Wainaina-Wozna (2013) recommended that schools implement programs to raise awareness of the issues of parental incarceration and promote positive and nondiscriminatory school environments.

Even if parental incarceration does not causally impact on children's life chances, there are important clinical considerations for working with children whose parents are incarcerated. In courts and clinics, children with a history of parental incarceration tend to have more disadvantaged backgrounds and more problem behaviors than other children in these settings. Phillips et al. (2002) found that, among youth in a mental health clinic, those with a history of parental incarceration were more likely than others to have been exposed to parental substance abuse, extreme poverty, and abuse or neglect. In a sample of adjudicated youth, Dannerbeck (2005) found that youth with a history of parental incarceration were more likely than other youth to have experienced severely ineffective parenting, child abuse, or neglect, and were more likely to have parents who abuse drink or drugs or have a mental illness. In clinics and courts, professionals should be aware that a history of parental incarceration could be associated with multiple other difficulties. As Kemper and Rivara (1993) suggested, it might therefore be appropriate for professionals, such as child health workers, to include questions about parental incarceration as part of a comprehensive assessment of children's needs. If a history of parental incarceration is apparent, this could indicate the need for more in-depth assessment and appropriate support services where necessary.

The research reported in this book shows that children with incarcerated parents are likely to have raised levels of problem behavior in adolescence that often continues into adulthood. Moreover, as we have shown previously (Murray & Farrington, 2008b), boys in England with incarcerated parents were at increased risk for comorbid antisocial and internalizing problems. Unfortunately, comorbidity of problems such as conduct disorder and depression indicate more serious social maladjustment for individuals (Goodwin & Hamilton, 2003; Marmorstein & Iacono, 2003). Early intervention, perhaps in the school context where comorbidity problems are particularly manifest (Marmorstein & Iacono, 2003), may be essential to prevent severe and long-lasting social and emotional difficulties among children with incarcerated parents.

The effectiveness of such policy reforms should be carefully evaluated in demonstration projects using randomized controlled trials and in systematic reviews. Policies and programs that are found to reduce harmful effects of parental incarceration and improve children's outcomes should be implemented on a large scale. Single agencies are unlikely to have the necessary resources to deliver the comprehensive support that is needed by families and children of prisoners (Rossman, 2003). A critical policy issue is coordinating the multiple agencies involved, including the criminal justice system, social services, health services, and schools (Nickel et al., 2009). Connecting these systems is challenging even when their objectives are complementary. However, security and welfare goals are sometimes at odds, and because of their different priorities, fragmented services, limited resources, and failures to share information between organizations, many states in the United States have significant service gaps (Parke & Clarke-Stewart, 2003; Rossman, 2003). Thus, a major policy challenge is to coordinate agencies to develop and implement programs that adequately support children of incarcerated parents.

IMPLICATIONS FOR FUTURE RESEARCH

John Hagan and Ronit Dinovitzer (1999) rightly argued that "the implication of not having better and more systematic research on the collateral effects of incarceration is that we are making penal policy in a less than fully, indeed poorly, informed fashion" (p. 152). We have brought together evidence from four large, long-term studies on parental incarceration, and a major systematic review to help this debate, but there are limitations to these studies that should be addressed in future research.

The main limitations of the studies in this book were as follows. None were based on an experimental design from which tighter causal conclusions could be drawn. None included in-depth qualitative questions with families about their experiences of parental incarceration; in particular, they did not collect information about the stigma that families may have experienced as a result of parental incarceration. The studies with the richest interview data (our English and American studies) had the smallest numbers of participants, meaning that subgroup comparisons provided low statistical power for investigating differences in effects of parental incarceration on children within those studies. We matched the studies in our cross-national comparisons as closely as possible, but of course measurement differences or other cross-national differences (apart from those we highlighted in our discussions) may account for the pattern of findings observed. Although it was an enormous strength to include long-term follow-up of children over several decades, the findings of such long-term studies necessarily refer to the historical period in which children grew up. Children with incarcerated parents today may experience quite different effects from children in the studies reported here.

Further research is needed to confirm the causal and varied effects postulated here, and identify the precise mechanisms involved. Our first recommendation for future research on the effects of parental incarceration is that randomized experiments—in which convicted parents who would normally be incarcerated are randomly assigned either to incarceration (as usual) or to alternative sentences (e.g., community service)—should be used wherever possible. Randomization, with large enough samples, ensures that children with incarcerated parents and comparison children are similar on observed and unobserved factors before incarceration, making any difference afterward attributable to the incarceration itself. A few randomized experiments have been conducted on the effects of incarceration on ex-prisoner outcomes (Barton & Butts, 1990; Bergman, 1976; Killias, Aebi, & Ribeaud, 2000; Schneider, 1986). For example, Killias et al. (2000) invited people sentenced to prison for up to 2 weeks in Switzerland to participate in a study in which they were randomly assigned either to serve their sentence in prison as usual or to serve a community sentence. Among the 123 randomly assigned participants, those who received prison sentences had higher rates of rearrest 2 years later and more unfavorable attitudes toward the criminal justice system than those in the control group. However, no differences were observed with respect to employment or social and private life, and also effects seemed to dissipate in the long term (Killias, Gilliéron, Villard, & Poglia, 2010).

If similar experiments were conducted focusing on convicted parents, and included interviews with families and children, the causal effects of parental incarceration (of a short duration) could be estimated with greater confidence than has been possible to date. Randomized studies would have to focus on short-term incarceration so that the alternative punishment condition was of comparable severity. The combination of circumstances that made the experiment by Killias and colleagues feasible (despite various forms of opposition to its implementation) was a Swiss legal provision for introducing (and thereby evaluating) new forms of punishment for limited periods of time (for instance, alternatives to incarceration) and the commitment to evidence-based policy by the director of the local corrections services and the Minister of Justice (Killias et al., 2010). One can imagine many practical, political, and ethical obstacles to conducting randomized studies of incarceration. However, these difficulties may not be as absolute as they first seem (Killias & Villetaz, 2008). A few studies now show that they can be overcome, and the benefits of randomized experiments imply that opportunities to conduct them should be taken wherever possible (Killias & Villetaz, 2008).

This discussion of randomized experiments relates to our second research recommendation—that families and children of prisoners be included in all program evaluations with offenders. The effects of treatment programs on families and children may be of critical importance, not only for the program's success in reducing reoffending, but also, vitally, in terms of overall program costs and benefits; consequences for families and children of offenders must be included in these calculations. The recommendation to evaluate family and child outcomes could be stretched to evaluations of all corrections policies, as Comfort, Nurse, McKay, and Kramer (2011) suggested:

> All penal policies [should] be accompanied by a "Family and Children Impact Statement" that would explicitly describe the likely repercussions of criminal justice laws and practices on incarcerated people's kin, provide justification for the degree of harm imposed on children, and discuss how negative effects could be avoided or mitigated. (p. 845)

A third recommendation is to use natural experiments to estimate effects of incarceration on their families and children. In natural experiments, researchers do not have control over the events being studied, but naturally occurring events simulate the conditions of a randomized experiment. For example, Charles Loeffler (2013) took advantage of the random assignment of felony cases to judges in Chicago, and the differential propensity of judges to sentence people to prison, to estimate the effects of incarceration on ex-prisoner recidivism. Similar studies might include outcomes for families or children of prisoners. The occurrence of prison amnesties—as in France on Bastille day, when thousands of prisoners have been granted pardons and released early from prison in the past—provide opportunities for investigating the effects of reducing prison sentence lengths on prisoners and their families. Any such "exogenous" change, caused by events outside the control of study participants, might provide an opportunity to separate out the effects of incarceration from other influences in people's lives.

The fourth need for future research is to mount new prospective longitudinal surveys, starting before parental incarceration takes place. Only by collecting data on children's experiences from both before and after parental incarceration can it be understood how children's problem behavior develops dynamically over time and to what extent children's outcomes are attributable to parental incarceration itself versus preexisting factors. New studies should be prospective and longitudinal, with large samples and repeated assessments to analyze development and change over time and the mediators and moderators of change. Some key questions for future research following children through time are: How do the effects of parental incarceration develop from the point of arrest, through trial, during incarceration, and after release? What are the effects of repeated parental incarcerations compared with the first incident? Do the effects of parental incarceration on children increase linearly the longer parents are held in prison? New studies should measure and test key theoretical mechanisms (e.g., attachment, strain, learning, and stigma) that might link parental incarceration and undesirable child outcomes. Further work is required on whether parental incarceration might represent a protective factor for some children, and under what circumstances. To advance knowledge on these issues, it is critical for future studies to take account of children's lives before parental incarceration. Nearly all studies to date have started after parental incarceration first occurred, and this makes it extremely difficult to disentangle effects of parental incarceration from other influences in children's lives.

The costs of this type of research may be considerable, but given the number of children who experience parental incarceration, their high-risk status, and the long-term risks associated with parental incarceration, failure to conduct this research might be even more costly. In Chapter 7, we presented unique data on changes in boys' behaviors and their social environments through several years from before to after parental incarceration in the Pittsburgh Youth Study. In new studies, it would be necessary to involve enough high-risk families such that parental incarceration occurs frequently during the course of the study and can be analyzed quantitatively. This might be done by recruiting a cohort of arrested or convicted parents with noncustodial sentences (who are at risk for future offending and incarceration) or by including a large number of families with known correlates of incarceration, perhaps living in high-risk neighborhoods.

A new prospective study might be combined with an experimental intervention aimed at reducing the risk of future parental incarceration (Loeber & Farrington, 2008). For example, a cohort of convicted parents receiving noncustodial sentences could be randomly assigned to receive additional employment programs, drug rehabilitation programs, or cognitive–behavioral therapy (aimed at reducing the chances of future offending and incarceration) or services as usual. Combining such experimental interventions with a longitudinal study would provide the opportunity to research both the effects of incarceration as it usually occurs (in quasi-experimental analyses) while also gaining knowledge about the effects of prevention programs aimed at reducing incarceration. Evidence also needs to be produced on the effects of intervention programs to reduce the undesirable effects of parental incarceration when it does occur. Knowledge could be drawn from other areas of child development (e.g., research on reducing the effects of parental mental illness and the effects of parental divorce on children). Qualitative and quantitative research should be used to investigate additional support needs of prisoners' families. Systematic evaluation of intervention programs should be conducted to test how effectively they reduce adverse outcomes for children of prisoners.

The research reported on in this book spanned four countries and several generations, highlighting how the effects of parental incarceration on children may vary across social and penal contexts. As Kruttschnitt (2011) argued, natural variation in U.S. state prison policies could also be used by researchers to examine how provision of programs to prisoners, visitation rules, and even sentence length influence children's reactions to parental incarceration.

The bottom line of our research is that children whose parents are incarcerated are a highly vulnerable group who often experience multiple challenges and adversities both before and after their parent is incarcerated. In certain contexts, parental incarceration may exacerbate their difficulties and contribute to long-lasting adverse outcomes, including crime in the next generation. Although some "pains" of incarceration are unavoidable for those closely involved, social and penal reform should aim to reduce the long-lasting harms left in its wake. A shift in culture and policy is needed to bring lawbreakers back into the community and realize the true potential of all their children. We end this book with the words of an English mother caring for her son whose father is in prison:

> I told him that sometimes good people do bad things and that maybe, people we think of as bad, might also do good things now and again— that those lines which we draw between good and bad are not quite as crisp and clear as we like to think they are, that he is a different person from his father and that he can use the experience of having a father in prison to help him make better choices than his father made and that when his dad comes out of prison, hopefully he can make better choices too. But my son will not believe what I told him, unless you, as professionals, believe it too; unless in your dealings with prisoners and their families you show compassion, humanity, understanding and positivity, avoid stereotyping, treat people as individuals, listen without prejudice. . . . [P]lease show my son that you care about him, that you understand, that you believe in positive change.

APPENDIX A: MEASURES
IN THE ENGLISH STUDY

PARENTAL CONVICTIONS

In the Cambridge Study in Delinquent Development in England, convictions of boys' biological mothers and fathers were identified from searches of the central Criminal Record Office (National Identification Bureau) in London. The Criminal Record Office contains records of all relatively serious offenses committed in Great Britain and Ireland and also acts as a repository for records of minor juvenile offenses committed in London. The following offenses were excluded: breaches of probation, minor motoring offenses, and minor nonindictable offenses not normally recorded unless the offender already had a Criminal Record Office file. Because every boy had at least one parent whose records were searched, no case was counted as "not known" on parental criminality (West & Farrington, 1973).

> In order to obtain identifying particulars that would enable these searches to be conducted, the full name and date of birth of each birth family member, including maiden names of mothers and wives, were obtained during interviews. These particulars were checked against, and frequently supplemented by, information from medical and social service records and from birth certificates and marriage certificate. (Farrington, Barnes, & Lambert, 1996, p. 51)

Convictions by both juvenile and adult courts were included, although it was realized that the juvenile records of the parents' generation were incomplete. Osborn and West (1979) listed several reasons for this:

> In pre-war years juvenile findings of guilt were not always notified to central records. Forty-two of the fathers were known to have spent their early years abroad, so that any convictions they may have had would not necessarily appear in English records . . . [and] the Criminal Record Office used to destroy the files of minor offenders after a period of 10 years without further convictions. . . . There is no means of knowing how many names had been deleted before 1964. (p. 121)

PARENTAL INCARCERATION

Cases of parental incarceration were identified from parents' criminal records that had been retrieved from the central Criminal Record Office in London (described previously). The original cards recording criminal convictions of boys' mothers and fathers were reexamined for the present research to identify cases of parental incarceration following conviction. Because parents had to be convicted for a relatively serious offense to have a criminal record card, social worker files, which recorded occasions of parent–child separation, were also reexamined to identify further cases of parental incarceration for minor offenses or on remand (up to the boys' 15th birthdays). Parents had to have been incarcerated for at least 1 month to appear in social worker files. Four cases were coded as "no parent incarcerated" because parents had only been held in custody for 1 day (in lieu of a fine, as shown on criminal records).

According to these criteria, 20 boys' fathers had been to prison, two boys' mothers had been to prison, and one boy's mother and father had been to prison in the boys' first 10 years of life. The mean time that these boys' parents were incarcerated during the boys' first 10 years of life was 9.6 months ($SD = 14.2$). According to social worker files, none of these boys were permanently separated from their parent before the parent's incarceration. Seventeen boys had a parent incarcerated before their births and not again afterward.

Ideally, boys experiencing parental incarceration would have been split into further categories—for example, according to their age at the time of parental incarceration (e.g., 0–5 compared with 5–10) or according to whether the boy's mother or father was incarcerated. However, this would have resulted in groups of extremely small numbers. Therefore, for the purposes of this research, it was decided to consider boys who experienced parental incarceration of mothers or fathers at any age (between 0 and 10) in one category. The reason why cases of parental incarceration beyond boys' 11th birthdays ($n = 6$ up to age 18) were not included in the main analyses was so that adolescent outcomes were genuinely predicted by the explanatory variables and also so that other age 10 predictors could be used as suitable controls.

BOYS' ANTISOCIAL OUTCOMES

Criminal convictions of the study males were measured from searches of the central Criminal Record Office in London. When the boys were juveniles, this information was supplemented by searches of various local authority Children's Departments, nearby police, court, and probation offices and occasionally from teachers (West, 1969; West & Farrington, 1973). Convictions were classified according to the age of the study male at the time of the offenses. *Juvenile convictions* refer to convictions for offenses committed between ages 10 and 16 (inclusive); *young adult convictions* refer to convictions for offenses committed between ages 17 and 24 (inclusive); and *adult convictions* refer to convictions for offenses committed between ages 25 and 40 (inclusive). Three men who had died were excluded from counts of young adult convictions, and eight men who had died were excluded from counts of adult convictions. In total, 85 study males were convicted as juveniles, 114 as young adults, and 80 as adults.

By age 32, 18 study males had emigrated outside Great Britain or Ireland. Applications were made to search their criminal records in the eight countries where they had settled, and searches were actually carried out in four countries. Because most males did not emigrate until their 20s, and because the emigrants had rarely been convicted in England, it is likely that the criminal records of the males are quite complete.

Juvenile convictions were defined as findings of guilt for offenses normally registered in the Criminal Record Office. Juvenile convictions included four types, classified by West and Farrington (1973) as follows: (a) crimes of dishonesty, consisting of theft, unauthorized taking of motor vehicles, burglary, fraud, handling stolen property, and being equipped to steal; (b) aggressive crimes, consisting of robbery, assault, insulting or threatening behavior, or carrying an offensive weapon; (c) damage to property, consisting of willful or malicious damage, or arson; and (d) sex offenses (of which there were very few), consisting of assault on female, unlawful sexual intercourse, indecent exposure, and indecent telephone messages. Offenses that were excluded from counts of conviction in the study were offenses "taken into consideration," breaches of probation and conditional discharge, nonattendance at school, or being beyond control, minor offenses dealt with at the same time as delinquency offenses, and other minor offenses.

Adult convictions were also defined by findings of guilt for offenses normally registered in the Criminal Records Office. This meant that study males had to have been convicted for a relatively serious offense to have a criminal record; offenses of common assault, traffic infractions, and drunkenness were excluded from these records. Although adult convictions were measured over many years (from when study males were ages 17–40), "standard list offenses" recorded during those times did not change much. One change during the period of study was that disqualified driving became a standard list offense.

Self-reported delinquency and violence were measured in interviews with cohort members at ages 18 to 19 and at age 32. To measure delinquency at age 18, during interviews study males were shown seven cards one by one, each bearing a written description of a delinquent act, and invited to say how often they had committed each of the acts in the previous 3 years (West & Farrington, 1977). The 97 boys (out of

389) who admitted the most delinquent acts were defined as self-reported delinquents.

To measure violence at age 18, youths were asked in interviews about fighting they had been involved in over the previous 3 years. *Fights* were defined as "incidents in which at least one blow was deliberately aimed at and connected with another person" (West & Farrington, 1977, p. 81). The interviewer tried to find out how many fights each youth had been involved in, how often he had started fights (in the sense of striking the first blow), and how often (in days) he had carried or used weapons in fights. Each of the four acts was scored 1 to 4. Scores were summed to give a maximum of 16, and boys scoring 10 or above were classified by West and Farrington (1977) as self-reported violent ($n = 79$ out of 389).

At age 32, men were asked if they had committed any of 10 offenses in the previous 5 years, including stealing something over £5 or more from work, tax evasion, burglary, unauthorized taking of a vehicle, theft from a vehicle, shoplifting, obtaining government benefits by fraud, vandalism, theft from machines, and stealing checks or credit cards and obtaining money with them (Farrington, 2000b, pp. 238–239). Overall, 22.5% of men (85 out of 378) admitted at least one offense at age 32.

Antisocial personality reflecting features of conduct disorder, antisocial personality disorder, and psychopathy were derived from interviews with the boys themselves, parents, teachers, and official records. For details of these measures, including intercorrelations, see Farrington (1991).

The combined scale of antisocial personality at age 14 comprised 12 items: convicted, self-reported delinquency, steals outside home, regular smoking, had sex, bully, lies frequently, lacks concentration/restless, daring, frequently disobedient, hostile to police, and truant (alpha or Kuder-Richardson 20 [KR20], which are equivalent for dichotomous data = .75). At age 18 the antisocial personality scale (referring to the previous 3 years) comprised 14 items: convicted, self-reported delinquency, self-reported violence, involvement with an antisocial group, taken drugs, heavy smoking, heavy drinking, drunk driving, irresponsible sex, heavy gambling, an unstable job record, an antiestablishment attitude, tattooed, and impulsive (KR20 = .74). At age 32 the antisocial personality scale (referring to the previous 5 years) comprised 12 items: convicted, self-reported delinquency, involved in fights, taken drugs, heavy drinking, poor relationship with parents, poor relationship with wife, divorced or child elsewhere, unemployed frequently, antiestablishment, tattooed, and impulsive (KR20 = .71). At age 48 the antisocial personality scale (referring to the previous 5 years) comprised 11 items: convicted, self-reported delinquency, involved in fights, taken drugs, heavy drinking, poor relation with female partner, ever divorced or separated, unemployed for over 10 months, antiestablishment, impulsive, tattooed ($\alpha = .51$).

BOYS' OTHER LIFE OUTCOMES

In other publications we have reported the relationship between parental incarceration and other (nonantisocial) outcomes for boys in the Cambridge Study during adolescence and early adulthood (Murray & Farrington, 2005, 2008a). To consider very long-term effects, in this book we report only on measures of educational attainment, drug use, mental health and overall "poor life success" in the most recent wave of interviews (at age 48, except for educational attainment measured at age 18).

Educational attainment at age 18 referred to no school examinations having been taken or passed. *Drug use at age 48* referred to the use of cannabis or other drugs during the previous 5 years. Poor mental health was measured at age 48 using the 30-item General Health Questionnaire (GHQ; Goldberg & Williams, 1988). The GHQ measures potential psychiatric cases of anxiety and depression, with reference to symptoms over the last few weeks. Respondents are asked to indicate on a 4-point scale whether they have recently "lost much sleep over worry," for example. Of study males still alive at age 48 ($n = 394$), 87% ($n = 342$) completed the GHQ. The reliability (α) of the GHQ at age 48 was .92, based on 339 cases with complete data.

Poor life success at age 48 was a combined scale, based on accommodation history, cohabitation history, employment history, involvement in fights, alcohol use, drug use, self-reported offending, anxiety–depression, and convictions over the previous 5 years (Farrington et al., 2006).

PARENT–CHILD SEPARATIONS FOR OTHER REASONS

Children separated from parents because of parental incarceration were compared with two comparison groups of boys who experienced separation from a parent for other reasons: (a) boys who experienced separation caused because of parental death or hospitalization (of the parent or son) and (b) boys who experienced separation for "other reasons" (usually because of parental disharmony). These are the same groups of boys used in previous analyses of the effects of parent–child separation in the Cambridge Study (West & Farrington, 1973, 71–72), except that they do not include the children whose parents were incarcerated. Separations were originally measured during psychiatric social worker interviews in which mothers were asked if their boys had ever been separated from one or both parents. The interview instruction guide directed that all separations, except for "odd days," should be noted and that the duration and circumstances should be specified, as well as the age of the child at the time of separation. Because some answers were vague or casual, "and there was reason to believe that certain separations, for instance those due to a father's incarceration, tended to be suppressed" (West, 1969, p. 61), notes on separations were often incomplete. Therefore, after 1964, subsequent social workers repeated these questions, which increased the number of separations recollected by mothers (West, 1969).

> The social workers also kept in touch with a variety of outside agencies, such as health visitors, the local Family Service Unit and the local children's officers, in order to supplement the data about the families, and especially about the small minority who were uncooperative or reluctant to divulge information. Visiting of parents ceased when the boys were 14–15 and began to leave school. (West & Farrington, 1973, p. 23)

"The study sample did not include any inmates of local authority children's homes, so the number of boys from broken families was relatively small" (West, 1969, p. 60). For the present research, boys defined as separated from their parents by hospitalization or death, or for other reasons, had to have been separated for at least 1 month from their operative parent up to age 10 (see West & Farrington, 1973, p. 71).

OTHER CHILDHOOD ADVERSITIES

Individual, parenting, and family risk factors were measured when boys were ages 8 to 11. The most important risk factors for antisocial outcomes in the Cambridge Study were selected for examination in the present study. Their importance as predictors of antisocial outcomes has been demonstrated elsewhere (see Farrington, 2003a). Childhood adversities were mostly measured by psychiatric social worker interviews and questionnaires with boys' parents, but also from school records, interviews, and questionnaires with the boys themselves and ratings by their peers. Social workers were given a schedule of topics to be covered in these interviews, but there were no fixed rules about how the information was to be sought or the order in which topics were to be dealt with. Every effort was made to have at least one of the interviews with the mother apart from other members of the household. In the first set of interviews, mothers were seen on their own in about 40% of cases. The mother was the primary informant, but fathers were interviewed in 70.8% of cases, although in nearly half of these cases the father was not seen except in the presence of the mother (West, 1969).

Many variables were originally measured in only three or four categories and were dichotomized into the worst quarter versus the remainder in the Cambridge Study. The dichotomization of childhood adversity scores equated the sensitivity of their measurement with the dichotomous parental incarceration variable. As well as equating sensitivity, dichotomous variables simplify the presentation of results and do not necessarily cause a decrease in measured strength of association (Farrington & Loeber, 2000). Moreover, the dichotomous scores facilitated calculating the number of risk factors boys were exposed to.

Boys' junior attainment was measured using arithmetic, English and verbal reasoning tests. These were measures used by the schools in grading the children for secondary school selection at ages 10 to 11. Boys who scored "low" on these tests ($n = 90$) were coded "1" (*low junior attainment*); the remainder ($n = 296$) were coded "0" (*low-average to high attainment*; missing = 25).

IQ was measured using Raven's Progressive Matrices test (Raven, 1956, as cited in West, 1969), administered to whole classes of boys when they were ages 8–9 and 10–11. The Progressive Matrices test measures nonverbal intelligence, which is believed to be relatively independent of educational experience. The scores of the study males at ages 8 to 9 were distributed very similarly to a normal population of the same age range (West, 1969). The dichotomized IQ variable was based on the average IQ score at ages 8 to 9 and at ages 10 to 11 (scores of 0.5 were rounded down). Scores of 90 or below ($n = 103$) were coded "1" (*low IQ*) and the remainder ($n = 308$) were coded "0" (*low-average to high IQ*; missing = 0).

Daring was based on parents' and peers' ratings of the boy's propensity to take risks. At ages 8 to 9, psychiatric social workers asked boys' parents about the boys' adventurousness—whether they were boys who took risks,

> for instance in climbing, exploring and crossing the road, or whether he was noticeably cautious or physically timid. On the basis of the impressions gained in talking with parents the [psychiatric social workers] categorized the boys as "daring," "average" or "cautious." (West & Farrington, 1973, p. 104)

The final daring score was based on a combination of the parent's rating at ages 8 to 9 and a peer rating of the boy's "daring" at ages 10 to 11. Each was measured on a 3-point scale and summed (if a score was not known on one measure, the other score was doubled for the summed score). Boys with scores of 4–6 ($n = 121$) were coded "1" (*daring*); the remainder ($n = 287$) were coded "0" (*not daring*; missing = 3).

Family size was measured by parents' reports and was checked against school records. Family size was defined as the number of biological children who survived at least 1 year, born to the biological parents before the study male's 10th birthday. Siblings living away were also counted, when their existence was known, provided only that they had once been members of the boy's nuclear family. Boys who had four or more other siblings ($n = 99$) were coded "1" (*coming from large families*), and boys with fewer siblings ($n = 312$) were coded "0" (*coming from small–medium-sized families*; missing = 0).

Socioeconomic status was defined by the occupation of the father on the Registrar General's scale. In nearly all cases (94%), the family breadwinner at that time (usually the father) had a working-class occupation (Categories III, IV, or V on the Registrar General's scale, describing skilled, semiskilled or unskilled manual workers). This compared with a national figure of 78% of married males of classifiable occupation, ages 35 to 44 years, at that time (based on 1961 Census figures; see Occupational Tables, 1966, as cited in West, 1969, p. 18). For the present research, as in previous analyses of the Cambridge Study, a combined measure of social class was used, based on the lower of the father's occupational statuses when boys were ages 8–9 and 10–11. Retired persons were classified on their last job, and members of the forces on nearest civilian equivalent. Chronically unemployed and unskilled were placed in "V Manual." Widows were coded on their husband's last job if recently deceased or otherwise on their own last job. Those classed as *unskilled manual workers* (Category V on the Registrar General's scale; $n = 79$) were coded as "1" (*low socioeconomic status*), and all others were coded as "0" ($n = 332$; missing $= 0$).

It should be noted that it was recognized early in the study that the Registrar General's scale of socioeconomic class had several weaknesses:

> The classification is not up to date, and does not always reflect the current status or level of earnings of a particular job. When it is applied to a neighborhood sample, in which the range of occupations is rather limited, the proportions of cases allocated to the different classes become too unbalanced for effective statistical comparisons. (West & Farrington, 1973, p. 43)

Family income was measured during interviews with parents by psychiatric social workers when boys were ages 8 to 9. Social workers attempted to record the following for each family: the father's earnings, the mother's earnings, contributions from other members of the household, the mother's housekeeping allowance, amounts of family allowances and national assistance, as well as regular financial commitments such as rent or any special payments. Also the presence or absence of specified items in the household e.g., cars, refrigerators, televisions, telephones, washing machines) was noted by the social workers, using tick-boxes.

An overall impressionistic classification was made by the psychiatric social workers

> on the basis of reported income, but taking into account the size of the family and style of living. Generally, families with £1000 per year net to spend would be classed comfortable. Those with £15 or less per week for 2 adults and 4 children would be classed as inadequate. (West, 1969, p. 18)

However, these measures should be treated with some caution, as the "psychiatric social workers who interviewed the boys' parents found many of them rather sensitive and unreliable on the topic of family income, and many mothers were either vague or genuinely ignorant of their husband's total earnings" (West, 1969, p. 17). "Where information was not forthcoming, or was obviously unreliable, the [psychiatric social workers] judged by appearances, taking note of visible possessions and style of living" (West, 1969, p. 17).

> As a check on consistency of standards, all records of income were read and reclassified by other members of the research team, and discrepant cases were referred back to the PSWs [psychiatric social workers] for confirmation or reconsideration. Sixteen cases left unclassified by the PSWs were allocated later, using data about the situation at age 8–9 obtained from outside agencies and subsequent enquiries. Despite the rough and ready nature of these assessments, they did appear to reflect realistic and important differences between families. (West & Farrington, 1973, pp. 26–27)

Overall, 93 boys were coded "1" (*from "poor" families*), and 318 were coded "0" (*from "adequate to comfortable" income families*; missing = 0).

Poor parenting attitude and discipline of mothers and fathers were measured based on definitions used by the McCords (McCord, McCord, & Zola, 1959; West, 1969). Psychiatric social workers rated each of the parents, over the course of their interviews, using detailed descriptions of what each parenting attitude and discipline style consisted of (further details can be found in West, 1969). Overall, parenting attitudes reflected combined scales of cruel, passive, or neglecting attitudes, and harsh or erratic discipline. Parenting attitudes were originally coded as follows: 1 = *loving, normal*; 2 = *loving, anxious, or overprotective*; and 3 = *cruel, passive or neglecting*. Discipline quality was originally coded as follows: 1 = *normal*; 2 = *spoilt or disinterested*; and 3 = *harsh*. Discipline was originally coded as follows: 1 = *normal*; 2 = *lax or strict*; 3 = *erratic or very strict*. Scores of attitude, discipline quality, and discipline were then summed. To dichotomize the maternal attitude variable, scores of 4 or more were coded "1" ($n = 119$), and scores below four were coded "0" ($n = 264$; missing = 28). Fathers' attitudes were scored in the same way, but using a score of 6 as the cutoff point. Sons of fathers with poor attitudes (scores of 6 or more) were scored "1" ($n = 77$), and sons of fathers with more loving attitudes (scores of 5 or less) were scored "0" ($n = 290$; missing = 44).

Neuroticism of fathers and mothers, measured when boys were ages 8 to 9, refers to combined measures of parents' nervousness and psychiatric treatment (and neuroticism in the case of mothers). Neuroticism of mothers was also measured at ages 10–11 using a shortened version of the neuroticism scale of the Cornell Medical Index (CMI; see Gibson, Hanson, & West, 1967, as cited in West, 1969). The CMI consists of a series of mental and physical symptoms that the respondents are asked to ring "yes" or "no" according to whether they suffer from the symptom. Nervousness of operative parents was assessed by psychiatric social workers during interviews and was rated on past history as well as on reactions during the whole period of contact from intake to November 1964. "Presence of any of the classic neurotic symptoms (e.g. chronic anxiety, tension states, depression, phobias, hypochondriasis, somatic complaints of emotional origin, and psycho-somatic diseases clearly associated with emotional tension) warranted a positive rating" (West, 1969, p. 90). Fathers were scored on a 3-point scale for nervousness and "3" or "1" according to whether they had been psychiatrically treated or not (respectively). Nervousness and psychiatric treatment scores were summed, and combined scores of 2 or more ($n = 81$) were coded "1," and scores of 1 ($n = 288$) were coded "0" (missing = 42). In the case of mothers, neuroticism was also scored on a 3-point scale and added to the summed score of nervousness and psychiatric treatment. Scores of 6 or more ($n = 125$) were coded "1," and scores of 5 or less ($n = 262$) were coded "0" (missing = 24).

The prospective relationships between the childhood adversities described previously and antisocial, delinquent, and violent outcomes in the Cambridge Study are reported in Farrington (2000b) and Farrington (2001). Independent predictors of study males' outcomes (either antisocial personalities at ages 18 or 32; being convicted at ages 21–40, or self-reporting violence at ages 27–32) included (from the previous list): low IQ, low junior attainment, a neurotic mother, poor child-rearing, a disrupted family, large family size, low social class, and a convicted parent (Farrington, 2000b; Farrington, 2001).

APPENDIX B: MEASURES
IN THE SWEDISH STUDY

PARENTAL CRIMINALITY AND INCARCERATION

Parental convictions and incarceration (up to when children were age 19) were identified from the criminal records of children's fathers or, "if the information about the father was meager, from criminal records of the child's mother" (Janson, 1975, p. 15).[1] If the participant was adopted at birth, then the adoptive parent's records were searched, although adoption was very rare in Sweden in the 1950s; before reaching adulthood, about 1% of the cohort members were adopted. Parental criminal records were collected from the National Police Board (*Rikspolisstyrelsen*) for three time periods separately: before 1953, 1953 to 1959, and 1960 to 1972, corresponding to before cohort children's births, when they were ages 0 to 6, and when they were ages 7 to 19. For each time period, there is information about how many times the parent (usually the father) was sentenced unconditionally (incarcerated) or given alternative sentences following conviction. Cases of pretrial incarceration could not be identified from these records, although rates of pretrial incarceration in Sweden in the 1950s were very low. In 1957, 417 persons were remanded in custody in the whole of Sweden; of these, only 17 were still in custody at the end of the year (personal communication, Carl-Gunnar Janson, 2005).

There are two main limitations to the data on parental incarceration in Project Metropolitan. First, criminal records of both parents were not searched for each child, and it is not known exactly how many records pertain to fathers or mothers. Second, the records are believed to only refer to parents identified at birth. However, changes in family structure were relatively rare in Sweden in the 1950s; by 1968, when the children were about age 15, only 9% of children's parents had divorced or separated. Additionally nothing is known about the length of parental incarceration among the Project Metropolitan cohort.

---

[1]Unfortunately, data on the sex of the parent whose criminal records were searched are not held in Project Metropolitan archives. Also, Project Metropolitan data have been de-identified. Therefore, it would be impossible to establish the sex of parents whose criminal records were searched. The best interpretation of the notes kept on parental criminality in Project Metropolitan is that the vast majority of criminal records referred to fathers, but a few mothers were also included.

CHILDREN'S CRIME

Cohort members' delinquency was measured from records of the Child Welfare Committee until children were age 15 and from police records of offenses collected each year until the end of 1983 (when the cohort members were age 30). Records cover offenses committed in the whole of Sweden. In Sweden at that time, the Child Welfare Committee had sole responsibility for responding to offenders under the age of 15 (Janson, 1984). Child Welfare Committee delinquency data covered six categories: stealing, violence or vandalism, narcotics or alcohol abuse, drunkenness or thinner abuse, maladjustment, and "other." Crimes recorded in Swedish police data included the following: stealing, violent crimes, vandalism, fraud, traffic crimes, narcotic crimes, and "other" (see Wikström, 1987). They referred to offenses "cleared up" by the police that were believed to have been committed by members of this sample up to 1983. Traffic offenses were excluded from these analyses to make them comparable with results from England. By March 1983, 59 females and 139 males had died (Janson, 1984). Although dead cohort members were not excluded from figures on offending, this only has a minimal effect on their criminal career patterns of the cohort (Farrington & Wikström, 1994). By 1983, 219 males and 347 females had left Sweden to live abroad, but 78 males and 100 females returned to Sweden before April 1983. The net emigration is 141 males and 247 females (or 1.8% and 3.4%, respectively; Janson, 1984). Unlike in the Cambridge Study, foreign criminal records of these cohort members were not searched. Assuming that all other cohort members' criminal records were complete, the total follow-up rate (excluding those who had died) is 97% (14,531 out of 14,919). Chronic offenders in the Swedish cohort were identified as the 5% of cohort members with the most number of offenses between 19 and 30.

FAMILY SOCIAL CLASS

Social class in Sweden was measured by the occupation of the head of the family in 1963. This was the same measure used by Farrington and Wikström (1994) to match children in Project Metropolitan and the Cambridge Study. Occupations were taken from the 1963 Swedish population register and refer to the head of the family except when the information was missing for the husband but not for the wife and when the husband had a working-class occupation but the wife had an upper-middle-class occupation or higher. The family is that which the cohort member was registered as living with in 1963, whether the child was registered with their parent(s) or with other people. The occupational classification was developed by the National Central Bureau of Statistics in its official reports on general elections from 1911 to 1956. In the present study, *working class* refers to combined categories of working class ($n = 5,722$) and no occupation, or no information on occupation ($n = 412$; following Farrington & Wikström, 1994). *Middle upper class* refers to combined categories of lower middle class ($n = 6,396$), and upper middle class ($n = 2,587$).

APPENDIX C: MEASURES IN THE DUTCH STUDY

CRIME DATA

In Transfive, each generation's offending behavior was measured using conviction data, collected from computerized, paper, and microfilmed archives of the Dutch Criminal Records Documentation Service ("judicial documentation"). These are complete conviction data, apart from the filmed archive that may miss some convictions for sample members born in the Almelo jurisdiction before 1967; this applies to no more than 3% of respondents in G3 and G4. Registrations that resulted in a conviction were counted. Acquittals and so-called technical dismissals (i.e., dismissals of the case by the public prosecutor because of insufficient evidence and the case being expected to result in acquittal) were not counted. Cases for which there was no disposition or that resulted in a policy dismissal (i.e., dismissal of the case because the prosecutor deemed it unfeasible to prosecute, for example, because the perpetrator had already paid damages) were counted, as they had been registered by the judicial authorities.

Information on parental offending and incarceration (the independent variables) is taken from the same criminal record sources. In our analyses, serious offenses are counted as all offenses with a maximum penalty of at least 4 years incarceration—that is, property, arson, violent, drugs, and weapons offenses. Violent offenses were counted according to Statistics Netherlands definitions, consisting of all sex crimes (i.e., rape, sexual assault, lewdness); crimes against life (i.e., murder and manslaughter); and threats, assaults, physical injury, robbery, and extortion.

MARRIAGE DATA

Information on marriages is taken from the GBA (*Gemeentelijke Basis Administratie* or municipal registries), the Netherlands centralized computerized population registration system, and for respondents who died before 1994 from the *Persoonskaarten* (person cards), the card archive that was the forerunner of the GBA system.

APPENDIX D: MEASURES
IN THE AMERICAN STUDY

PARENTAL CRIMINAL JUSTICE INVOLVEMENT

It is very difficult to conduct systematic searches of criminal records in the United States because records are compiled by various criminal justice agencies at the local, state, and federal levels. This problem was overcome in the Pittsburgh Youth Study by asking about parental criminal justice contact in questionnaires administered to the boy's caretaker (usually the mother). Information on biological and stepmothers' and fathers' arrests, convictions, and incarcerations at any time in the past were collected in the Family Criminal History Questionnaire, administered at the start of the study and when the youngest and oldest samples were ages approximately 14 and 17, respectively. These questionnaires recorded all police contacts of the boy's relatives, the relative's age at the time of police contact, and the result of the police contact, which was coded as *incarceration, conviction without incarceration,* or *arrest without conviction or incarceration.* This information was supplemented from the Caretaker History Questionnaire, which recorded the male and female most responsible for caring for the boy and the reason for any changes in caretaker each year. Additional reports of parental incarceration were gathered from this questionnaire. When multiple sources reported criminal justice involvement of the same parent at the same age, these reports were consolidated. Demographic data from the year before parental incarceration were used to determine whether the parent had been living in the boy's home. Individuals with no recorded information on parental incarceration, conviction, or arrest were classified as having parents with no criminal justice involvement.

We explored the possibility of conducting searches of parents' criminal records in local court records to test the validity of parental reports of criminal justice system involvement, but this was not possible because permission to search these records had never been granted by participants' parents, and it would have been extremely difficult to make renewed contact for this purpose. Another study that compared youth reports and official data on parental incarceration found that the two sources were often inconsistent, possibly because youths did not remember events that occurred early in their lives or were not told the truth about their parent's incarceration, or because the official records only pertained to occasions of incarceration in Oregon and might be incomplete (Kjellstrand, 2009). To our knowledge, all other major longitudinal surveys of the effects of parental incarceration in the

United States have used questionnaire measures of parental criminal justice contact, normally administered to parents (Foster & Hagan, 2007, 2009; Geller, Cooper, Garfinkel, Schwartz-Soicher, & Mincy, 2012; Huebner & Gustafson, 2007; R. Johnson, 2009; Roettger, Swisher, Kuhl, & Chavez, 2011; Wakefield & Wildeman, 2011; Wildeman, 2010). It is important to be aware of possible underreporting in these and the current study (Western, Lopoo, & McLanaghan, 2004). Previous analyses in the Pittsburgh Youth Study demonstrated the validity of parental reports about the boys' arrests using juvenile court data (Farrington, Jolliffe, Loeber, Stouthamer-Loeber, & Kalb, 2001). As a basic check on parental reports about parental criminal justice system involvement, we examined them in relation to parents' levels of lifetime antisocial behavior (measurement of parental antisocial behavior is described next). Parents who had ever had contact with the criminal justice system had significantly higher antisocial behavior scores (M = 1.4) than parents who had no contact (M = 0.7; $p < .001$), giving some confidence about these reports. However, there still might be inaccuracy or underreporting in these data.

YOUTH PROBLEM BEHAVIOR

Theft. Theft was measured using multiple informants and data sources: youth self-report (adapted Self-Reported Delinquency Scale—Elliott, Huizinga, & Ageton, 1985; Self-Reported Antisocial Behavior Scale—Loeber, Stouthamer-Loeber, van Kammen, & Farrington, 1989), caretaker reports (Child Behavior Checklist; Achenbach & Edelbrock, 1983), teacher reports (Teacher's Report Form; Edelbrock & Achenbach, 1984), and court records. Predictive validity of these measures has been demonstrated for both Black and White youth (Farrington, Loeber, Stouthamer-Loeber, van Kammen, & Schmidt, 1996). We used data on moderate and serious theft, which is characterized by acts of stealing a bicycle or skateboard from the street, stealing things worth more than $5, joyriding, purse snatching, dealing in stolen goods, stealing from a car, breaking and entering, or auto theft. The summed frequency of these acts was scored from 0 (*no acts of theft*) to 10 (*10 or more acts*) in each year.

Marijuana use. Frequency of youth marijuana use was based on youths' self-reported number of days using marijuana each year. This number was divided by 36.5 (and rounded) to produce a score from 0 (*no marijuana use*) to 10 (*highest frequency of marijuana use*).

Depression. This construct is the sum of 13 items on the Recent Mood and Feelings Questionnaire (Angold, Costello, Messer, & Pickles, 1995; Messer et al., 1995) administered to the youth. The items covered criteria for a diagnosis of major depression according to the *Diagnostic and Statistical Manual of Mental Disorders* (3rd ed., rev.; *DSM–III–R*; American Psychiatric Association, 1987). Previous analyses have shown the questionnaire has good psychometric properties: Using a cutpoint of eight or more symptoms predicted clinically diagnosed depression with 60% sensitivity and 85% specificity (Angold et al., 1995).

Academic performance. This construct combines the caretaker's (Child Behavior Checklist; Achenbach & Edelbrock, 1983), teacher's (Teacher's Report Form; Edelbrock & Achenbach, 1984), and youth's (Youth Self-Report; Achenbach & Edelbrock, 1987) evaluations of the youth's performance in reading, math, writing and spelling; caretakers and youths also evaluated up to three other subjects. Academic performance was scored on a 4-point scale, ranging from *above average* to *failing*.

Criminal records. Criminal conviction records held at the FBI were searched for adult study males. We included in the dichotomous outcome variable (convicted vs. not convicted) any record of conviction between ages 19 and 30 years (all study males had reached age 30 at the time of the search). We excluded most status offenses, noncriminal trespassing, most violations of ordinances, harassment, drunkenness, and motor vehicle law violations to make results more comparable with the other studies in this book.

OTHER FAMILY AND PEER INFLUENCES

Parent lifetime antisocial behavior. This construct is based on the Georgia Child Center Questionnaire developed by Benjamin Lahey, which asks about lifetime occurrence of 20 behaviors such as "acting without thinking about consequences," "lying," and "stealing." This was administered when the youngest and oldest samples were ages approximately 7 and 14, respectively. The highest score of the biological mother or father (ranging from 0 to 7) was used to measure the highest level of parental antisocial behavior that the child was exposed to.

Parent lifetime substance use problem. This construct combines information on whether absent or present fathers or mothers have ever had substance use problems (i.e., alcohol or drug problems; Loeber et al., 1998, p. 68). This was measured when the youngest and oldest samples were ages approximately 7 and 14, respectively.

Caretaker stress. This construct summarizes caretakers' perceptions of their stress levels and ability to handle problems and was made from 14 items of the Perceived Stress Scale ($\alpha = .83$ youngest sample; $\alpha = .83$ oldest sample; Loeber et al., 1998). We use this as a proxy for the various forms of family social and economic strain associated with parental criminal justice system involvement.

Parental supervision. This construct combines caretaker and youth reports of the extent of the caretaker's knowledge of the youth's activities. It was made from four items from each informant's Supervision/Involvement Scale. An example item is "Do your parent(s) know who you are with when you are away from home?" ($\alpha = .63$ youngest sample; $\alpha = .75$ oldest sample; Loeber et al., 1998, p. 65).

Parent–child communication. This construct combines information from the parent and the boy on the Revised Parent–Adolescent Communication Form (Loeber et al., 1998, p. 66). It measures, on a 3-point frequency scale, how often the boy (28 items) and the parent (30 items) communicate directly or indirectly about emotions, disagreements, and problems. An example item for the boys is "Do you tell your mother/father about your personal problems?" Recent analyses showed excellent internal reliability of the scale in early adolescence ($\alpha = .97$ youngest sample; $\alpha = .98$ oldest sample).

Boy not involved in the family. This construct combines caretaker and youth reports of the degree to which the youth was involved in planning and participating in family activities. It was made from four items from each informant's Supervision/Involvement Scale ($\alpha = .61$ youngest sample; $\alpha = .73$ oldest sample; Loeber et al., 1998, p. 66).

Relationship with peers. This construct is made from a single caretaker item (Child Behavior Checklist; Achenbach & Edelbrock, 1983), a single teacher item (Teacher's Report Form; Edelbrock & Achenbach, 1984), and a single youth item (Youth Self-Report; Achenbach & Edelbrock, 1987) regarding the youth's tendency to get along with his peers.

Peer delinquency. This construct is based on youth self-reports and summarizes the participation of the youth's friends in delinquent activities, such as stealing and vandalism, based on items corresponding to those in the Self-Reported Delinquency Scale and the Substance Use Scale (Elliott, Huizinga, & Ageton, 1985). An example item is "How many of them (i.e., friends) have gone into or tried to go into a building to steal something?" ($\alpha = .79$ youngest sample; $\alpha = .90$ oldest sample; Loeber et al., 1998, p. 71).

APPENDIX E: TECHNICAL NOTES ON THE SYSTEMATIC REVIEW

ASSESSMENT OF METHODOLOGICAL QUALITY

The methodological quality of studies included in the review was assessed on the Cambridge Quality Checklists, which were developed to evaluate the quality of risk factor studies in systematic reviews (Murray, Farrington, & Eisner, 2009) and have been shown to have high reliability (Jolliffe, Murray, Farrington, & Vannick, 2012). Each study was coded "yes" or "no" according to whether it had the following five characteristics (for further details about this checklist, scoring instructions, and rationale for cutpoints, see Jolliffe et al., 2012; Murray, Farrington, & Eisner, 2009):

1. An adequate sampling method: use of either random or total sampling methods.
2. An adequate response rate: response and retention rates $\geq 70\%$ and differential attrition between children of incarcerated parents and the comparison group $\leq 10\%$.
3. An adequate sample size: 400 or more.
4. A good measure of parental incarceration: Children with incarcerated parents were identified by sampling parents in a jail or prison, or by using official criminal records to determine whether parents were incarcerated, or by asking parents themselves about their own history of incarceration. (Note: if children themselves reported whether their parents were incarcerated, this was not coded as a good measure because it is possible that many children are not told the truth about the whereabouts of their incarcerated parent.)
5. A good measure of the child outcome: reliability coefficient $\geq .75$ and reasonable face validity odds ratio (OR) criterion validity coefficient $\geq .3$ OR more than one instrument or information source used to assess the outcome OR official records of arrest, conviction, or incarceration were used to measure an antisocial outcome OR clinical diagnosis was used to measure mental health problems OR standardized test or grade scores were used to measure educational performance.

As recommended by Murray, Farrington, and Eisner (2009), in addition to coding the five items above, and coding the basic study design (prospective, retrospective, or cross-sectional), we also coded the covariates that were controlled in each study. Most studies controlled at least some covariates either by matching or using statistical modeling techniques (e.g., in regression analyses). We coded the total number of covariates that were controlled in each study (excluding demographic covariates such as child sex, race, and social class) and whether parental criminality or antisocial behavior was controlled for (e.g., by including the number of prior parental criminal convictions as a covariate in multiple regression analysis). We also coded whether studies controlled for a pretest of children's outcomes before parental incarceration—for example, by adjusting for pretest scores in regression analyses or by analyzing change scores. Arguably parental criminality is the most important confounding variable to take into account when investigating the association between parental incarceration and children's outcomes, and analysis of change (control for children's outcomes before parental incarceration) helps rule out the possibility that children with incarcerated parents had raised levels of problem behavior before their parent was incarcerated.

EFFECT SIZES

OR was used as the effect size to represent the association between parental incarceration and children's outcomes for five reasons. First, many primary studies reported results using ORs. Second, many measures of both parental incarceration and children's outcomes were dichotomous (e.g., incarcerated or not, convicted or not). Third, the OR is easily and often used as an effect size in meta-analysis and can be estimated from other commonly reported statistics. Fourth, the OR is unaffected by differential base rates (the marginal distributions of the predictor or the outcome), giving greater comparability across studies and types of outcome. Also, as described in Chapter 3 in this book, an OR is easily interpretable.

If studies reported only other statistics, such as Cohen's d, or mean differences and standard deviations (from which d can be calculated), we converted them into ORs using the formulas presented in Lipsey and Wilson (2001). An OR based on d is interpretable like any other OR: the increase (or decrease) in odds associated with parental incarceration. However, it is necessary to interpret the underlying continuous variable, which was used to calculate d, as dichotomous. For example, Stroble (1997) compared mean depression scores between children with incarcerated parents and children without incarcerated parents. In this study, $d = 0.3$, and we converted this into an OR = 1.8. This can be interpreted as showing that parental incarceration was associated with 1.8 times the odds of high depression scores compared with no parental incarceration. When the underlying continuous distribution is approximately normal, d is an appropriate metric for summarizing the relationship between the two variables and can be converted to an OR without problem. However, we note that if the distribution is skewed (e.g., standard deviation > mean), d is reduced because of the high standard deviation, and an OR based on d is likely to be conservative or too small.

Wherever possible, covariate-adjusted ORs were extracted from study results. Covariate-adjusted ORs indicate how many times greater (or smaller) the odds of the outcome is for children with incarcerated parents compared with other children, while taking into account effects of covariates. For example, by comparing children of prisoners and children of parents with other criminal justice sentences, the resulting OR shows how more or less likely children of prisoners are to experience the outcome, while taking into account parental crime and conviction. Covariate-adjusted ORs can be calculated directly from 2×2 tables comparing outcomes for children with incarcerated parents and matched controls; or extracted directly from logistic regression results; or converted from other effect sizes such as d, where covariates are taken into account in the calculation of d.

MULTIPLE RESULTS FROM SINGLE STUDIES

One issue that must be dealt with in meta-analysis is the assumption of statistical independence of results. Studies sometimes have multiple results reported for the same outcome for the same sample (e.g., in multiple publications). Using more than one result from the same sample in a meta-analysis can lead to underestimating error variance and inflating significance tests. To isolate independent results for use in each meta-analysis, first we identified independent samples by doing the following:

1. Separate meta-analyses were conducted for antisocial behavior, mental health, drug use, and educational performance. Thus, only if a study reported multiple results for a single outcome would we need to address independence of findings further.
2. Samples of boys and girls were coded separately and used as the unit of analysis. (This was done even if combined results, for boys and girls together, were also reported.) Thus, only if a study reported multiple results either for boys or for girls for any particular outcome would we need to address independence of findings further. Although there might be some dependence between effect sizes derived for boys and girls in the same study, we assume that they are independent in these analyses.
3. Two studies reported results separately for main study participants and their siblings. For each study, we coded the main

participants and their siblings separately (as two different samples) because different types of analyses were performed on each group.

4. Within a study, when more than one sample of children with incarcerated parents was compared to a single comparison group, the results from these multiple comparisons were averaged, and the average effect size was used in the analysis. For example, if a study compared both children of incarcerated mothers and children of incarcerated fathers with a single comparison group, the mean OR (and mean variance) from these two comparisons was used in analysis.[1]

5. Within a study, if a single group of children with incarcerated parents was compared with multiple comparison groups, we selected or combined the comparison groups to calculate a single effect size for each analysis. Comparison groups were selected or combined to produce a single effect size reflecting the maximum control of covariates. In studies that included a comparison group of children separated from parents for reasons other than parental incarceration, results from that comparison were coded separately for specific analysis.

Sometimes, even for a particular outcome investigated in a single sample, multiple results were still reported—for example, at different time points. When this occurred, we did the following, in order, until we identified a single effect size for the sample:

1. If an outcome was measured at multiple time points, the measure longest after parental incarceration was selected for analysis, unless attrition since the previous measure was over 10%. For example, a measure of conviction at ages 30 to 40 would be selected instead of a measure of conviction at ages 20 to 30, so long as the later measure did not have more than 10% attrition since the earlier measure.

2. If there were multiple covariate-adjusted effect sizes, the effect size reflecting maximum control for covariates was selected for analysis. For example, if one effect size estimated the effects of parental incarceration while controlling for family income and another effect size controlled for family income and parental criminality, the latter effect size was selected. Effect sizes that estimated change in children's outcomes from before to after

---

[1] It was not possible to pool the groups of children of prisoners before calculating an effect size in these studies.

parental incarceration (i.e., controlling for preincarceration child outcome scores) were always selected in preference to effect sizes that did not estimate change in children's outcomes.

3. Measures of an outcome with higher reliability or validity were selected in preference to measures with lower reliability or validity.

4. For antisocial behavior, measures of criminal behavior were selected in preference to measures of antisocial behavior that did not necessarily involve breaking the law. Measures of antisocial behavior that were closer to official delinquency (e.g., the Delinquency subscale on the Child Behavior Checklist) were selected instead of other measures (e.g., a "total externalizing" score). Measures of crime in general (e.g., conviction for any offense) were selected in preference to measures of specific types of crime (e.g., conviction for violence). Effect sizes based on conviction records were used in preference to self-reports. Measures using children's own reports were chosen in preference to measures based on other people's reports (e.g., caregivers' or teachers' reports) because parents and teachers may not know about children's delinquent behaviors. Children's self-reports were also selected in preference to measures of arrest.

5. For outcomes of mental health, drug use, and educational performance, more generic measures were selected in preference to subtypes of the outcome. For example, for mental health, measures of general internalizing problems were selected in preference to measures of depression or anxiety specifically. If a result for general internalizing problems was not reported but results for more than one specific internalizing problem (e.g., both depression and anxiety) were reported, these were combined into one effect size. If multiple results for educational performance were reported, standardized test scores were selected in preference to other measures of educational performance.

6. If there were still multiple results for a single type of outcome, results were combined to produce one summary effect size.

For some of the moderator variables that we investigated (e.g., whether it was the mother or the father who was incarcerated), multiple relevant results were reported for a single sample (i.e., one result for maternal incarceration and one result for paternal incarceration). Where this was the case, separate effect sizes were calculated for each category of the moderator (i.e., one effect size for maternal incarceration and one for paternal incarceration), following Steps 1 through 6 described previously. For analysis of that moderator, the result for the category that was most rare (i.e., maternal incarceration in this example) was selected for analysis. In all other analyses, the average effect size was used (i.e., for maternal incarceration and paternal incarceration combined).

Following these procedures for handling multiple comparisons, multiple measures of outcomes, and multiple results on moderator variables, each sample counted only once in each meta-analysis.

REFERENCES

Academy of Medical Sciences. (2007). *Identifying the environmental causes of disease: How should we decide what to believe and when to take action?* London, England: Academy of Medical Sciences.

Achenbach, T. M., & Edelbrock, C. S. (1983). *Manual for the Child Behavior Checklist and Revised Child Behavior Profile.* Burlington, VT: University of Vermont, Department of Psychiatry.

Achenbach, T. M., & Edelbrock, C. S. (1987). *Manual for the Youth Self-Report and Profile.* Burlington, VT: University of Vermont, Department of Psychiatry.

Agnew, R. (1992). Foundation for a general strain theory of crime and delinquency. *Criminology, 30,* 47–88. doi:10.1111/j.1745-9125.1992.tb01093.x

Altman, D. G., & Bland, J. M. (2003). Interaction revisited: The difference between two estimates. *British Medical Journal, 326,* 219. doi:10.1136/bmj.326.7382.219

Amato, P. R. (1993). Children's adjustment to divorce: Theories, hypotheses, and empirical support. *Journal of Marriage and the Family, 55,* 23–38. doi:10.2307/352954

Amato, P. R. (2001). Children of divorce in the 1990s: An update of the Amato and Keith (1991) meta-analysis. *Journal of Family Psychology, 15,* 355–370. doi:10.1037/0893-3200.15.3.355

Amato, P. R., & Keith, B. (1991a). Parental divorce and adult well-being: A meta-analysis. *Journal of Marriage and the Family, 53,* 43–58. doi:10.2307/353132

Amato, P. R., & Keith, B. (1991b). Parental divorce and the well-being of children: A meta-analysis. *Psychological Bulletin, 110,* 26–46. doi:10.1037/0033-2909.110.1.26

American Psychiatric Association. (1987). *Diagnostic and statistical manual of mental disorders* (3rd ed., rev.). Washington, DC: Author.

Amira, Y. (1992). We are not the problem: Black children and their families within the criminal justice system. In R. Shaw (Ed.), *Prisoners' children: What are the issues?* (pp. 86–98). London, England: Routledge.

Angold, A., Costello, E. J., Messer, S. C., & Pickles, A. (1995). Development of a short questionnaire for use in epidemiological studies of depression in children and adolescents. *International Journal of Methods in Psychiatric Research, 5,* 237–249.

Appleyard, K., Egeland, B., van Dulman, M. H. M., & Sroufe, L. A. (2005). When more is not better: The role of cumulative risk in child behavior outcomes. *Journal of Child Psychology and Psychiatry, 46,* 235–245. doi:10.1111/j.1469-7610.2004.00351.x

Arditti, J. A. (2005). Families and incarceration: An ecological approach. *Families in Society: The Journal of Contemporary Social Services, 86,* 251–260. Retrieved from http://www.familiesinsociety.org/

Arditti, J. A., Lambert-Shute, J., & Joest, K. (2003). Saturday morning at the jail: Implications of incarceration for families and children. *Family Relations, 52,* 195–204. doi:10.1111/j.1741-3729.2003.00195.x

Arditti, J. A., Smock, S. A., & Parkman, T. (2005). "It's been hard to be a father": A qualitative exploration of incarcerated fatherhood. *Fathering, 3,* 267–288. doi:10.3149/fth.0303.267

Aronson, E., Phoebe, C. E., Carlsmith, J. M., & Gonzales, M. H. (1990). *Methods of research in social psychology* (2nd ed.). Singapore: McGraw-Hill.

Ashworth, A. (2000). *Sentencing and criminal justice* (3rd ed.). London, England: Butterworths.

Bandura, A., Ross, D., & Ross, S. A. (1961). Transmission of aggression through imitation of aggressive models. *Journal of Abnormal and Social Psychology, 63,* 575–582. doi:10.1037/h0045925

Baron, R. M., & Kenny, D. A. (1986). The moderator–mediator variable distinction in social psychological research: Conceptual, strategic, and statistical considerations. *Journal of Personality and Social Psychology, 51,* 1173–1182. doi:10.1037/0022-3514.51.6.1173

Barton, W. H., & Butts, J. A. (1990). Viable options: Intensive supervision programs for juvenile delinquents. *Crime and Delinquency, 36,* 238–256. doi:10.1177/0011128790036002004

Baunach, P. J. (1985). *Mothers in prison.* New Brunswick, NJ: Transaction Books.

Becker, H. S. (1963). *Outsiders: Studies in the sociology of deviance.* New York, NY: Free Press.

Belsky, J., & Fearon, R. M. P. (2002). Infant–mother attachment security, contextual risk, and early development: A moderational analysis. *Development and Psychopathology, 14,* 293–310. doi:10.1017/S0954579402002067

Bergman, G. R. (1976). *The evaluation of an experimental program designed to reduce recidivism among second felony criminal offenders.* Detroit, MI: Wayne State University.

Bernstein, N. (2005). *All alone in the world: Children of the incarcerated.* New York, NY: New Press.

Besemer, S., van der Geest, V., Murray, J., Bijleveld, C. C. J. H., & Farrington, D. P. (2011). The relationship between parental imprisonment and offspring offending in England and the Netherlands. *British Journal of Criminology, 51,* 413–437. doi:10.1093/bjc/azq072

Bijleveld, C. C. J. H., & Wijkman, M. (2009). Intergenerational continuity in convictions: A five-generation study. *Criminal Behaviour and Mental Health, 19,* 142–155. doi:10.1002/cbm.714

Bijleveld, C. C. J. H., Wijkman, M., & Stuifbergen, J. A. M. (2007). *198 Boefjes?* [198 Rascals?]. Leiden, the Netherlands: NSCR.

Blumstein, A. (2011). Bringing down the U.S. prison population. *The Prison Journal, 91*(Suppl. 3), 12S–26S. doi:10.1177/0032885511415218

Blumstein, A., & Beck, A. J. (1999). Population growth in U.S. prisons, 1980–1996. In M. Tonry & J. Petersilia (Eds.), *Crime and justice: A review of research* (Vol. 26, pp. 17–61). Chicago, IL: University of Chicago Press.

Blumstein, A., & Beck, A. J. (2005). Reentry as a transient state between liberty and recommitment. In J. Travis & C. Visher (Eds.), *Prisoner reentry and crime in America* (pp. 50–79). New York, NY: Cambridge University Press. doi:10.1017/CBO9780511813580.003

Bocknek, E., Sanderson, J., & Britner, P. (2009). Ambiguous loss and posttraumatic stress in school-age children of prisoners. *Journal of Child and Family Studies, 18,* 323–333. doi:10.1007/s10826-008-9233-y

Boswell, G. (2002). Imprisoned fathers: The children's view. *Howard Journal of Criminal Justice, 41,* 14–26. doi:10.1111/1468-2311.00222

Boswell, G., & Wedge, P. (2002). *Imprisoned fathers and their children.* London, England: Jessica Kingsley.

Bottoms, A. (2002). The divergent development of juvenile justice policy and practice in England and Scotland. In M. K. Rosenheim, F. E. Zimring, D. S. Tanenhaus, & B. Dohrn (Eds.), *A century of juvenile justice* (pp. 413–504). Chicago, IL: University of Chicago Press.

Boutellier, J. C. J. (2008). *Solidariteit en slachtofferschap. De morele betekenis van criminaliteit in een postmoderne cultuur* [Solidarity and victimisation. The moral meaning of crime in a post-modern culture]. Amsterdam, the Netherlands: Amsterdam University Press.

Bowlby, J. (1969). *Attachment and loss: Vol. 1. Attachment.* London, England: Hogarth Press and the Institute of Psycho-Analysis.

Bowlby, J. (1973). *Attachment and loss: Vol. 2. Separation, anxiety and anger.* London, England: Hogarth Press and the Institute of Psycho-Analysis.

Bowlby, J. (1980). *Attachment and loss: Vol. 3. Loss, sadness and depression.* London, England: Hogarth Press and the Institute of Psycho-Analysis.

Braithwaite, J. (1999). Restorative justice: Assessing optimistic and pessimistic accounts. In M. Tonry (Ed.), *Crime and justice: A review of research* (Vol. 25, pp. 1–127). Chicago, IL: Chicago University Press. doi:10.1086/449287

Braithwaite, J., & Mugford, S. (1994). Conditions of successful reintegration ceremonies: Dealing with juvenile offenders. *British Journal of Criminology, 34,* 139–171.

Braman, D. (2004). *Doing time on the outside: Incarceration and family life in urban America.* Ann Arbor: University of Michigan Press.

Braman, D., & Wood, J. (2003). From one generation to the next: How criminal sanctions are reshaping family life in urban America. In J. Travis & M. Waul (Eds.), *Prisoners once removed: The impact of incarceration and reentry on children, families, and communities* (pp. 157–188). Washington, DC: Urban Institute.

Bretherton, I. (1997). Bowlby's legacy to developmental psychology. *Child Psychiatry and Human Development, 28,* 33–43. doi:10.1023/A:1025193002462

Bronfenbrenner, U. (1979). *The ecology of human development*. Cambridge, MA: Harvard University Press.

Brown, C. S., & Bigler, R. S. (2005). Children's perceptions of discrimination: A developmental model. *Child Development, 76*, 533–553. doi:10.1111/j.1467-8624.2005.00862.x

Bryggan. (2013). *Bryggan*. Retrieved from http://www.riksbryggan.se/english.html

Buruma, Y. (2007). Dutch tolerance: On drugs, prostitution, and euthanasia. In M. Tonry & C. Bijleveld (Eds.), *Crime and justice: A review of research* (Vol. 35, pp. 73–113). Chicago, IL: University of Chicago Press. doi:10.1086/650185

Chamberlain, P., & Reid, J. B. (1998). Comparison of two community alternatives to incarceration for chronic juvenile offenders. *Journal of Consulting and Clinical Psychology, 66*, 624–633. doi:10.1037/0022-006X.66.4.624

Cho, R. M. (2009). The impact of maternal imprisonment on children's educational achievement: Results from children in Chicago public schools. *The Journal of Human Resources, 44*, 772–797. doi:10.1353/jhr.2009.0003

Christian, J. (2005). Riding the bus: Barriers to prison visitation and family management strategies. *Journal of Contemporary Criminal Justice, 21*, 31–48. doi:10.1177/1043986204271618

Clear, T. R. (2007). *Imprisoning communities: How mass incarceration makes disadvantaged neighborhoods worse*. New York, NY: Oxford University Press. doi:10.1093/acprof:oso/9780195305791.001.0001

Clear, T. R., Rose, D. R., & Ryder, J. A. (2001). Incarceration and the community: The problem of removing and returning offenders. *Crime and Delinquency, 47*, 335–351. doi:10.1177/0011128701047003003

Cohen, P. (1996). Childhood risks for young adult symptoms of personality disorder: Method and substance. *Multivariate Behavioral Research, 31*, 121–148. doi:10.1207/s15327906mbr3101_7

Comfort, M. (2007). Punishment beyond the legal offender. *Annual Review of Law and Social Science, 3*, 271–296. doi:10.1146/annurev.lawsocsci.3.081806.112829

Comfort, M., Nurse, A. M., McKay, T., & Kramer, K. (2011). Taking children into account. *Criminology & Public Policy, 10*, 839–850. doi:10.1111/j.1745-9133.2011.00750.x

Comfort, M. L. (2003). In the tube at San Quentin: The "secondary prisonization" of women visiting inmates. *Journal of Contemporary Ethnography, 32*, 77–107. doi:10.1177/0891241602238939

Condry, R. (2007). *Families shamed: The consequences of crime for relatives of serious offenders*. Cullompton, England: Willan.

Cook, T. D., & Campbell, D. T. (1979). *Quasi-experimentation: Design and analysis issues for field settings*. Chicago, IL: Rand-McNally.

Cook, T. D., & Shadish, W. R. (1994). Social experiments: Some developments over the past fifteen years. *Annual Review of Psychology, 45*, 545–580. doi:10.1146/annurev.ps.45.020194.002553

Council of Europe. (1997). *Recommendation 1340 (1997) on the social and family effects of detention*. Strasbourg, France: Parliamentary Assembly, Council of Europe.

Cummings, E. M., Davies, P. T., & Campbell, S. B. (2000). *Developmental psychopathology and family process: Theory, research, and clinical implications*. New York, NY: Guilford Press.

Cunningham, A., & Baker, L. (2003). *Waiting for mommy: Giving a voice to the hidden victims of imprisonment*. London, Ontario, Canada: Centre for Children and Families in the Justice System.

Dallaire, D. H. (2007). Children with incarcerated mothers: Developmental outcomes, special challenges and recommendations. *Journal of Applied Developmental Psychology, 28*, 15–24. doi:10.1016/j.appdev.2006.10.003

Dannerbeck, A. M. (2005). Differences in parenting attributes, experiences, and behaviors of delinquent youth with and without a parental history of incarceration. *Youth Violence and Juvenile Justice, 3*, 199–213. doi:10.1177/1541204005276260

Deater-Deckard, K., Dodge, K. A., Bates, J. E., & Pettit, G. S. (1996). Physical discipline among African American and European American mothers: Links to children's externalizing behaviors. *Developmental Psychology, 32*, 1065–1072. doi:10.1037/0012-1649.32.6.1065

de Haan, W. (1986). Explaining expansion: The Dutch case. In B. Rolston & M. Tomlinson (Eds.), *The expansion of European prison systems* (Working Papers in European Criminology, No. 7, pp. 1–15). Belfast, Ireland: The European Group for the Study of Deviance and Social Control.

DeHart, D., & Altshuler, S. (2009). Violence exposure among children of incarcerated mothers. *Child and Adolescent Social Work Journal, 26*, 467–479. doi:10.1007/s10560-009-0184-y

Derzon, J. (2010). The correspondence of family features with problem, aggressive, criminal, and violent behavior: A meta-analysis. *Journal of Experimental Criminology, 6*, 263–292. doi:10.1007/s11292-010-9098-0

Downes, D. (1988). *Contrasts in tolerance: Post-war penal policy in the Netherlands and England and Wales*. Oxford, England: Clarendon Press.

Downes, D. (1992a). The case for going Dutch. *Tijdschrift voor Criminologie, 34*, 198–209.

Downes, D. (1992b). The case for going Dutch: The lessons of post-war penal policy. *The Political Quarterly, 63*, 12–24. doi:10.1111/j.1467-923X.1992.tb00880.x

Downes, D., & Mitchel, P. (1982). The origins and consequences of Dutch penal policy since 1945: A preliminary analysis. *The British Journal of Criminology, 22*, 325–362.

Downes, D., & van Swaaningen, R. (2007). The road to dystopia? Changes in the penal climate of the Netherlands. In M. Tonry & C. C. J. H. Bijleveld (Eds.), *Crime and justice: A review of research* (Vol. 35, pp. 31–71). Chicago, IL: University of Chicago Press.

Eddy, J. M., Martinez, C. R., Schiffmann, T., Newton, R., Olin, L., Leve, L., . . . Shortt, J. W. (2008). Development of a multisystemic parent management training intervention for incarcerated parents, their children and families. *Clinical Psychologist, 12*, 86–98. doi:10.1080/13284200802495461

Eddy, J. M., & Poehlmann, J. (2010). *Children of incarcerated parents: A handbook for researchers and practitioners*. Washington, DC: Urban Institute.

Eddy, J. M., & Reid, J. B. (2003). The adolescent children of incarcerated parents. In J. Travis & M. Waul (Eds.), *Prisoners once removed: The impact of incarceration and reentry on children, families, and communities* (pp. 233–258). Washington, DC: Urban Institute.

Edelbrock, C., & Achenbach, T. (1984). The teacher version of the Child Behavior Profile: I. Boys aged 6–11. *Journal of Consulting and Clinical Psychology, 52*, 207–217. doi:10.1037/0022-006X.52.2.207

Elliott, D. S., Huizinga, D., & Ageton, S. S. (1985). *Explaining delinquency and drug use*. Beverly Hills, CA: Sage.

Emery, R. E. (1999). *Marriage, divorce, and children's adjustment* (2nd ed.). Thousand Oaks, CA: Sage.

Farrington, D. P. (1991). Antisocial personality from childhood to adulthood. *The Psychologist, 4*, 389–394.

Farrington, D. P. (1997). Human development and criminal careers. In M. Maguire, R. Morgan, & R. Reiner (Eds.), *The Oxford handbook of criminology* (2nd ed., pp. 361–408). Oxford, England: Oxford University Press.

Farrington, D. P. (2000a). Explaining and preventing crime: The globalization of knowledge: The American Society of Criminology 1999 presidential address. *Criminology, 38*, 1–24. doi:10.1111/j.1745-9125.2000.tb00881.x

Farrington, D. P. (2000b). Psychosocial predictors of adult antisocial personality and adult convictions. *Behavioral Sciences & the Law, 18*, 605–622. doi:10.1002/1099-0798(200010)18:5<605::AID-BSL406>3.0.CO;2-0

Farrington, D. P. (2001). Predicting adult official and self-reported violence. In G.-F. Pinard & L. Pagani (Eds.), *Clinical assessment of dangerousness: Empirical contributions* (pp. 66–88). Cambridge, England: Cambridge University Press.

Farrington, D. P. (2003a). Key results from the first forty years of the Cambridge Study in Delinquent Development. In T. P. Thornberry & M. D. Krohn (Eds.), *Taking stock of delinquency: An overview of findings from contemporary longitudinal studies* (pp. 137–183). New York, NY: Kluwer/Plenum. doi:10.1007/0-306-47945-1_5

Farrington, D. P. (2003b). Methodological quality standards for evaluation research. *Annals of the American Academy of Political and Social Science, 587*, 49–68. doi:10.1177/0002716202250789

Farrington, D. P. (2004). Conduct disorder, aggression, and delinquency. In R. M. Lerner & L. Steinberg (Eds.), *Handbook of adolescent psychology* (2nd ed., pp. 627–664). New York, NY: Wiley.

Farrington, D. P., Barnes, G. C., & Lambert, S. (1996). The concentration of offending in families. *Legal and Criminological Psychology, 1*, 47–63. doi:10.1111/j.2044-8333.1996.tb00306.x

Farrington, D. P., Coid, J. W., Harnett, L., Jolliffe, D., Soteriou, N., Turner, R., & West, D. J. (2006). *Criminal careers up to age 50 and life success up to age 48: New findings from the Cambridge Study in Delinquent Development* (Research Study No. 299). London, England: Home Office.

Farrington, D. P., Coid, J. W., & Murray, J. (2009). Family factors in the intergenerational transmission of offending. *Criminal Behaviour and Mental Health, 19*, 109–124. doi:10.1002/cbm.717

Farrington, D. P., Jolliffe, D., Loeber, R., Stouthamer-Loeber, M., & Kalb, L. M. (2001). The concentration of offenders in families, and family criminality in the prediction of boys' delinquency. *Journal of Adolescence, 24*, 579–596. doi:10.1006/jado.2001.0424

Farrington, D. P., Langan, P. A., & Tonry, M. (Eds.). (2004). *Cross-national studies in crime and justice* (NCJ 200988). Washington, DC: U.S. Department of Justice, Bureau of Justice Statistics.

Farrington, D. P., & Loeber, R. (1989). Relative improvement over chance (RIOC) and phi as measures of predictive efficiency and strength of association in 2 x 2 tables. *Journal of Quantitative Criminology, 5*, 201–213. doi:10.1007/BF01062737

Farrington, D. P., & Loeber, R. (2000). Some benefits of dichotomization in psychiatric and criminological research. *Criminal Behaviour and Mental Health, 10*, 100–122. doi:10.1002/cbm.349

Farrington, D. P., Loeber, R., & Stouthamer-Loeber, M. (2003). How can the relationship between race and violence be explained. In D. F. Hawkins (Ed.), *Violent crime: Assessing race & ethnic differences* (pp. 213–237). Cambridge, England: Cambridge University Press. doi:10.1017/CBO9780511499456.014

Farrington, D. P., Loeber, R., Stouthamer-Loeber, M., van Kammen, W. B., & Schmidt, L. (1996). Self-reported delinquency and a combined delinquency seriousness scale based on boys, mothers, and teachers: Concurrent and predictive validity for African-Americans and Caucasians. *Criminology, 34*, 493–517. doi:10.1111/j.1745-9125.1996.tb01217.x

Farrington, D. P., & Murray, J. (Eds.). (2014). *Labeling theory: Empirical tests* (*Advances in criminological theory*, Vol. 18). New Brunswick, NJ: Transaction.

Farrington, D. P., Piquero, A. R., & Jennings, W. G. (2013). *Offending from childhood to late middle age: Recent results from the Cambridge Study in Delinquent Development*. New York, NY: Springer. doi:10.1007/978-1-4614-6105-0

Farrington, D. P., & Welsh, B. C. (2007). *Saving children from a life of crime: Early risk factors and effective interventions*. Oxford, England: Oxford University Press.

Farrington, D. P., & Wikström, P.-O. H. (1994). Criminal careers in London and Stockholm: A cross-national comparative study. In E. G. M. Weitekamp & H.-J. Kerner (Eds.), *Cross-national longitudinal research on human development and criminal behavior* (pp. 65–89). Dordrecht, the Netherlands: Kluwer. doi:10.1007/978-94-011-0864-5_2

Fearon, R. P., Bakermans-Kranenburg, M. J., Van Ijzendoorn, M. H., Lapsley, A., & Roisman, G. I. (2010). The significance of insecure attachment and disorganization in the development of children's externalizing behavior: A meta-analytic study. *Child Development, 81*, 435–456. doi:10.1111/j.1467-8624.2009.01405.x

Ferraro, K. J., Johnson, J. M., Jorgensen, S. R., & Bolton, F. G., Jr. (1983). Problems of prisoners' families: The hidden costs of imprisonment. *Journal of Family Issues, 4*, 575–591. doi:10.1177/019251383004004004

Fishman, S. H. (1983). The impact of incarceration on children of offenders. *Journal of Children in Contemporary Society, 15*, 89–99. doi:10.1300/J274v15n01_11

Foster, H., & Hagan, J. (2007). Incarceration and intergenerational social exclusion. *Social Problems, 54*, 399–433. doi:10.1525/sp.2007.54.4.399

Foster, H., & Hagan, J. (2009). The mass incarceration of parents in America: Issues of race/ethnicity, collateral damage to children, and prisoner reentry. *Annals of the American Academy of Political and Social Science, 623*, 179–194. doi:10.1177/0002716208331123

Foucault, M. (1977). *Discipline and punish: The birth of the prison*. Middlesex, England: Penguin.

Friday, P. C. (1976). Sanctioning in Sweden: An overview. *Federal Probation, 40*, 48–55.

Friedman, S., & Esselstyn, T. C. (1965). The adjustment of children of jail inmates. *Federal Probation, 29*, 55–59. Retrieved from http://www.uscourts.gov/Federal Courts/ProbationPretrialServices/FederalProbationJournal.aspx

Fritsch, T. A., & Burkhead, J. D. (1981). Behavioral reactions of children to parental absence due to imprisonment. *Family Relations, 30*, 83–88. doi:10.2307/584240

Gabel, K., & Johnston, D. (Eds.). (1995). *Children of incarcerated parents*. New York, NY: Lexington Books.

Gabel, S. (2003). Behavioral problems in sons of incarcerated or otherwise absent fathers: The issue of separation. In O. Harris & R. R. Miller (Eds.), *Impacts of incarceration on the African American family* (pp. 105–119). New Brunswick, NJ: Transaction.

Geller, A. (2013). Paternal incarceration and father–child contact in fragile families. *Journal of Marriage and Family, 75*, 1288–1303. doi:10.1111/jomf.12056

Geller, A., Cooper, C., Garfinkel, I., Schwartz-Soicher, O., & Mincy, R. (2012). Beyond absenteeism: Father incarceration and child development. *Demography, 49*, 49–76. doi:10.1007/s13524-011-0081-9

Geller, A., Garfinkel, I., & Western, B. (2011). Paternal incarceration and support for children in fragile families. *Demography, 48*, 25–47. doi:10.1007/s13524-010-0009-9

Giordano, P. C. (2010). *Legacies of crime: A follow-up of the children of highly delinquent girls and boys*. Cambridge, England: Cambridge University Press. doi:10.1017/CBO9780511810046

Glaze, L. E., & Maruschak, L. M. (2008). *Parents in prison and their minor children* (NCJ 222984). Washington, DC: U.S. Department of Justice, Bureau of Justice Statistics.

Glaze, L. E., & Parks, E. (2012). *Correctional populations in the United States, 2011* (NCJ 239972). Washington, DC: U.S. Department of Justice, Bureau of Justice Statistics.

Glover, J. (2009). *Every night you cry: The realities of having a parent in prison*. Ilford, England: Barnardo's.

Goffman, E. (1963). *Stigma: Notes on the management of spoiled identity*. Harmondsworth, England: Penguin.

Goldberg, D., & Williams, P. (1988). *A user's guide to the General Health Questionnaire*. Windsor, England: NFER-Nelson.

Goodwin, R. D., & Hamilton, S. P. (2003). Lifetime comorbidity of antisocial personality disorder and anxiety disorders among adults in the community. *Psychiatry Research, 117*, 159–166. doi:10.1016/S0165-1781(02)00320-7

Gottschalk, M. (2010). Cell blocks & red ink: Mass incarceration, the great recession & penal reform. *Daedalus, 139*(3), 62–73. doi:10.1162/DAED_a_00023

Guo, G., Roettger, M. E., & Cai, T. (2008). The integration of genetic propensities into social-control models of delinquency and violence among male youths. *American Sociological Review, 73*, 543–568. doi:10.1177/000312240807300402

Hagan, J., & Dinovitzer, R. (1999). Collateral consequences of imprisonment for children, communities and prisoners. In M. Tonry & J. Petersilia (Eds.), *Crime and justice: A review of research* (Vol. 26, pp. 121–162). Chicago, IL: University of Chicago Press.

Hairston, C. F. (1998). The forgotten parent: Understanding the forces that influence incarcerated fathers' relationships with their children. *Child Welfare, 77*, 617–639.

Hairston, C. F. (2003). Prisoners and their families: Parenting issues during incarceration. In J. Travis & M. Waul (Eds.), *Prisoners once removed: The impact of incarceration and reentry on children, families, and communities* (pp. 259–282). Washington, DC: Urban Institute.

Hames, C. C., & Pedreira, D. (2003). Children with parents in prison: Disenfranchised grievers who benefit from bibliotherapy. *Illness, Crisis & Loss, 11*, 377–386. doi:10.1177/1054137303256589

Harm, N. J., & Phillips, S. D. (1998). Helping children cope with the trauma of parental arrest. *Interdisciplinary Report on At-Risk Children and Families, 1*, 35–36.

Harris, O., & Miller, R. R. (Eds.). (2002). *Impacts of incarceration on the African American family*. New Brunswick, NJ: Transaction.

Harris, Y. R., Graham, J. A., & Carpenter, G. J. O. (Eds.). (2010). *Children of incarcerated parents: Theoretical, developmental, and clinical issues*. New York, NY: Springer.

Healey, K., Foley, D., & Walsh, K. (2000). *Parents in prison and their families: Everyone's business and no-one's concern*. Brisbane, Queensland, Australia: Catholic Prison Ministry.

Henggeler, S. W., Schoenwald, S. K., Borduin, C. M., Rowland, M. D., & Cunningham, P. B. (1998). *Multisystemic treatment of antisocial behavior in children and adolescents.* New York, NY: Guilford Press.

Hess, L. E. (1995). Changing family patterns in Western Europe: Opportunity and risk factors for adolescent development. In M. Rutter & D. J. Smith (Eds.), *Psychosocial disorders in young people: Time trends and their causes* (pp. 104–193). Chichester, England: Wiley.

Hetherington, E. M., & Stanley-Hagan, M. (1999). The adjustment of children with divorced parents: A risk and resiliency perspective. *Journal of Child Psychology and Psychiatry, 40,* 129–140. doi:10.1111/1469-7610.00427

Hinshaw, S. P., & Cicchetti, D. (2000). Stigma and mental disorder: Conceptions of illness, public attitudes, personal disclosure, and social policy. *Development and Psychopathology, 12,* 555–598. doi:10.1017/S0954579400004028

Hissel, S., Bijleveld, C., & Kruttschnitt, C. (2011). The well-being of children of incarcerated mothers: An exploratory study for the Netherlands. *European Journal of Criminology, 8,* 346–360. doi:10.1177/1477370811415755

Hodgins, S., & Janson, C.-G. (2002). *Criminality and violence among the mentally disordered: The Stockholm Metropolitan Project.* Cambridge, England: Cambridge University Press. doi:10.1017/CBO9780511489280

Huebner, B. M., & Gustafson, R. (2007). The effect of maternal incarceration on adult offspring involvement in the criminal justice system. *Journal of Criminal Justice, 35,* 283–296. doi:10.1016/j.jcrimjus.2007.03.005

International Centre for Prison Studies. (2013). *World prison brief.* London, England: Author.

Jacobs, A. L. (1995, October). *Protecting children and preserving families: A cooperative strategy for nurturing children of incarcerated parents.* Paper presented at the Family to Family Initiative Conference (Annie E. Casey Foundation), Baltimore, MD.

Jaffee, S. R., Moffitt, T. E., Caspi, A., & Taylor, A. (2003). Life with (or without) father: The benefits of living with two biological parents depend on the father's antisocial behavior. *Child Development, 74,* 109–126. doi:10.1111/1467-8624.t01-1-00524

James, D. J., & Glaze, L. E. (2006, September). *Mental health problems of prison and jail inmates* (Special Report NCJ 213600). Washington, DC: U.S. Department of Justice, Bureau of Justice Statistics.

Janson, C.-G. (1975). *Project Metropolitan: A description of its data archive* (Research Report No. 2, p. 18). Stockholm, Sweden: University of Stockholm, Department of Sociology.

Janson, C.-G. (1984). *Project Metropolitan: A presentation and progress report* (Research Report No. 21, p. 151). Stockholm, Sweden: University of Stockholm, Department of Sociology.

Janson, C.-G. (2000). Project Metropolitan. In C.-G. Janson (Ed.), *Seven Swedish longitudinal studies in the behavioral sciences* (pp. 140–171). Stockholm, Sweden: Forskningsradsnamuden.

Janson, C.-G. (2004). Youth justice in Sweden. In M. Tonry & A. N. Doob (Eds.), *Crime and justice: A review of research* (Vol. 31, pp. 391–442). Chicago, IL: University of Chicago Press.

Janson, C.-G., & Wikström, P.-O. H. (1995). Growing up in a welfare state: The social class–offending relationship. In J. Hagan (Ed.), *Delinquency and disrepute in the life course: Current perspectives on aging and the life cycle* (Vol. 4, pp. 191–215). Greenwich, CT: JAI Press.

Johnson, E. I., & Waldfogel, J. (2002). Parental incarceration: Recent trends and implications for child welfare. *The Social Service Review, 76*, 460–479. doi:10.1086/341184

Johnson, E. I., & Waldfogel, J. (2004). Children of incarcerated parents: Multiple risks and children's living arrangements. In M. Pattillo, D. Weiman, & B. Western (Eds.), *Imprisoning America: The social effects of mass incarceration* (pp. 97–131). New York, NY: Russell Sage.

Johnson, R. (2005). Brave new prisons: The growing social isolation of modern penal institutions. In A. Liebling & S. Maruna (Eds.), *The effects of imprisonment* (pp. 255–284). Cullompton, England: Willan.

Johnson, R. (2009). Ever-increasing levels of parental incarceration and the consequences for children. In S. Raphael & M. Stoll (Eds.), *Do prisons make us safer? The benefits and costs of the prison boom* (pp. 177–206). New York, NY: Russell Sage.

Johnston, D. (1995). Effects of parental incarceration. In K. Gabel & D. Johnston (Eds.), *Children of incarcerated parents* (pp. 59–88). New York, NY: Lexington Books.

Jolliffe, D., Murray, J., Farrington, D. P., & Vannick, C. (2012). Testing the Cambridge Quality Checklists on a review of disrupted families and crime. *Criminal Behaviour and Mental Health, 22*, 303–314. doi:10.1002/cbm.1837

Jones, A. D., & Wainaina-Wozna, A. E. (Eds.). (2013). *Children of prisoners: Interventions and mitigations to strengthen mental health.* Huddersfield, England: University of Huddersfield. doi:10.5920/cop.hud.2013

Junger-Tas, J. (1995). Sentencing in the Netherlands: Context and policy. *Federal Sentencing Reporter, 7*, 293–299. doi:10.2307/20639820

Kampfner, C. J. (1995). Post-traumatic stress reactions in children of imprisoned mothers. In K. Gabel & D. Johnston (Eds.), *Children of incarcerated parents* (pp. 89–102). New York, NY: Lexington Books.

Kazdin, A. E., Kraemer, H. C., Kessler, R. C., Kupfer, D. J., & Offord, D. R. (1997). Contributions of risk-factor research to developmental psychopathology. *Clinical Psychology Review, 17*, 375–406. doi:10.1016/S0272-7358(97)00012-3

Kelemenis, I. (1999). *Between captivity and freedom.* Unpublished doctoral dissertation, Oxford University, England.

Kemper, K. J., & Rivara, F. P. (1993). Parents in jail. *Pediatrics, 92*, 261–264.

Kenworthy, L. (1999). Do social-welfare policies reduce poverty? A cross-national assessment. *Social Forces, 77*, 1119–1139. doi:10.2307/3005973

Killias, M., Aebi, M. F., & Ribeaud, D. (2000). Does community service rehabilitate better than short-term imprisonment? Results of a controlled experiment. *Howard Journal of Criminal Justice, 39,* 40–57. doi:10.1111/1468-2311.00152

Killias, M., Gilliéron, G., Villard, F., & Poglia, C. (2010). How damaging is imprisonment in the long-term? A controlled experiment comparing long-term effects of community service and short custodial sentences on re-offending and social integration. *Journal of Experimental Criminology, 6,* 115–130. doi:10.1007/s11292-010-9093-5

Killias, M., & Villetaz, P. (2008). The effects of custodial vs. noncustodial sanctions on reoffending: Lessons from a systematic review. *Psicothema, 20,* 29–34. Retrieved from http://www.psicothema.es/

Kjellstrand, J. M. (2009). *Children with incarcerated parents: A longitudinal study of the effect of parental incarceration on adolescent externalizing behaviors.* Unpublished doctoral dissertation, Portland State University, Portland, OR.

Kjellstrand, J. M., & Eddy, J. M. (2011a). Mediators of the effect of parental incarceration on adolescent externalizing behaviors. *Journal of Community Psychology, 39,* 551–565. doi:10.1002/jcop.20451

Kjellstrand, J. M., & Eddy, J. M. (2011b). Parental incarceration during childhood, family context, and youth problem behavior across adolescence. *Journal of Offender Rehabilitation, 50,* 18–36. doi:10.1080/10509674.2011.536720

Klein, R. G., & Pine, D. S. (2002). Anxiety disorders. In M. Rutter & A. Taylor (Eds.), *Child and adolescent psychiatry* (4th ed., pp. 486–509). Oxford, England: Blackwell.

Kobak, R. (1999). The emotional dynamics of disruptions in attachment relationships: Implications for theory, research, and clinical intervention. In J. Cassidy & P. R. Shaver (Eds.), *Handbook of attachment: Theory, research and clinical applications* (pp. 21–43). New York, NY: Guilford Press.

Kraemer, H. C., Kazdin, S. E., Offord, D., & Kuper, D. (2001). How do risk factors work together? Mediators, moderators and independent, overlapping and proxy risk factors. *The American Journal of Psychiatry, 158,* 848–856.

Kraemer, H. C., Lowe, K. K., & Kupfer, D. J. (2005). *To your health: How to understand what research tells us about risk.* New York, NY: Oxford University Press.

Kruttschnitt, C. (2011). Is the devil in the details? Crafting policy to mitigate the collateral consequences of parental incarceration. *Criminology & Public Policy, 10,* 829–837. doi:10.1111/j.1745-9133.2011.00732.x

Lemert, E. M. (1967). *Human deviance, social problems, and social control.* Englewood Cliffs, NJ: Prentice-Hall.

Li, Y. P., Propert, K. J., & Rosenbaum, P. R. (2001). Balanced risk set matching. *Journal of the American Statistical Association, 96*(455), 870–882. doi:10.1198/016214501753208573

Liang, K.-Y., & Zeger, S. L. (1986). Longitudinal data analysis using generalized linear models. *Biometrika, 73,* 13–22. doi:10.1093/biomet/73.1.13

Liebling, A., & Maruna, S. (Eds.). (2005). *The effects of imprisonment*. Cullompton, England: Willan.

Light, R. (1994). *Black and Asian prisoners' families*. Bristol, England: Bristol Centre for Criminal Justice.

Lipsey, M. W., & Derzon, J. H. (1998). Predictors of violent or serious delinquency in adolescence and early adulthood: A synthesis of longitudinal research. In D. P. Farrington & R. Loeber (Eds.), *Serious and violent juvenile offenders: Risk factors and successful interventions* (pp. 86–105). Thousand Oaks, CA: Sage.

Lipsey, M. W., & Wilson, D. B. (2001). *Practical meta-analysis*. Thousand Oaks, CA: Sage.

Lipsitz, S. R., Laird, N. M., & Harrington, D. P. (1991). Generalized estimating equations for correlated binary data: Using the odds ratio as a measure of association. *Biometrika, 78*, 153–160. doi:10.1093/biomet/78.1.153

Loeber, R., & Farrington, D. P. (2008). Advancing knowledge about causes in longitudinal studies: Experimental and quasi-experimental methods. In A. M. Liberman (Ed.), *The long view of crime: A synthesis of longitudinal research* (pp. 257–279). New York, NY: Springer. doi:10.1007/978-0-387-71165-2_8

Loeber, R., Farrington, D. P., Stouthamer-Loeber, M., & van Kammen, W. B. (1998). *Antisocial behavior and mental health problems: Explanatory factors in childhood and adolescence*. Mahwah, NJ: Erlbaum.

Loeber, R., Farrington, D. P., Stouthamer-Loeber, M., & White, H. R. (2008). *Violence and serious theft: Development and prediction from childhood to adulthood*. New York, NY: Routledge.

Loeber, R., & Stouthamer-Loeber, M. (1986). Family factors as correlates and predictors of juvenile conduct problems and delinquency. In M. Tonry & N. Morris (Eds.), *Crime and Justice: A review of research* (Vol. 7, pp. 29–149). Chicago, IL: University of Chicago Press. doi:10.1086/449112

Loeber, R., Southamer-Loeber, M., van Kammen, W. B., & Farrington, D. P. (1989). Development of a new measure of self-reported antisocial behavior for young children: Prevalence and reliability. In M. Klein (Ed.), *Cross-national research in self-reported crime and delinquency* (Vol. 50, pp. 203–225). Boston, MA: Kluwer Academic. doi:10.1007/978-94-009-1001-0_10

Loeffler, C. E. (2013). Does imprisonment alter the life course? Evidence on crime and employment from a natural experiment. *Criminology, 51*, 137–166. doi:10.1111/1745-9125.12000

Loper, A. B., & Tuerk, E. H. (2006). Parenting programs for incarcerated parents: Current research and future directions. *Criminal Justice Policy Review, 17*, 407–427. doi:10.1177/0887403406292692

Mackintosh, V. H., Myers, B. J., & Kennon, S. S. (2006). Children of incarcerated mothers and their caregivers: Factors affecting the quality of their relationship. *Journal of Child and Family Studies, 15*, 579–594. doi:10.1007/s10826-006-9030-4

Main, M., Kaplan, N., & Cassidy, J. (1985). Security in infancy, childhood, and adulthood: A move to the level of representation. *Monographs of the Society for*

Research in Child Development, 50(1–2, Serial No. 209), 66–104. doi:10.2307/3333827

Major, B., & O'Brien, L. T. (2005). The social psychology of stigma. *Annual Review of Psychology, 56*, 393–421. doi:10.1146/annurev.psych.56.091103.070137

Marmorstein, N. R., & Iacono, W. G. (2003). Major depression and conduct disorder in a twin sample: Gender, functioning, and risk for future psychopathology. *Journal of the American Academy of Child & Adolescent Psychiatry, 42*, 225–233. doi:10.1097/00004583-200302000-00017

Marnell, G. (1972). Comparative correctional systems: United States and Sweden. *Criminal Law Bulletin, 7*, 748–760.

Martin, J. P., & Webster, D. (1971). *The social consequences of conviction.* London, England: Heinemann Educational.

Maruna, S., & LeBel, T. P. (2002). Revisiting ex-prisoner re-entry: A buzzword in search of a narrative. In S. Rex & M. Tonry (Eds.), *Reform and punishment: The future of sentencing* (pp. 158–180). Cullompton, England: Willan.

Massoglia, M., & Warner, C. (2011). The consequences of incarceration: Challenges for scientifically informed and policy-relevant research. *Criminology & Public Policy, 10*, 851–863. doi:10.1111/j.1745-9133.2011.00754.x

Matthews, J. (1983). *Forgotten victims: How prison affects the family.* London, England: National Association for the Care and Resettlement of Offenders.

McCord, W., McCord, J., & Zola, I. K. (1959). *Origins of crime: A new evaluation of the Cambridge-Somerville Youth Study.* New York, NY: Columbia University Press.

McCubbin, H. I., Dahl, B. B., Lester, G. R., & Ross, B. (1977). The prisoner of war and his children: Evidence for the origin of second generational effects of captivity. *International Journal of Sociology of the Family, 7*, 25–36.

McDermott, K., & King, R. D. (1992). Prison rule 102: Stand by your man. In R. Shaw (Ed.), *Prisoners' children: What are the issues?* (pp. 50–73). London, England: Routledge.

McDougall, C., Cohen, M. A., Swaray, R., & Perry, A. (2003). The costs and benefits of sentencing: A systematic review. *Annals of the American Academy of Political and Social Science, 587*, 160–177. doi:10.1177/0002716202250807

McEvoy, K., O'Mahony, D., Horner, C., & Lyner, O. (1999). The home front: The families of politically motivated prisoners in Northern Ireland. *The British Journal of Criminology, 39*, 175–197. doi:10.1093/bjc/39.2.175

Menting, A. T. A. (2012). *A fresh start from arrested motherhood: A randomized trial of parent training for mothers being released from incarceration.* Utrecht, the Netherlands: Utrecht University.

Merton, R. (1938). Social structure and anomie. *American Sociological Review, 3*, 672–682. doi:10.2307/2084686

Messer, S. C., Angold, A., Costello, E. J., Loeber, R., van Kammen, W., & Stouthamer-Loeber, M. (1995). Development of a short questionnaire for use in epidemiological studies of depression in children and adolescents: Factor composition and structure across development. *International Journal of Methods in Psychiatric Research, 5,* 251–262.

Miller, H. V., & Barnes, J. C. (2013). Genetic transmission effects and intergenerational contact with the criminal justice system: A consideration of three dopamine polymorphisms. *Criminal Justice and Behavior, 40,* 671–689. doi:10.1177/0093854812468434

Morgan, S. L., & Winship, C. (2007). *Counterfactuals and causal inference: Methods and principles for social research.* New York, NY: Cambridge University Press. doi:10.1017/CBO9780511804564

Morris, N. (1966). Lessons from the adult correctional system of Sweden. *Federal Probation, 30,* 3–13.

Morris, P. (1965). *Prisoners and their families.* Woking, England: Unwin Brothers.

Moses, M. C. (1995). *Keeping incarcerated mothers and their daughters together: Girl Scouts beyond bars* (NCJ 182335). Washington, DC: National Institute of Justice (Program Focus).

Mulready-Jones, A. (2011). *Hidden children: A study into services for children of incarcerated parents in Sweden and the United States.* Retrieved from http://www.wcmt. org.uk/reports/814_1.pdf

Mumola, C. J. (2000). *Incarcerated parents and their children* (Special Report). Washington, DC: U.S. Department of Justice, Bureau of Justice Statistics.

Murray, J. (2005). The effects of imprisonment on families and children of prisoners. In A. Liebling & S. Maruna (Eds.), *The effects of imprisonment* (pp. 442–492). Cullompton, England: Willan.

Murray, J. (2007). The cycle of punishment: Social exclusion of prisoners and their children. *Criminology & Criminal Justice, 7,* 55–81. doi:10.1177/1748895807072476

Murray, J., Blokland, A., Theobald, D., & Farrington, D. P. (2014). Long-term effects of conviction and incarceration on men in the Cambridge Study in Delinquent Development. In D. P. Farrington & J. Murray (Eds.), *Labeling theory: Empirical tests* (*Advances in criminological theory*, Vol. 18, pp. 209–235). New Brunswick, NJ: Transaction.

Murray, J., & Farrington, D. P. (2005). Parental imprisonment: Effects on boys' antisocial behaviour and delinquency through the life-course. *Journal of Child Psychology and Psychiatry, 46,* 1269–1278. doi:10.1111/j.1469-7610.2005.01433.x

Murray, J., & Farrington, D. P. (2006). Evidence-based programs for children of prisoners. *Criminology & Public Policy, 5,* 721–735. doi:10.1111/j.1745-9133.2006.00412.x

Murray, J., & Farrington, D. P. (2008a). The effects of parental imprisonment on children. In M. Tonry (Ed.), *Crime and justice: A review of research* (Vol. 37, pp. 133–206). Chicago, IL: University of Chicago Press. doi:10.1086/520070

Murray, J., & Farrington, D. P. (2008b). Parental imprisonment: Long-lasting effects on boys' internalizing problems through the life-course. *Development and Psychopathology, 20,* 273–290. doi:10.1017/S0954579408000138

Murray, J., Farrington, D. P., & Eisner, M. P. (2009). Drawing conclusions about causes from systematic reviews of risk factors: The Cambridge Quality Checklists. *Journal of Experimental Criminology, 5*, 1–23. doi:10.1007/s11292-008-9066-0

Murray, J., Farrington, D. P., & Sekol, I. (2012). Children's antisocial behavior, mental health, drug use, and educational performance after parental incarceration: A systematic review and meta-analysis. *Psychological Bulletin, 138*, 175–210. doi:10.1037/a0026407

Murray, J., Farrington, D. P., Sekol, I., & Olsen, R. F. (2009). Effects of parental imprisonment on child antisocial behaviour and mental health: A systematic review. *Campbell Systematic Reviews, 4*. doi:10.4073/csr.2009.4

Murray, J., Janson, C.-G., & Farrington, D. P. (2007). Crime in adult offspring of prisoners: A cross-national comparison of two longitudinal samples. *Criminal Justice and Behavior, 34*, 133–149. doi:10.1177/0093854806289549

Murray, J., Loeber, R., & Pardini, D. (2012). Parental involvement in the criminal justice system and the development of youth theft, depression, marijuana use, and poor academic performance. *Criminology, 50*, 255–302. doi:10.1111/j.1745-9125.2011.00257.x

Murray, J., & Murray, L. (2010). Parental incarceration, attachment and child psychopathology. *Attachment & Human Development, 12*, 289–309. doi:10.1080/14751790903416889

Myers, B. J., Smarsh, T. M., Amlund-Hagen, K., & Kennon, S. (1999). Children of incarcerated mothers. *Journal of Child and Family Studies, 8*, 11–25. doi:10.1023/A:1022990410036

Nagin, D. S., Cullen, F., & Jonson, C. L. (2009). Imprisonment and reoffending. In M. Tonry (Ed.), *Crime and justice: A review of research* (Vol. 38, 115–200). doi:10.1086/599202

Najafi, M., Akochkian, S., & Nikyar, H. R. (2007). Being child of prisoners of war: The case of mental health status. *Iranian Journal of Pediatrics, 18*, 154–158. http://journals.tums.ac.ir/abs/8012

Naudeau, S. (2005). *Positive development among children of incarcerated parents: A focus on character.* Unpublished doctoral dissertation, Tufts University, Medford, MA.

Nesmith, A., & Ruhland, E. (2008). Children of incarcerated parents: Challenges and resiliency, in their own words. *Children and Youth Services Review, 30*, 1119–1130. doi:10.1016/j.childyouth.2008.02.006

Newburn, T. (2002). Atlantic crossings: 'Policy transfer' and crime control in the USA and Britain. *Punishment and Society, 4*, 165–194. doi:10.1177/14624740222228536

Nickel, J., Garland, C., & Kane, L. (2009). *Children of incarcerated parents: An action plan for federal policy.* New York, NY: Council of State Governments Justice Center.

Nieuwbeerta, P., Nagin, D. S., & Blokland, A. (2009). Assessing the impact of first-time imprisonment on offenders' subsequent criminal career development: A matched samples comparison. *Journal of Quantitative Criminology, 25,* 227–257. doi:10.1007/s10940-009-9069-7

Nijnatten, C. (1998). *Detention and development: Perspectives of children of prisoners.* Mönchengladbach, Germany: Forum Verlag Godesberg.

Nurse, A. M. (2002). *Fatherhood arrested: Parenting from within the juvenile justice system.* Nashville, TN: Vanderbilt University Press.

Office for National Statistics. (2013). *Statistical bulletin: Annual mid-year population estimates for England and Wales, 2012.* London, England: Office for National Statistics.

Olds, D., Henderson, C. R., Cole, R., Eckenrode, J., Kitzman, H., Luckey, D., . . . Powers, J. (1998). Long-term effects of nurse home visitation on children's criminal and antisocial behavior: 15-year follow-up of a randomized controlled trial. *JAMA, 280,* 1238–1244. doi:10.1001/jama.280.14.1238

Olsson, S. E. (1993). *Social policy and welfare state in Sweden.* Lund, Sweden: Arkiv.

Osborn, S. G., & West, D. J. (1979). Conviction records of fathers and sons compared. *The British Journal of Criminology, 19,* 120–133. http://bjc.oxfordjournals.org/

Pager, D., Western, B., & Sugie, N. (2009). Sequencing disadvantage: Barriers to employment facing young black and white men with criminal records. *Annals of the American Academy of Political and Social Science, 623,* 195–213. doi: 10.1177/0002716208330793

Parke, R., & Clarke-Stewart, K. A. (2003). The effects of parental incarceration on children: Perspectives, promises, and policies. In J. Travis & M. Waul (Eds.), *Prisoners once removed: The impact of incarceration and reentry on children, families, and communities* (pp. 189–232). Washington, DC: Urban Institute.

Patterson, G. R. (1995). Coercion as a basis for early age of onset for arrest. In J. McCord (Ed.), *Coercion and punishment in long-term perspectives* (pp. 81–105). Cambridge, England: Cambridge University Press.

Petersilia, J. (2003). *When prisoners come home: Parole and prisoner reentry.* Oxford, England: Oxford University Press.

Petersilia, J. (2005). From cell to society: Who is returning home? In J. Travis & C. Visher (Eds.), *Prisoner reentry and crime in America* (pp. 15–49). Cambridge, England: Cambridge University Press. doi:10.1017/CBO9780511813580.002

Petrosino, A., Boruch, R. F., Farrington, D. P., Sherman, L. W., & Weisburd, D. (2003). Toward evidence-based criminology and criminal justice: Systematic reviews, the Campbell Collaboration, and the Crime and Justice Group. *International Journal of Comparative Criminology, 3,* 42–61.

Pettit, B., & Western, B. (2004). Mass imprisonment and the life course: Race and class inequality in US incarceration. *American Sociological Review, 69,* 151–169. doi:10.1177/000312240406900201

Phillips, S. D., Burns, B. J., Wagner, H. R., Kramer, T. L., & Robbins, J. M. (2002). Parental incarceration among adolescents receiving mental health services. *Journal of Child and Family Studies, 11,* 385–399. doi:10.1023/A:1020975106679

Phillips, S. D., & Gates, T. (2011). A conceptual framework for understanding the stigmatization of children of incarcerated parents. *Journal of Child and Family Studies, 20,* 286–294. doi:10.1007/s10826-010-9391-6

Phillips, S. D., & Zhao, J. (2010). The relationship between witnessing arrests and elevated symptoms of posttraumatic stress: Findings from a national study of children involved in the child welfare system. *Children and Youth Services Review, 32,* 1246–1254. doi:10.1016/j.childyouth.2010.04.015

Piehl, A. M., & Dilulio, J. J., Jr. (1995). "Does prison pay?" revisited: Returning to the crime scene. *The Brookings Review, 13,* 20–25.

Piquero, A. R., Farrington, D. P., & Blumstein, A. (2007). *Key issues in criminal career research: New analyses of the Cambridge Study in Delinquent Development.* Cambridge, England: Cambridge University Press. doi:10.1017/CBO9780511499494

Poehlmann, J. (2005a). Children's family environments and intellectual outcomes during maternal incarceration. *Journal of Marriage and Family, 67,* 1275–1285. doi:10.1111/j.1741-3737.2005.00216.x

Poehlmann, J. (2005b). Representations of attachment relationships in children of incarcerated mothers. *Child Development, 76,* 679–696. doi:10.1111/j.1467-8624.2005.00871.x

Poehlmann, J., Dallaire, D., Loper, A. B., & Shear, L. D. (2010). Children's contact with their incarcerated parents: Research findings and recommendations. *American Psychologist, 65,* 575–598. doi:10.1037/a0020279

Pratt, J. (2008). Scandinavian exceptionalism in an era of penal excess: Part I: The nature and roots of Scandinavian exceptionalism. *The British Journal of Criminology, 48,* 119–137. doi:10.1093/bjc/azm072

Raphael, S. (2014). The effects of conviction and incarceration on future employment outcomes. In D. P. Farrington & J. Murray (Eds.), *Labeling theory: Empirical tests* (*Advances in criminological theory,* Vol. 18, pp. 237–262). New Brunswick, NJ: Transaction.

Rezmovic, E. L. (1979). Methodological considerations in evaluating correctional effectiveness: Issues and chronic problems. In L. B. Sechrest, S. O. White, & E. D. Brown (Eds.), *The rehabilitation of criminal offenders: Problems and prospects* (pp. 163–209). Washington, DC: National Academies of Science.

Rhee, S. H., & Waldman, I. D. (2002). Genetic and environmental influences on antisocial behavior: A meta-analysis of twin and adoption studies. *Psychological Bulletin, 128,* 490–529. doi:10.1037/0033-2909.128.3.490

Richards, M. (1992). The separation of children and parents: Some issues and problems. In R. Shaw (Ed.), *Prisoners' children: What are the issues?* (pp. 3–12). London, England: Routledge.

Richards, M., McWilliams, B., Allcock, L., Enterkin, J., Owens, P., & Woodrow, J. (1994). *The family ties of English prisoners: The results of the Cambridge Project on Imprisonment and Family Ties.* Cambridge, England: Centre for Family Research, University of Cambridge.

Robertson, O. (2007). *The impact of parental imprisonment on children.* Geneva, Switzerland: Quakers United Nations Office.

Robertson, O., Sharratt, K., Pascaru, G., Bieganski, J., Kearney, H., Sommerland, N., . . . Cheung, R. (2012). Stakeholder perspectives on the needs of children of prisoners in Europe. *Scientific Annals of the "Alexandru Ioan Cuza" University of Iasi: Social Work Series, 5,* 98–114.

Rodgers, B., & Pryor, J. (1998). *Divorce and separation: The outcomes for children.* York, England: Joseph Rowntree Foundation.

Roettger, M. E. (2008). *Three essays on social inequality and the U.S. criminal justice system.* Unpublished doctoral dissertation, University of North Carolina at Chapel Hill.

Roettger, M. E., & Swisher, R. R. (2011). Associations of fathers' history of incarceration with sons' delinquency and arrest among black, white, and Hispanic males in the United States. *Criminology, 49,* 1109–1147. doi:10.1111/j.1745-9125.2011.00253.x

Roettger, M. E., Swisher, R. R., Kuhl, D. C., & Chavez, J. (2011). Paternal incarceration and trajectories of marijuana and other illegal drug use from adolescence into young adulthood: Evidence from longitudinal panels of males and females in the United States. *Addiction, 106,* 121–132. doi:10.1111/j.1360-0443.2010.03110.x

Rosenbaum, P. R., & Rubin, D. B. (1983). The central role of the propensity score in observational studies for causal effects. *Biometrika, 70,* 41–55. doi:10.1093/biomet/70.1.41

Rosenfeld, R., & Messner, S. F. (2009). The crime drop in comparative perspective: The impact of the economy and imprisonment on American and European burglary rates. *The British Journal of Sociology, 60,* 445–471. doi:10.1111/j.1468-4446.2009.01251.x

Rossman, S. B. (2003). Building partnerships to strengthen offenders, families, and communities. In J. Travis & M. Waul (Eds.), *Prisoners once removed: The impact of incarceration and reentry on children, families, and communities* (pp. 343–379). Washington, DC: Urban Institute.

Rutter, M. (1995a). Causal concepts and their testing. In M. Rutter & D. J. Smith (Eds.), *Psychosocial disorders in young people: Time trends and their causes* (pp. 686–761). Chichester, England: Wiley.

Rutter, M. (1995b). Clinical implications of attachment concepts: Retrospect and prospect. *Journal of Child Psychology and Psychiatry and Allied Disciplines, 36,* 549–571. doi: 10.1111/j.1469-7610.1995.tb01311.x

Rutter, M. (2003). Crucial paths from risk indicator to causal mechanism. In B. B. Lahey, T. E. Moffitt, & A. Caspi (Eds.), *Causes of conduct disorder and juvenile delinquency* (pp. 3–24). New York, NY: Guilford Press.

Rutter, M., Giller, H., & Hagell, A. (1998). *Antisocial behavior by young people.* Cambridge, England: Cambridge University Press.

Rutter, M., & Sroufe, L. A. (2000). Developmental psychopathology: Concepts and challenges. *Development and Psychopathology, 12*, 265–296. doi:10.1017/S0954579400003023

Sack, W. H. (1977). Children of imprisoned fathers. *Psychiatry: Journal for the Study of Interpersonal Processes, 40*, 163–174.

Sack, W. H., & Seidler, J. (1978). Should children visit their parents in prison? *Law and Human Behavior, 2*, 261–266. doi:10.1007/BF01039083

Sack, W. H., Seidler, J., & Thomas, S. (1976). The children of imprisoned parents: A psychosocial exploration. *American Journal of Orthopsychiatry, 46*, 618–628. doi:10.1111/j.1939-0025.1976.tb00960.x

Salomon, R. A. (1976). Lessons from the Swedish criminal justice system: A reappraisal. *Federal Probation, 40*, 40–48.

Sampson, R. J. (2011). The incarceration ledger: Toward a new era in assessing societal consequences. *Criminology & Public Policy, 10*, 819–828. doi:10.1111/j.1745-9133.2011.00756.x

Sanders, M. R., Markie-Dadds, C., Tully, L. A., & Bor, W. (2000). The Triple P-Positive Parenting Program: A comparison of enhanced, standard and self-directed behavioral family intervention for parents of children with early onset conduct problems. *Journal of Consulting and Clinical Psychology, 68*, 624–640. doi:10.1037/0022-006X.68.4.624

Schneider, A. L. (1986). Restitution and recidivism rates of juvenile offenders: Results from four experimental studies. *Criminology, 24*, 533–552. doi:10.1111/j.1745-9125.1986.tb00389.x

Schneller, D. P. (1975). Prisoners' families a study of some social and psychological effects of incarceration on the families of negro prisoners. *Criminology, 12*, 402–412. doi:10.1111/j.1745-9125.1975.tb00646.x

Scott, S., Spender, Q., Doolan, M., Jacobs, B., & Aspland, H. (2001). Multi-centre controlled trial of parenting groups for childhood antisocial behaviour in clinical practice. *BMJ: British Medical Journal, 323*, 194–198. doi:10.1136/bmj.323.7306.194

Shadish, W. R., Cook, T. D., & Campbell, D. T. (2002). *Experimental and quasi-experimental designs for generalized causal inference*. Boston, MA: Houghton Mifflin.

Sharp, S. F., Marcus-Mendoza, S. T., Bentley, R. G., Simpson, D. B., & Love, S. R. (1997/1998). Gender difference in the impact of incarceration on the children and families of drug offenders. *Journal of the Oklahoma Criminal Justice Research Consortium, 4*.

Shaw, R. (1987). *Children of imprisoned fathers*. London, England: Hodder and Stoughton.

Shaw, R. (1992a). Imprisoned fathers and the orphans of justice. In R. Shaw (Ed.), *Prisoners' children: What are the issues?* (pp. 41–49). London, England: Routledge.

Shaw, R. (Ed.). (1992b). *Prisoners' children: What are the issues?* London, England: Routledge.

Sherman, L. W. (1993). Defiance, deterrence and irrelevance: A theory of the criminal sanction. *Journal of Research in Crime and Delinquency, 30,* 445–473. doi:10.1177/0022427893030004006

Sherman, L. W., & Strang, H. (2007). *Restorative justice: The evidence.* London, England: Smith Institute.

Sherman, L. W., Strang, H., Angel, C., Woods, D., Barnes, G. C., Bennett, S., & Inkpen, N. (2005). Effects of face-to-face restorative justice on victims of crime in four randomized, controlled trials. *Journal of Experimental Criminology, 1,* 367–395. doi:10.1007/s11292-005-8126-y

Shlafer, R. J., Poehlmann, J., Coffino, B., & Hanneman, A. (2009). Mentoring children with incarcerated parents: Implications for research, practice, and policy. *Family Relations, 58,* 507–519. doi:10.1111/j.1741-3729.2009.00571.x

Siegel, J. A. (2011). *Disrupted childhoods: Children of women in prison.* New Brunswick, NJ: Rutgers University Press.

Sigle-Rushton, W., & McLanahan, S. (2004). Father absence and child wellbeing: A critical review. In D. P. Moynihan, L. Rainwater, & T. Smeeding (Eds.), *The future of the family* (pp. 116–155). New York, NY: Russell Sage Foundation.

Simmons, C. W. (2000). *Children of incarcerated parents.* Sacramento: California Research Bureau.

Singleton, N., Meltzer, H., Gatward, R., Coid, J., & Deasy, D. (1998). *Psychiatric morbidity among prisoners in England and Wales.* London, England: The Stationery Office.

Skinner, D., & Swartz, L. (1989). The consequences for preschool children of a parent's detention: A preliminary South African clinical study of caregivers' reports. *Journal of Child Psychology and Psychiatry, and Allied Disciplines, 30,* 243–259. doi:10.1111/j.1469-7610.1989.tb00238.x

Slotboom, A.-M., Bijleveld, C. C. J. H., Day, S., & van Giezen, A. (2008). *Gedetineerde Vrouwen in Nederland; Over Import-en Deprivatiefactoren bij Detentieschade* [Detained women in the Netherlands; about import and deprivation factors in detention damage]. Amsterdam, the Netherlands: Vrije Universiteit.

Smith, C. A., & Farrington, D. P. (2004). Continuities in antisocial behavior and parenting across three generations. *Journal of Child Psychology and Psychiatry, and Allied Disciplines, 45,* 230–247. doi:10.1111/j.1469-7610.2004.00216.x

Smith, C. A., & Stern, S. B. (1997). Delinquency and antisocial behavior: A review of family processes and intervention research. *The Social Service Review, 71,* 382–420. doi:10.1086/604263

Smith, D. J. (2002). Crime and the life course. In R. Morgan, R. Reiner, & M. Maguire (Eds.), *The Oxford handbook of criminology* (3rd ed., pp. 702–745). Oxford, England: Oxford University Press.

Social Exclusion Unit. (2002). *Reducing re-offending by ex-prisoners*. London, England: Author.

Springer, D. W., Lynch, C., & Rubin, A. (2000). Effects of a solution-focused mutual aid group for Hispanic children of incarcerated parents. *Child & Adolescent Social Work Journal, 17*, 431–442. doi:10.1023/A:1026479727159

Sroufe, L. A. (2005). Attachment and development: A prospective, longitudinal study from birth to adulthood. *Attachment & Human Development, 7*, 349–367. doi:10.1080/14616730500365928

Stroble, W. L. (1997). *The relationship between parental incarceration and African-American high school students' attitudes towards school and family*. Unpublished doctoral dissertation, College of William and Mary, Williamsburg, VA.

Swann, C. A., & Sylvester, M. S. (2006). The foster care crisis: What caused caseloads to grow? *Demography, 43*, 309–335. doi:10.1353/dem.2006.0019

Swedish Prison and Probation Service. (2013). *Barn till föräldrar i fängelse* [Children or parents in prison]. Retrieved from http://www.kriminalvarden.se/sv/Startsida-skolportal1/Nina/Barn-till-foraldrar-i-fangelse/

Swisher, R. R., & Roettger, M. E. (2012). Father's incarceration and youth delinquency and depression: Examining differences by race and ethnicity. *Journal of Research on Adolescence, 22*, 597–603. doi:10.1111/j.1532-7795.2012.00810.x

Swisher, R. R., & Waller, M. R. (2008). Confining fatherhood: Incarceration and paternal involvement among nonresident White, African American, and Latino fathers. *Journal of Family Issues, 29*, 1067–1088. doi:10.1177/0192513X08316273

Tak, P. J. (2001). Sentencing and punishment in the Netherlands. In M. Tonry & R. S. Frase (Eds.), *Sentencing and sanctions in Western countries* (pp. 151–187). Oxford, England: Oxford University Press.

Thane, P. (2011). Unmarried motherhood in twentieth-century England. *Women's History Review, 20*, 11–29. doi:10.1080/09612025.2011.536383

Thornberry, T. P., Freeman-Gallant, A., Lizotte, A. J., Krohn, M. D., & Smith, C. A. (2003). Linked lives: The intergenerational transmission of antisocial behavior. *Journal of Abnormal Child Psychology, 31*, 171–184. doi:10.1023/A:1022574208366

Tonry, M. (1996). *Sentencing matters*. New York, NY: Oxford University Press.

Tonry, M. (1998). Intermediate sanctions in sentencing guidelines. In M. Tonry (Ed.), *Crime and justice: A review of research* (Vol. 23, pp. 199–253). Chicago, IL: University of Chicago Press.

Tonry, M. (2001). Punishment policies and patterns in Western Countries. In M. Tonry & R. S. Frase (Eds.), *Sentencing and sanctions in western countries* (pp. 3–28). Oxford, England: Oxford University Press.

Tonry, M. (2003). Reducing the prison population. In M. Tonry (Ed.), *Confronting crime: Crime control policy under new labour* (pp. 211–223). Cullompton, England: Willan.

Tonry, M. (2004). *Punishment and politics: Evidence and evaluation in the making of English crime control policy*. Cullompton, England: Willan.

Tonry, M., & Bijleveld, C. C. J. H. (2007). Crime, justice, and criminology in the Netherlands. In M. Tonry & C. C. J. H. Bijleveld (Eds.), *Crime and justice: A review of research* (Vol. 35, pp. 1–30). Chicago, IL: University of Chicago Press.

Tonry, M., & Petersilia, J. (1999a). American prisons. In M. Tonry (Ed.), *Crime and justice: A review of research* (Vol. 26, pp. 1–23). Chicago, IL: University of Chicago Press.

Tonry, M., & Petersilia, J. (Eds.). (1999b). *Crime and justice: A review of research* (Vol. 26). Chicago, IL: University of Chicago Press.

Travis, J., McBride, E. C., & Solomon, A. L. (2005). *Families left behind: The hidden costs of incarceration and reentry.* Washington, DC: Urban Institute Justice Policy Center.

Travis, J., & Waul, M. (2003a). Prisoners once removed: The children and families of prisoners. In J. Travis & M. Waul (Eds.), *Prisoners once removed: The impact of incarceration and reentry on children, families, and communities* (pp. 1–29). Washington, DC: Urban Institute.

Travis, J., & Waul, M. (Eds.). (2003b). *Prisoners once removed: The impact of incarceration and reentry on children, families, and communities.* Washington, DC: Urban Institute.

Trice, A. D., & Brewster, J. (2004). The effects of maternal incarceration on adolescent children. *Journal of Police and Criminal Psychology, 19,* 27–35. doi:10.1007/BF02802572

Turanovic, J. J., Rodriguez, N., & Pratt, T. C. (2012). The collateral consequences of incarceration revisited: A qualitative analysis of the effects on caregivers of children of incarcerated parents. *Criminology, 50,* 913–959. doi: 10.1111/j.1745-9125.2012.00283.x

Uggen, C., & Manza, J. (2002). Democratic contraction? Political consequences of felon disenfranchisement in the United States. *American Sociological Review, 67,* 777–803. doi:10.2307/3088970

Uggen, C., Manza, J., & Behrens, A. (2004). 'Less than the average citizen': Stigma, role transition and the civic reintegration of convicted felons. In S. Maruna & R. Immarigeon (Eds.), *After crime and punishment: Ex-offender reintegration and desistance from crime* (pp. 258–290). Cullompton, England: Willan.

Uggen, C., Wakefield, S., & Western, B. (2005). Work and family perspectives on reentry. In J. Travis & C. Visher (Eds.), *Prisoner reentry and crime in America* (pp. 209–243). Cambridge, England: Cambridge University Press. doi:10.1017/CBO9780511813580.008

United Nations General Assembly. (1989). *The convention on the rights of the child.* New York, NY: United Nations.

van de Rakt, M., Murray, J., & Nieuwbeerta, P. (2012). The long-term effects of paternal imprisonment on criminal trajectories of children. *Journal of Research in Crime and Delinquency, 49,* 81–108. doi:10.1177/0022427810393018

Van Wormer, K. S., & Bartollas, C. (2000). *Women and the criminal justice system.* Needham Heights, MA: Allyn & Bacon.

Vasey, M. W., & Ollendick, T. H. (2000). Anxiety. In A. J. Sameroff, M. Lewis, & S. M. Miller (Eds.), *Handbook of developmental psychopathology* (2nd ed., pp. 511–529). New York, NY: Kluwer Academic/Plenum. doi:10.1007/978-1-4615-4163-9_27

Vaughn, B., Byron, E., Sroufe, L. A., & Waters, E. (1979). Individual differences in infant–mother attachment at twelve and eighteen months: Stability and change in families under stress. *Child Development, 50,* 971–975. doi:10.2307/1129321

Wakefield, S., & Wildeman, C. (2011). Mass imprisonment and racial disparities in childhood behavioral problems. *Criminology & Public Policy, 10,* 793–817. doi:10.1111/j.1745-9133.2011.00740.x

Wakefield, S., & Wildeman, C. (2014). *Children of the prison boom: Mass incarceration and the future of American inequality.* New York, NY: Oxford University Press.

Walker, N. (1980). *Punishment, danger and stigma: The morality of criminal justice.* Oxford, England: Blackwell.

Walker, N. (1983). Side-effects of incarceration. *British Journal of Criminology, 23,* 61–71. Retrieved from http://bjc.oxfordjournals.org/

Walmsley, R. (2011). *World prison population list* (9th ed.). London, England: International Centre for Prison Studies.

Ward, D. A. (1972). Inmate rights and prison reform in Sweden and Denmark. *The Journal of Criminal Law, Criminology, and Police Science, 63,* 240–255. doi:10.2307/1142301

Ward, D. A. (1979). Sweden: The middle way to prison reform? In M. E. Wolfgang (Ed.), *Prisons: Present and possible* (pp. 89–167). Lexington, MA: Lexington.

Warren, S. L., Huston, L., Egeland, B., & Sroufe, L. A. (1997). Child and adolescent anxiety disorders and early attachment. *Journal of the American Academy of Child & Adolescent Psychiatry, 36,* 637–644. doi:10.1097/00004583-199705000-00014

Webster-Stratton, C. (1998). Preventing conduct problems in Head Start children: Strengthening parenting competencies. *Journal of Consulting and Clinical Psychology, 66,* 715–730. doi:10.1037/0022-006X.66.5.715

Weissman, M. M., Warner, V., Wickramaratne, P., Moreau, D., & Olfson, M. (1997). Offspring of depressed parents: 10 years later. *Archives of General Psychiatry, 54,* 932–940. doi:10.1001/archpsyc.1997.01830220054009

Weissman, M. M., Wickramaratne, P., Nomura, Y., Warner, V., Pilowsky, D., & Verdeli, H. (2006). Offspring of depressed parents: 20 years later. *The American Journal of Psychiatry, 163,* 1001–1008. doi:10.1176/appi.ajp.163.6.1001

West, D. J. (1969). *Present conduct and future delinquency: First report of the Cambridge Study in Delinquent Development.* London, England: Heinemann.

West, D. J. (1982). *Delinquency: Its roots, careers and prospects.* London, England: Heinemann.

West, D. J., & Farrington, D. P. (1973). *Who becomes delinquent?* London, England: Heinemann.

West, D. J., & Farrington, D. P. (1977). *The delinquent way of life*. London, England: Heinemann.

Western, B. (2002). The impact of incarceration on wage mobility and inequality. *American Sociological Review, 67*, 526–546. doi:10.2307/3088944

Western, B., Kling, J. R., & Weiman, D. F. (2001). The labor market consequences of incarceration. *Crime and Delinquency, 47*, 410–427. doi:10.1177/0011128701047003007

Western, B., Lopoo, L. M., & McLanaghan, S. (2004). Incarceration and the bonds between parents in fragile families. In M. Pattillo, D. Weiman, & B. Western (Eds.), *Imprisoning America: The social effects of mass incarceration* (pp. 21–45). New York, NY: Russell Sage.

Why does it cost so much for prisoners to keep in touch with their families? (2013, May 25). *Economist*, p. 10.

Wikström, P.-O. H. (1987). *Patterns of crime in a birth cohort: Age, sex and social class differences* (Project Metropolitan Research Report No. 24). Stockholm, Sweden: Stockholm University, Department of Sociology.

Wilbur, M. B., Marani, J. E., Appugliese, D., Woods, R., Siegel, J. A., Cabral, H. J., & Frank, D. A. (2007). Socioemotional effects of fathers' incarceration on low-income, urban, school-aged children. *Pediatrics, 120*, e678–e685. doi:10.1542/peds.2006-2166

Wildeman, C. (2009). Paternal imprisonment, the prison boom, and the concentration of disadvantage. *Demography, 46*, 265–280. doi:10.1353/dem.0.0052

Wildeman, C. (2010). Paternal Incarceration and children's physically aggressive behaviors: Evidence from the Fragile Families and Child Wellbeing Study. *Social Forces, 89*, 285–309. doi:10.1353/sof.2010.0055

World Bank. (2013). *Data: Population*. Retrieved from http://data.worldbank.org/

Zalba, S. R. (1964). *Women prisoners and their families*. Los Angeles, CA: Delmar.

Zeger, S. L., & Liang, K.-Y. (1992). An overview of methods for the analysis of longitudinal data. *Statistics in Medicine, 11*, 1825–1839. doi:10.1002/sim.4780111406

INDEX

Parental conviction
    in American study, 97, 106
    children's experiences of, 14
    in English study, 51, 54, 58
    in Swedish study, 65, 67, 70–71, 171
Parental criminality
    in American study, 95–97, 177–178
    as background issue, 23, 37
    and children's experiences, 13–14
    and delinquent development, 46
    in Dutch study, 80
    in English study, 161
    as predictor of children's offending,
        36–37
    in Swedish study, 66, 71, 72
    in systematic review, 129, 131,
        137–138
Parental incarceration
    in American study, 106
    among children in vulnerable
        populations, 6
    children's experiences of, 14–17
    before child's birth, 39
    in cross-national comparisons, 114,
        115
    in Dutch study, 79–80
    in English study, 50, 52, 161–162
    mediators of effects of, 103–106
    and other childhood adversities, 53
    as risk marker, 51, 53–54
    in Swedish study, 66, 171
    in systematic review, 131–134
Parental prison release
    children's experiences of, 17
    in studies, 38
Parental separation
    in English study, 45, 49, 51, 54, 59–60
    as mechanism of outcome, 39, 146
    non-incarceration, in English study,
        165–166
    in systematic review, 129, 141
Parenting programs, 153
Parent-management training programs,
    153
Parents
    adjustment of, after divorce, 23
    antisocial behavior of. See Antisocial
        behavior (of parents)
    caregiving by, prior to incarceration,
        18–19, 29

contact between children and
        incarcerated, 14–15, 19, 151
    drug use of, prior to incarceration, 29
    mental health problems of, 19, 29
    nervousness of, 169–170
    prison release of, 17, 38
    as repeat offenders, 19, 29
    visitation of children with
        incarcerated, 15, 151
Partners, of prisoners, 15–16
Peer delinquency, in American study,
    103–106, 180
Peers, children's relationships with,
    103–106, 180
Penal climate
    effect of, on children, 8
    effect of, on children's experiences, 19
    suggestions for changes in, 148–150
Perceived Stress Scale, 179
Persoonskaarten, 175
Petersilia, J., 149
Phillips, S. D., 155
Pittsburgh Youth Study. See American
    study
Poehlmann, J., 15, 25
Policymakers, 149–150
Population registration numbers
    (Sweden), 64
Posttraumatic stress symptoms, in
    children, 14, 126
Poverty, and incarceration, 26
Pratt, J., 116–117
Pratt, T. C., 16
Prevention programs, 158
Principles of Prison Administration Act
    (1953, Netherlands), 76–77
Prison conditions, children's concerns
    about, 17
Prisoners
    discrimination against families of, 28
    educational attainment of English, 29
    educational opportunities for, 26
    isolation of, from families, 118–119
    number of, in England, 5
    number of, in Netherlands, 5
    number of, in Sweden, 5
    number of, in United States, 4–5
    partners of, 15–16
    reintegration of, 153
    unemployment among English, 29
    voting rights of, 117

ABOUT THE AUTHORS

Joseph Murray, PhD, is a senior research associate and Wellcome Trust Research Career Development Fellow in the department of psychiatry at the University of Cambridge. His main research interests are in developmental criminology, cross-national comparisons, and crime and violence in low- and middle-income countries. He was awarded the University of Cambridge Manuel Lopez-Rey Graduate Prize in Criminology in 2002; the University of Cambridge Nigel Walker Prize for his PhD in 2007; a British Academy Postdoctoral Fellowship in 2006; a Darwin College Research Fellowship in 2007; and the Distinguished Young Scholar Award of the American Society of Criminology, Division of Corrections and Sentencing, in 2008.

Catrien C. J. H. Bijleveld, PhD, studied psychology and criminal law at Leiden University, earning her degree in statistical analysis of categorical time series. After working as an assistant professor at Leiden University she moved to the WODC Research and Documentation Center of the Netherlands Ministry of Justice. In 2001, she moved to NSCR in Leiden, and became professor of criminological research methods at the Vrije University in Amsterdam. Her main research interests are in the areas of criminal careers, female offenders, the intergenerational transmission of offenders, genocide, and sex offending. She is the author of several textbooks and the editor of other volumes on crime and justice in the Netherlands and on the association between employment and offending.

David P. Farrington, OBE, is Professor Emeritus of psychological criminology and Leverhulme Trust Emeritus Fellow at the Institute of Criminology at Cambridge University. He received the Stockholm Prize in Criminology in 2013. His major research interest is in developmental criminology, and he is director of the Cambridge Study in Delinquent Development, which is a prospective longitudinal survey of over 400 London males from ages 8 to 56. In addition to more than 600 published journal articles and book chapters on criminological and psychological topics, he has published nearly 100 books, monographs, and government publications.

Rolf Loeber, PhD, is a professor of psychiatry, psychology, and epidemiology at the University of Pittsburgh. He is director of the Life History Program and is principal investigator of two longitudinal studies, the Pittsburgh Youth Study and the Pittsburgh Girls Study. He has published in the fields of juvenile antisocial behavior and delinquency, substance use, and mental health problems. He is an elected member of the Koninklijke Academie van Wetenschappen (Royal Academy of Sciences) in the Netherlands and the Royal Irish Academy in Ireland.